Praise for *What I Couldn't Tell My Therapist*

"If you are looking for a firsthand experience of how a master therapist conducts intensive psychodynamic therapy, you will find it in this fascinating, beautifully written account of three engaging clinical cases that capture and keep your interest throughout. Enthusiastically recommended!"
—Stanley B. Messer, PhD, Distinguished Professor Emeritus and former Dean, Graduate School of Applied and Professional Psychology, Rutgers University

"This is a wonderful book of therapy situations. Gutsy, honest, and revealing, it gives insight into human emotional suffering and psychodynamic processes. I recommend it for all who want to learn about working with anger, guilt, and sadness related to mistreatment and with feelings toward the therapist."
—Leslie S. Greenberg, Distinguished Research Professor Emeritus, Department of Psychology, York University

"In *What I Couldn't Tell My Therapist*, Michelle May beautifully intertwines her own experiences along with those of her patients to provide powerful lessons on how to effect change in our own lives."
—Alan Gordon, LCSW, author of *The Way Out*

"I urge anyone interested in Davanloo's ISTDP to read Michelle M. May's new book. It is particularly suited for students of ISTDP who are struggling to learn the metapsychology of the unconscious and apply this difficult technique to patients with challenging conditions, including medically unexplained symptoms. May, through both clinical and personal experiences, makes it abundantly clear how unlocking the unconscious heals these conditions when applied properly."
—Robert. J. Neborsky, MD, Voluntary Clinical Professor of Psychiatry, UCSD and UCLA (Hon.) Schools of Medicine, and coauthor of *Mastering Intensive Short-Term Dynamic Psychotherapy*

"This is a poignant and intimate exploration of the powerful relationship between emotions and medical disorders. May has given us an insightful view into the intricacies of ISTDP therapy and how people can recover from great suffering."

—Howard Schubiner, MD, author of *Unlearn Your Pain*

"Seamlessly integrating theoretical constructs with clinical material, this magnificently humane and nonpathologizing volume shines brilliantly with May's optimistic belief in our innate resilience and capacity to self-repair even in the face of deep woundedness and addiction—if we are blessed enough to have a gifted therapist to whom, over time, we can reveal our most private and painful truths."

—Martha Stark, MD, Faculty, Harvard Medical School, and award-winning author of nine books, including *Relentless Hope*

"Through detailed descriptions of her own treatment process and that of two clients, Michelle May covers the spectrum of therapeutic processes, challenges, and changes one can encounter when using the intensive short-term dynamic psychotherapy model in working with individuals with attachment trauma. The book is an excellent primer for people entering therapy and can be therapeutic in and of itself. I highly recommend it."

—Allan Abbass, MD, FRCPC, Professor of Psychiatry and Psychology, Dalhousie University, and author of *Reaching through Resistance* and *Hidden from View*

"May candidly shares her personal experiences and insights, allowing readers to connect with the heartfelt narratives. She also provides a profound understanding of the intricate and personal processes involved in ISTDP, creating an intersection between science and humanity. Her words will deeply resonate with readers, touching them directly as they delve into the book."

—Nima Ghorbani, PhD, Professor of Clinical Psychology, University of Tehran; Certified Supervisor of ISTDP; and author of *Joyful Madness* and *Self-Narrated by Self* (in Persian)

"A poignant and psychologically sound read highlighting three lives, including the author's, which adds a compelling depth. Authentically relatable, the book shows the complexity of shared human suffering and challenges and how best to overcome them by discovering the truths about ourselves. I highly recommend it for readers who want to improve their lives for lasting change and for clinicians alike."

—Tami Chelew, LMFT, President, International Experiential Dynamic Psychotherapy Association

"This courageous book reveals what most therapists want to avoid—their own history of trauma! Through three captivating stories, May navigates the reader to the heart of emotional difficulties in a fiercely loving, respectful, and insightful way. It flips the script on the usual therapist-client encounters and shows us that, while different, we are all fundamentally made of the same essence."

—Ange Cooper, DClinPsy, RPsych, Assistant Professor, Dalhousie University

"May makes the concepts of intensive dynamic therapy understandable and accessible through realistic depictions of therapy, including her own. I recommend this book to anyone who wants to know what psychodynamic psychotherapy is *really* like. It will be especially helpful for trainees to improve their skill with dynamic interventions and to foster greater acceptance of themselves, their patients, and the therapeutic process as perfectly imperfect."

—Deborah Pollack, PhD, Associate Professor of Psychology, Utica University, and Clinical Assistant Professor, SUNY Upstate Medical University

"Michelle's unwavering commitment to honesty in exploring her own trauma and journey to health is inspiring. On top of this, she demonstrates her clinical wisdom in empathically responding to her own patients' struggles. What really strikes the reader is the human connection between Michelle and her patients and how crucial this is for healing. An important book not only for therapists but for anyone interested in how to recover from trauma."

—Jonathan J. Entis, PhD, Teaching Associate in Psychiatry, Harvard Medical School

"This book is replete with great examples of being present, observing what is said and unsaid in both patient and therapist, and actively intervening or using silence to encourage the patient to reveal herself more and align with the therapist in a positive working relationship. Michelle uses verbal interchanges from her practice, as well as her own therapy, to highlight how to take theory and bring it into the consultation room in a very relatable and authentic way."

—Ronald C. Albucher, MD, President-Elect, International Experiential Dynamic Therapy Association, and Volunteer Clinical Assistant Professor, Department of Psychiatry and Behavioral Sciences, UC San Francisco School of Medicine

"A daringly honest reflection of addressing substance use and chronic pain. May takes the reader on an engaging journey through clinical stories woven through her personal experiences, conveying useful psychodynamic concepts that make this a compelling and important read. I would recommend *What I Couldn't Tell My Therapist* to all my patients."

—Taylor Nichols, MD, emergency medicine and addiction medicine physician and Assistant Clinical Professor, UC San Francisco

"By sharing the story of three relatable individuals in therapy, including herself, May reveals how we unconsciously repeat destructive patterns and maladaptive behaviors long after we experience trauma. Ultimately, she shows that we can heal and live with agency as our true selves when we do the work to make our unconscious conscious."

—Sunita Merriman, DDS, author of *Stripping: My Fight to Find Me*

"Michelle M. May reveals the most important aspect of providing good psychotherapy, the ability of the psychotherapist to do for themselves what they ask of others. As a reader you will see through the eyes of a master therapist the process of psychotherapy, which entails precise observation and the delivery of effective interventions while maintaining the therapeutic bond once the patient commits to their own transformation."

—Kristin Osborn, LMHC, Associate in Psychiatry, Harvard Medical School, and coauthor of *Paraverbal Communication in Psychotherapy*

"Michelle M. May's unique perspective offers a profoundly felt sense of the vulnerability and bravery required in transformative psychotherapy. Her extensive session vignettes, both from her own therapy and from her work with clients, shed light on the intimate process that makes it possible to expose the parts of ourselves that we most wish to hide."

—Susan Warren Warshow, LCSW, founder of the DEFT Institute and author of *A Therapist's Handbook to Dissolve Shame and Defense*

"With this book, Michelle M. May joins the ranks of the great therapy storytellers, including Yalom, Havens, and Greenberg. Her narratives shed light on the moment-by-moment clinical thinking of an advanced dynamic therapist, and she takes the reader even deeper by sharing her own experience and development as a person *in* therapy. As the book balances engagingly told clinical tales with clear explanations of complex psychodynamic concepts, it will be an absorbing and educational read for both advanced and novice clinicians."

—Maury Joseph, PsyD, ISTDP Training Program Faculty, New Washington School of Psychiatry, and Certified Trainer and Supervisor, International Experiential Dynamic Therapy Association

What I Couldn't Tell My Therapist

What I Couldn't Tell My Therapist

The Truths We Told to Heal Our Lives

MICHELLE M. MAY

Seven Leaves Press

Copyright © 2024 by Michelle M. May

All rights reserved. No part of this publication may be reproduced, distributed, or transmitted in any form or by any means, including photocopying, recording, or other electronic or mechanical methods, without the prior written permission of the publisher, except in the case of brief quotations embodied in critical reviews and certain other noncommercial uses permitted by copyright law. For permission requests, write to the publisher, addressed "Attention: Permissions Department."

Seven Leaves Press
www.sevenleavespress.com

Ordering Information
Quantity sales. Special discounts are available on quantity purchases by corporations, associations, and others. For details, contact the "Special Sales Department" at the address above.

Orders by US trade bookstores and wholesalers. Please contact BCH: (800) 431-1579 or visit www.bookch.com for details.

Printed in the United States of America

Cataloging-in-Publication Data

Names: May, Michelle M., author.
Title: What I couldn't tell my therapist : the truths we told to heal our lives / Michelle M. May.
Description: Includes bibliographical references. | Kensington, MD: Seven Leaves Press, 2024.
Identifiers: LCCN: 2024905753 | ISBN: 979-8-9901879-0-0 (paperback) | 979-8-9901879-1-7 (ebook)
Subjects: LCSH May, Michelle M. | Psychoanalysts—United States—Anecdotes. | Psychoanalysis—Anecdotes. | Insight in psychotherapy. | BISAC BIOGRAPHY & AUTOBIOGRAPHY / Memoirs | SELF HELP / General | PSYCHOLOGY / Psychotherapy / Counseling
Classification: LCC BF175 .M39 2024 | DDC 158.1—dc23

First Edition

28 27 26 25 24   1 2 3 4 5 6 7 8 9 10

To those who have yet to find a way out

Contents

Introduction — 1
1. Walter: 16,801 Days of Pot — 5
2. Emma: Complexity Guaranteed — 9
3. Michelle: Pleasing and Other Games — 15
4. Walter: Finding the Threshold — 19
5. Michelle: The Lies My Defenses Told — 25
6. Emma: Wallflower — 31
7. Michelle: Clawing Out — 37
8. Walter: The Question No One Asks — 41
9. Michelle: The Eyes — 49
10. Emma: The Abused Body — 57
11. Michelle: The Post-its — 65
12. Walter: Shame and Other Games — 71
13. Michelle: Memory Boils and Other Betrayals — 81
14. Emma: Whose Fault Is It Anyway? — 89
15. Michelle: The Insertion — 99
16. Walter: The Suicide — 107
17. Michelle: The Only Savior — 113
18. Emma: The Cool Girl — 121
19. Michelle: Too Much — 129
20. Walter: My Juice and Other Breakthroughs — 135
21. Michelle: Out of the Box — 145
22. Emma: Ghosting — 151
23. Michelle: Set Changes — 159

24.	Walter: The Pot Plan	165
25.	Michelle: The New Name	171
26.	Emma: A Horse to Water	177
27.	Michelle: Milkboarding and Other Forms of Torture	181
28.	Walter: Intergenerational Use	187
29.	Michelle: I Love You, Opioids	193
30.	Emma: Hating the Unconscious	201
31.	Michelle: Moving On	205
32.	Walter: The Uselessness of Perfection	209
33.	Michelle: The Therapist with the Marshmallow Chair	213
34.	Emma: The Anger Thing	221
35.	Michelle: Cow Parts	227
36.	Walter: The Mistletoe	235
37.	Michelle: The Toxic Daughter	241
38.	Emma: To Feel or Not to Feel	249
39.	Michelle: Projective Identification and Other Potato Drops	253
40.	Emma: The Impossible Facade	263
41.	Walter: The Roof Overhead	265
Epilogue		267

Acknowledgments	269
Appendix	271
Grounding Techniques for Anxiety Regulation	271
Examples of Anxiety and Resulting Issues	272
Further Reading	279
Notes	283
About the Author	287

And I was lifted, wet and bloody, out of my mother, into the world, screaming

and enough.

—Ocean Vuong, *Time Is a Mother*

Introduction

I had originally intended to write about my grueling medical odyssey because I wanted to help those struggling with unexplained chronic pain. However, when I finished the draft, I realized that the pages were filled with lies, so I rewrote the book, which ended up being one of the most liberating acts of my life.

What I Couldn't Tell My Therapist is about how we silence ourselves to protect those we love and thus do violence to ourselves. We hurt ourselves in invisible ways. And what we cannot see, we cannot change.

How do we learn to do violence to ourselves? If our caregivers became anxious or pushed us away because of our feelings, our bodies learned to sound the alarm of anxiety as a warning sign that something is wrong in the relationship, so we developed strategies, or defenses, to reduce anxiety and hide our emotions, aiming to stay close to our caregivers. These defenses acted like loyal guards, working to make our caregivers comfortable and accepting of us. Yet this acceptance was incomplete, embracing only the parts of us that remained after we discarded what unsettled our caregivers. Defenses are not weaknesses in ourselves but strategies we used to protect those unable to tolerate our feelings and urges. Defenses are forged in the battle between who we are and who our caretakers, culture, and society want us to be.

Although defenses and anxiety served a purpose in our early years, they can lead to unnecessary suffering later in life. In fact, anxiety and harmful defenses create the reasons we go to therapy. What used to be beneficial has now, ironically, tragically, ridiculously, and maddeningly, become harmful. Our defenses were shaped by environments we didn't choose in our early years. To add insult to injury, these defenses often fail to adapt when our surroundings change or as we grow into adulthood. When they don't update, we unnecessarily suffer.

This book illuminates the concealed patterns of our anxiety and defenses, revealing the hidden sources of our suffering. Through interweaving sessions with two of my patients as well as my own experiences in and out of therapy, I show how we can reach into our depths, pull ourselves out, and find freedom from self-torture.

Many don't like to hear that unconscious dynamics exist. I certainly didn't like to hear it. In fact, when I learned how much the invisible puppet strings of my unconscious tugged me around, I was both angered by their power and humbled by my abundant blind spots. Only after I learned how my strings worked did I become hopeful I could loosen their hold.

Because unconscious anxiety and defenses operate covertly, my patients and I suffered from pain we could not understand or articulate. While we thought we could, we could not directly tell our therapists what ailed us, and we certainly could not say what caused our suffering. Thankfully, we had the privilege of learning that listening deeply and observing unconscious communication helps us emerge, that being with another in bold partnership helps us shed needless armor.

What I Couldn't Tell My Therapist is also about embracing how we are innately conflicted. When we try to avoid or oversimplify our humanity, we suffer. When we embrace our complexity, we free ourselves from the false promise of perfectionism.

Making the distinction between inevitable pain and undue suffering is important. Inevitable pain is caused by loss, conflict, change, regret, and certain injuries and diseases that come with being alive. This book offers ways to live through inevitable pain rather than promising a way around it. Undue suffering, on the other hand, is caused by both conscious and unconscious processes within us that do not necessarily need to occur. Undue suffering is caused by the lie that life's inevitable pain can be avoided. It cannot. This book illuminates how we unwittingly create undue suffering as we attempt to avoid life's inevitable pains. It also provides examples of how to find a way out of our self-induced suffering.

Reading this book might be emotionally challenging. As it helps you explore your own hidden inner processes, it will stir up and reveal unseen worlds. Thus, read it at whatever pace or in whatever order works for you. Some might prefer to read the chapters in the order they were written, while others might prefer to read the chapters according to the patient, for example, reading all of Walter's chapters first. It is designed to be read either way. I have included grounding techniques to help with anxiety in the appendix.

In this book, I explore the therapy of three people who, being white and born in the United States, inherently offer a limited scope of experiences and perspectives. It is crucial to acknowledge that these stories do not comprehensively encapsulate the diverse array of experiences present in society. People of color, for instance, encounter unique challenges, including a potential cultural stigma surrounding therapy-seeking. This book does not explicitly delve into those challenges, and it's important to recognize the broader need for an inclusive representation of experiences.

The session content is a distillation of many sessions to cover crucial clinical points. This is not a complete depiction of intensive dynamic therapy, nor is it a complete representation of any client or therapist. Intensive dynamic therapy is a robust and complex form of therapy that requires years of dedication from the therapist to learn. (For those interested, I have included reading recommendations in the back of the book.) The words *patient*, *client*, and *person* are used interchangeably throughout the book. While the dialogue is sometimes verbatim, it is most often an approximation. The clients in this book have given me permission to share their therapeutic experiences and weighed in on their stories. Many names and identifying information have been changed to protect confidentiality. While the therapy sessions in this book were video recorded, the rest of my life was not. Thus, the parts of this book that contain my story are an incomplete portrayal subject to multiple interpretations. You are seeing mine. I have done my best to ensure it is accurate by sharing these pages with family members, colleagues, my therapists, peers, and the clients in the book.

Hopefully this book helps you discover what hides behind your secrets, anxiety, and pain so you can find your path to relief.

1

Walter: 16,801 Days of Pot

Therapist Note: Fifty-six-year-old married, unemployed Caucasian male. Had over a decade of individual therapy for depression with the therapist who referred him. Reports he smokes "a lot of pot." Has severe anxiety and long-term, treatment-resistant depression. One adult son. Has never been hospitalized for psychiatric reasons. Reports no psychiatric medication.

Walter walked into my office with a loose stride and slumped shoulders. His face was red underneath deep wrinkles. He looked as if he had been carrying a heavy bag of rocks his entire life. When he finally sat down on the couch across from me, he looked out the window instead of at me.

Adrenaline shot through my chest. Could I help a man who hasn't responded to over a decade of therapy?

"How can I help?" I asked.

"I hear you, uh, do things very . . . differently," he sputtered. "At first, I wasn't sure about the kind of therapy you do or what kind of therapist you are, but the more I hear about it, I think there are good things for me . . ."

Walter trailed off as he looked down at his shoes. His head began to swing from side to side as if suddenly attached by a limp noodle.

He popped his head up. "I should start by saying I've been smoking pot every day since I was nine or ten!" he spat out.

He had smoked for forty-six years, which was twelve more than I'd been alive. Later, I calculated this to be 16,801 days of pot. My chest hurt at the thought of a young boy smoking joint after joint, day after day, until he was the man in front of me.

"Every day since you were nine or ten?" I asked.

Walter slowly nodded. "As you know," he continued, "I spent eleven years with my previous therapist. I really liked him. But I want something . . . more intense."

I waited.

"Yes, I want something more intense," Walter repeated to the window. He started to open his mouth again, but nothing came out.

"About five or six years ago," he finally managed, "I thought to myself, this is it. This is my life, and it's not going to change. I have no hope. It's not like I am going to kill myself, but it's just that . . ." He continued to stare out the window. I knew that therapy often fails because people talk to walls, carpets, plants, or bookshelves instead of their therapist. And then to the floor he shared, "I don't think anything can change."

"On the one hand," I said, interrupting his connection with the floor, "you want more intensive therapy, and on the other hand, there's no hope for change."

He wanted to die or at least anesthetize himself until he was dead. We needed to find out why. I waited for my next signal.

As Freud said, "He that has eyes to see and ears to hear may convince himself that no mortal can keep a secret. If his lips are silent, he chatters with his fingertips."[1] What Walter couldn't tell me could be seen in his unconscious communications. Not only did I need to listen to Walter's words, but I also needed to listen to and observe these unconscious communications—the defense mechanisms, renegade words, and anxiety signals in his body. Defenses and anxiety tell me what words cannot, what we cannot simply tell a therapist. Like beeps from a metal detector scanning the sand, defenses and anxiety point toward hidden and taboo thoughts, feelings, and urges. Guided by these beeps, we could look for what was covered up by Walter's depression and smoking. Would he sigh, lose muscle tension, stare vacantly, or change his tone of voice?

After I mirrored his contradiction of wanting help yet having no hope for change, Walter's head slumped to his collarbone. He didn't sigh or fidget. Instead, his body sagged. His anxiety was now too high. It needed to be regulated.

"I notice you seem limp. Is that how your body feels?" I asked Walter. His body abruptly bounced up again, his muscles engaging, which meant his anxiety was lower after I asked him to observe his body.

"Yes, yes, it did feel limp!" he said with enthusiasm. I felt warmth in my chest.

"When I said that you want more intensive therapy and there's no hope for change, your body went limp." I flopped my body over to demonstrate.

"Yes!" he laughed. Tension returned to his neck. With my simple observation of his body, Walter came to life.

But not for long. His body collapsed, his head dropping to the side.

"But I do want something more intense," he said to the floor.

Walter was in the right place if he wanted something more intense. As a team, we would work relentlessly to excavate him from his depressive shell. To do this, we would have to see how his unconscious processes worked by inviting him to do what he usually avoided. These processes had a leading role in determining his behavior, thoughts, feelings, memories, and, most importantly, his suffering.

Walter slowly picked up his head. His eyes landed on the wall behind me.

I was beginning to see signs and hear whispers of what caused Walter's depression and suffering. But what was driving such severe anxiety and depression? Why did he want to die?

2

Emma: Complexity Guaranteed

Therapist Note: Thirty-four-year-old single, employed Caucasian female. Says she is "unable to establish and sustain romantic relationships." Wants "better confidence and perspective on dating." Reports hopelessness, mild depression, anxiety, and low self-esteem. Has seen multiple therapists. Reports no substance use, no prior psychiatric hospitalizations, no medications.

Emma's short brown hair, parted exactly down the middle, hung like a thick curtain in front of her face. Her gaze was absorbed by her phone as she gripped it with white knuckles. "Hi, Emma?"

She looked up with a closed-mouth smile and shot up from the chair. I ushered her into my office, gesturing toward the couch.

"What's the problem you'd like my help with?"

I always wonder how people will react when I ask that question. It sounds like a McDonald's order: "Hello, what can I get you?" Yet the answer to my question has nothing to do with fries and a cheeseburger. People's answers tell me about their history of suffering.

"Well, I don't know if you can help me." Though she was in her midthirties, her tone sounded like that of a resentful teenager. She fidgeted with her nails and pulled at her cuticles. "I went to a few other therapists before you, and honestly, I wasn't sure if I wanted a therapist like you. I kind of wanted someone older who couldn't relate at all."

"Could *not*?"

"Right, could *not*. The last therapist told me she couldn't help me because I didn't have a diagnosis or whatever."

Excuse me? I thought. Heat rose in my chest.

"Excuse me?" I said out loud.

Emma flung her palms up toward the ceiling. "I know, right? She said I didn't have an official diagnosis, so insurance wouldn't cover therapy. I couldn't continue to see her after the first session. And that was that."

While I listened to Emma, the room began to spin. Did Emma activate something within me, causing the room to spin with high anxiety? What was going on with me?

"You're saying that the therapist you saw right before me said, basically, she couldn't help you because you didn't have a diagnosis like, say, depression, bipolar, or generalized anxiety disorder?" Halfway through my sentence, my dizziness subsided.

"Yeah. I mean, I'm screwed up but apparently not enough!"

Emma and her past therapist didn't know that while a diagnosis describes symptoms, it doesn't explain what causes them. For example, suppose I suffer from restlessness, fatigue, difficulty concentrating, irritability, and muscle tension. I might get the diagnosis "generalized anxiety disorder." Yet this label does me little good. If you had a cough, the doctor would not hand you a piece of paper that said, "Diagnosis: Cough. Expels air from lungs in sudden, involuntary sharp bursts." If they did, you'd be enraged. "Yes, Doctor! I know it's a cough. But what's causing it? A common cold? Pneumonia? COVID? And how do I treat it? How do I make it go away?" A mental health diagnosis only describes symptoms. It doesn't explain the causes or how to treat them.

Emma needed an explanation for what caused her problems. To find that explanation, I needed to look under the surface to see the unconscious dynamics that caused her symptoms.

"So what can I help you with?" I asked Emma again.

"Wait, no personal history?"

"Not yet. Since I don't know what you want my help with, I can't know what to do with that history yet." I didn't mention that her anxiety and defenses were how her unconscious was already telling me her history. I was watching it in action.

Instead of a verbal dissemination of her history, I had to help develop a conscious therapeutic alliance.[1]

A conscious therapeutic alliance is more than the therapist and client liking each other. This is not about "good vibes." It's much more.

Conscious Therapeutic Alliance

A conscious therapeutic alliance includes the following components:

1. The first component is identifying an internal emotional problem, which occurs when the patient does something that leads to their problem, even if they're unaware. For example, "I get so anxious, I end up screaming at my mother." An external problem, for example, is "I haven't found the right guy because I just haven't met him yet."
2. The second component is identifying the patient's positive goal, which is what they do want rather than what

they don't want. An example of a positive goal is "I want to feel good in my body." A negative goal is "I don't want to feel anxious anymore." Positive goals are the prizes at the end of a race.
3. The third component is making sure the patient's will is driving the therapy. Do they want to do good things for themselves? Or are they in therapy because someone else wants them there?
4. The fourth component is looking at a specific example of the patient's problem. The example can't be vague; otherwise, we'd get vague results.
5. The fifth component is using that specific example to start determining how the patient's unconscious processes work. What does the patient avoid? What triggers anxiety? What types of anxiety are in their body? What defenses contribute to their problem? We find out this information by seeing what happens when we ask the patient to face what they usually avoid.
6. The sixth component is determining and agreeing on the therapeutic task: What are we going to do together to help the patient?

Then we'd have a conscious therapeutic alliance.

But I have a confession. I've been misleading. I spoke of steps, of a linear approach to therapy. There are steps, but they rarely happen in order. Instead, I must follow the person in front of me. Each person is a unique flesh-and-blood puzzle. And it's not only one puzzle. It's two--the patient and me. The combinations of steps are endless. Complexity is guaranteed.

"Makes sense," Emma replied after I said there would be no history taking just yet. She began to pick at her nails, a defense that not only put a wall between us but also picked her apart. "Okay, well, I guess I've had a hard time sustaining any romantic relationships. I really have no confidence or hope for dating. My friends and parents and sisters want me to do online dating. I've tried, but I just can't anymore. I don't know what's wrong with me."

"Do *you* want to meet someone? Do online dating?" I asked, checking for her will. I needed to make sure her statement was not a *projection of will*, a defense when someone unknowingly (unconsciously) takes their healthy desire and puts it in someone else—for example, "My wife wants me to work on my drinking," "My past therapist said I don't know what I want to do with my life," "My friends think I have a problem and I should work on it." All these desires belong to someone other than the patient. The desire had to be Emma's for me to help her.

"Yes, I do," she said with a sigh. The sigh revealed inner conflict—unconscious feelings creating anxiety in the form of tension around her lungs, resulting in a sigh, regarding her wish to meet someone. Something stirred deep within her about meeting someone. Asking about her own desire, rather than her family's and friends' desire, made her metal detector beep.

"I want help to date," Emma continued. "But I also have like . . ." She paused and looked at the wall behind my head. "I also have these headaches, acid reflux, and TMJ. You know, TMJ, meaning temporomandibular joint or whatever. It's like inflammation, and sometimes my jaw locks. I've been to the doctor. Nothing's worked except my acid reflux medication." She rubbed her jaw.

Some people come to me when doctors can't find a medical cause for their symptoms. I specialize in helping patients with body symptoms such as headaches, irritable bowel syndrome, fibromyalgia, and acid reflux that are caused by psychological processes.[2] When I asked Emma if she had sought me out because of this, she told me she had come to see me only because no one else would see her.

"You certainly weren't my first choice."

I felt a jab in my chest. *Right. Got it.*

"I didn't know you could treat any of those things," Emma continued, "or that anyone could." She shook her head quickly, as if a bug had flown onto her forehead. "I just wanted to tell you. I get nervous about these issues. Like one time I got this headache after a cycling class, and I thought, What if this never goes away? I mean, what a nightmare. What if it never stopped? Can you imagine? I'd feel crazy!"

My body tensed. *I don't have to imagine.*

3

Michelle: Pleasing and Other Games

Years before seeing Emma and Walter, I sat on the floor of my closet, my phone pressed hard against my cheek. If I'd had a bird's-eye view, I would have noticed my white knuckles, which were as white as Emma's on the day I met her. My closet afforded me a quiet space in my studio apartment to call Dr. A, a potential new therapist. As I waited for him to answer, I felt a bubble of hope rise in my throat. I had never had intensive therapy. What would we uncover that I hadn't seen before? Could he even help me?

A month later, I drove to Dr. A's office for our first appointment. Instead of hope, tension riddled my body. I fervently scratched at a fake tattoo around my wrist. Why did I put it somewhere Dr. A could see? Why did I do something so thoughtless?

Dr. A greeted me and outstretched his arm toward a chair. I sat down and looked around the room.

"What would you like my help with?" he asked.

When he had ushered me in, his eyes were kind; now they seemed stern. I didn't like his sparse office. I didn't like the dust collecting on his books. I didn't like his not-so-comfy chair. Usually, therapy chairs are the pinnacle of comfort. Dr. A's chair was a comfort-refusing, bullshit-rejecting chair.

Even though Dr. A had asked the question, I told my answer to the floor.

"I want to learn about my defenses and my unconscious. I want to get to know myself as deeply as possible." It certainly wasn't a specific task, but I wanted to look at everything and anything.

"You look at the floor," he noted.

I tried to appear calm. I looked down at my wrist, where I had tried to rub off the temporary tattoo. I scratched at it lightly. "I'm trying to get more of this off." I stopped scratching at the tattoo and showed him, saying proudly, "It's not real."

"Why does it matter if it's real?" he asked calmly.

The room went fuzzy, as if the dust on his books had blown into the air.

I had signed up for this, but now that I was in the room, I wasn't sure I wanted to be there. I didn't want him to think I had a real tattoo, that I was the kind of person who my dad would look at and say, "Why would they do that to themselves?"

When I told Dr. A that I didn't want him to think I had a real tattoo, he looked at me with an expression that said to me, *Why not?* I decided to say whatever came to my mind.

"I don't know why I don't want you to think I have a real tattoo. My, uh, my dad doesn't like tattoos. This morning, when I was getting ready to come here, I tried to get all of it off, and I couldn't, and now it looks ridiculous." While one part of me said that I didn't know, the other part of me knew exactly why I didn't want Dr. A to think I had a real tattoo. The war inside me was on—the war between defenses that wanted me to keep my mouth shut and the healthy drive for honesty.

"But I am not your father," Dr. A replied. I wondered if he thought I was projecting, relating to him as I would my father. "What feelings are coming up toward me as we meet together today?"

There it was, the question. I had read transcripts, seen videos, and read books with this question. At this point, I was a novice therapist, just beginning to ask my own patients this question. I knew Dr. A would ask it, and I had told myself that it would be easy to answer. I was wrong. It was not easy.

I felt heat in my face. I hated that I blushed. Other than my stupid tomato face, I was good at appearing calm. I became red when embarrassed, excited, mad, or surprised. In middle school, my Spanish teacher called me out for having a crush: "Michelle likes Brad! Michelle likes Brad!" I turned full-on tomato. Everyone made fun of my stupid tomato face. I felt so anxious my nose went numb.

I wanted to put a bag over my head as I looked at Dr. A. I already liked him and wanted him to like me. I liked how serious he was. He got right down to business. I told him.

"Right, but that doesn't explain trying to remove your tattoo this morning for me," Dr. A responded.

"I don't know why I tried to remove it," I said as if pleading with him.

"Part of you must have already been in a relationship with me because you acted as if I would judge what's on your wrist."

Heat returned to my face. I scanned the carpet for answers. He looked where I looked, as if to say, *There's nothing there, and I'm here.* I pushed my body into his torturous chair.

"I see I'm avoiding you. The wall I'm putting up between us. I see it."

"So you see it. What feelings are coming up toward me then?"

I felt some strength in my arms. I was relieved a feeling was coming up in my body, but I also wanted to ignore it. I told myself I was doing a good job. I didn't want him to struggle with me. I didn't want to be difficult.

"Your jaw?" he asked. "You're tensing it." He touched his jaw as he clenched it.

My face flushed again. This was too weird. I knew what being a therapist was like. However, *this* seat, where the client sits, was harder. I told him as much and laughed. I hoped he would laugh with me. He didn't.

"I'm sorry I'm difficult," I added. "My life's really good. I don't have any problems. I just want to get to know myself better."

"And so what feelings are coming up toward me that make you put up this wall or look away and such?" Dr. A was relentlessly trying to get to the truth. He ignored my defense of denial that said everything was fine. Denial is a way to hypnotize us into a dream. Denial says, *What is, isn't!*

And then, I felt a familiar sensation: a tension headache. Suddenly, I realized how much Dr. A didn't know about me. He didn't know about the headache that lasted for six years. He didn't know about the pills. He didn't know what my scalp looked like underneath my hair.

While there was much Dr. A didn't know, I didn't know that through my anxiety and defenses, Dr. A was already witnessing my history that was hidden from me.

4

Walter: Finding the Threshold

As I watched Walter melt into a depression puddle, I felt a desire to zap him with magic energy I didn't have. I imagined myself clapping loudly in front of his face. *Walter! Wake up!* I suddenly wished I knew everything about him, that I already knew all his patterns.

As I felt an ache to be omniscient, I took a breath. I had fallen into this trap of thinking I should know everything about another human being too many times. I wish I could claim that this belief only occurred early in my career, but occasionally, I still fall into the trap of believing that I can—or should—know everything. It feels good when my own thoughts match reality, but they often don't. To learn more about Walter, I had to keep watching how he reacted to what I said and what I invited him to do. I couldn't guess, and I couldn't lie to myself or Walter. I must collect information both Walter and I could observe to get the truth about what caused his anxiety and depression.

"Is the pot something you want my help with?" I asked, checking into his desires. Therapists get burned out when they try to solve problems people don't actually want to solve.

"I know it should be something I want help with," Walter said, perking up again.

"But it isn't?"

"I know that sounds terrible!"

"Well, if it isn't, it isn't."

He paused and looked at me as though I was playing a trick on him. I wasn't.

"What is the problem *you* want my help with?" I asked again. "What do *you* want? Because therapy will go nowhere if you work on things you think others want you to work on."

I wanted to block any projection of his will. If Walter couldn't own his healthy drive, we couldn't succeed.

"I know I don't want to feel like this anymore!" Walter said, throwing his arms out. His face stretched into a pleading *You got to help me!*

"*This?*" I asked.

"Huh?" Walter looked at me, confused. Tension kept his body upright.

"*This* is vague. Since *this* isn't specific, we wouldn't know what to shoot for."

Since Walter's body held tension, his vagueness indicated anxiety about closeness. Vagueness is a defense, a beep of the metal detector. Vagueness hides specificity, which increases closeness. Compare how close you'd feel to someone if you asked them how their weekend went, and they said, "Fine," versus if they shared, "It was hard. I struggled a bit on Saturday because I didn't want to get out of bed. Thankfully, I managed to get out of bed and go for a nice walk." Sharing specific details increases closeness. Closeness increases feelings. Thus, if I ignored Walter's vagueness, I would be complicit in keeping a wall up between us. Barriers to intimacy like these contribute to the development or exacerbation of depression. The vagueness would also lead to a meandering and anchorless therapy where, before we know it, the time is up, and Walter's wondering why we wasted his precious time and money. If I don't specifically know what he wants, I can't help him.

"I think I do that all the time." The wrinkles deepened on his forehead.

"*That?*" I truly didn't know to what he was referring.

Walter let out a powerful laugh. "Ha! *That* is vague! Damn, there it goes again! Look at that! How fast that vagueness happens!" He seemed tickled we were noticing him in such detail, and more importantly, it helped him feel better. I felt a powerful warmth surge through my body.

"And so, what's the problem you want my help with? What do *you* want out of your therapy?" I said smiling.

"I don't want to feel depressed anymore. I don't have any energy. I want to . . . feel better! I want some hope! Some energy!" He said these words with the very power he craved.

He didn't mention his pot smoking because, apparently, he didn't want to work on it. Of course, pot might kill his energy; however, it wasn't clear yet. If it contributed to his depression, then we'd have to look at it since he wanted help with depression. While I had a hard time imagining that pot didn't contribute to his problem, I didn't say anything. It wouldn't help to say anything he wasn't ready to hear, especially about a beloved, precious, and intimate relationship with a drug. I knew this from my own beloved, precious, and intimate relationship with my drug.

"You want my help with anything that creates this depression and steals your energy? You want to understand what causes the slump so you can feel hopeful and get some energy back?"

"Yes."

Walter's body was starting to slump again.

If a client looks tense and moves around, we can explore feelings and try to unearth unconscious material. We can explore where the metal detector beeps. However, if they look limp or sound out of it, we check on and regulate their anxiety. Looking limp and sounding out of it are the beeps of the metal detector, though they signal that it is not yet safe to explore. I must monitor Walter's anxiety from moment to moment, staying in tune with his body.

"Did you just feel a little more depressed?"

"Yes! Yes, I did...it...uh..." This time, the perk up lasted only a few seconds. His voice started with enthusiasm and then whimpered out as depression crushed his fervor. His anxiety had increased again.

Walter's hand moved to his face, covering his eyes with his palm. He was now relating to the palm of his hand as he covered his eyes. His muscles still lacked tone.

"You want my help feeling energy, and you want a more intensive therapy?"

"Yes." His body remained the same.

"And right now, your body has become a little more depressed. Is that right?"

"Yes." His body remained the same.

"What do you feel in your body right now?"

"I'm nauseated," he said flatly, gazing into his palm. Nausea meant we needed to regulate his high anxiety.

"Does the nausea happen often?"

He nodded into his hand.

"Have you investigated it with a doctor?" I needed to rule out a medical diagnosis so Walter didn't go to a therapist for a medical issue only a doctor could treat. Conversely, people often go to a doctor for an issue only a therapist can treat.

"Yes, I've asked doctors," he said to his hand.

"And they didn't find anything?"

He shook his head back and forth with his hand still attached.

"Nausea is often a sign of high anxiety. It's a sign your anxiety is too high."

He finally removed his hand from his face and looked directly at me.

"Really?" A hint of optimism could be heard in his voice. He now had a label for this mysterious nausea.

As I watched the cycle of depression followed by the healthy drive for relief, I could feel a growing warmth for Walter.

I told Walter that nausea is a type of anxiety called *smooth muscle anxiety*. The smooth muscles are the ones we can't move on purpose. They line the gastrointestinal tract and exist in the urinary system, arteries, and veins.

"Nausea is whoa-wait-we-must-slow-down anxiety," I continued. "Let's listen to your body's message and slow down. Is there still nausea right now?"

He checked his body, straining to focus inward.

"Yes . . ."

Since explaining often helps to lower anxiety when it's too high, I went on.

"Nausea is a sign of high anxiety. Our bodies have a limit to how much feeling it can take without getting super anxious and feeling unsafe. Tension is under the threshold anxiety. Nausea, migraines, acid reflux, bowel issues, lightheadedness, blurry vision, hearing issues—those are all over the threshold."

"Yes, yes, yes . . ." he said eagerly. Tension was returning to his body, which meant his anxiety was getting regulated by my explanations. While some defenses are harmful, others serve a helpful purpose at certain times. I had used the defense of intellectualization, which is where we use the thinking part of our brain to process information. This defense is helpful when anxiety is over the threshold. Thinking and reflecting take the heat off the emotional part of the brain and help regulate anxiety. When Walter went over his body's anxiety threshold, I intellectualized to help him process. It succeeded. Tension returned to his muscles.

"Moving your feet or fidgeting with your hands," I continued. "That's when you're tense or sighing or moving around like this." I lifted myself off the couch and repositioned my body to show him. "That means you're under the threshold."

"Yeah, I do that a lot!" Walter said with a bright laugh. "Okay, over and under the threshold. I think I get it." He finished with a sigh, which was another sign of muscle tension.

"Do you want to see if we can figure out what's making you nauseated and depressed right now so you can be free from these symptoms? To look underneath these symptoms and this tension so you can have hope and energy?"

"Oh, god, yes," he replied to the floor, his feet shifting and then bouncing.

Walter seemed to hover right around his anxiety threshold—the point at which his body transitioned from too much anxiety (nausea and muscle limpness) to the optimal state of anxiety for change and growth (muscle tension). Knowing this threshold would help me benchmark Walter's progress. I had yet to ask him what lay beneath his anxiety. Whatever it was, we would help him face what he avoided. If we avoided his issues and feelings, therapy would become chitchat, and he would not experience enduring change.

Exploring what we avoid also inspires hope. And to a depressed person, hope is everything.

5

Michelle: The Lies My Defenses Told

As soon as I felt the tension headache, I wanted to tell Dr. A about my history of head pain. I didn't want to acknowledge that my hands were in the shape of claws or my jaw had an urge to bite. Instead, I wanted to tell Dr. A that I had a six-year-long headache.

"My head is killing me all of a sudden," I told Dr. A. "I have to tell you about my history with head pain."

"And your feelings here toward me that are making you put up these barriers?" Dr. A asked, brushing aside my wish for story time. One part of my body went up in flames of rage while another part of my body tried to snuff them out. I wanted to tell him about my head, yet if I did, I feared I would be difficult. If I changed the subject from my feelings toward him, I feared I would be doing the wrong thing. I didn't want to look weak or, even worse, like an avoidant therapist.

Also, I knew Dr. A was right to brush aside my wish to tell my story. My goal for therapy was to learn everything I could about myself, such as what feelings were hidden by my avoidance. Right now, Dr. A was taking that wish more seriously than I was.

Dr. A saw more clearly that my story, while true and important, was a way to avoid my feelings toward him in that moment. It can be hard to tell if a story has the purpose of covering anxiety-producing material. One way to discern if something we've experienced, thought, or done is a defense is if our anxiety drops. Avoiding what makes us anxious makes us feel comfortable. If our anxiety is too high, a defense helps bring our anxiety down to the optimal level. Yet if our anxiety is already at the optimal level, a defense slows the process. We avoid what we need to face. In my case, I was right below the line of my anxiety being too high. My level of anxiety told Dr. A I could face my emotions toward him, even if my defenses fought against it.

"But what if the story about your head is true?" you might ask. Well, one truth can be enlisted to cover up another truth. A true story can still help us avoid another truth.

"But what's the harm in the therapist hearing the story, even if it's a defense?" you might ask. In many cases, the therapist would be helping the patient avoid what they need to face. If they tell their stories rather than face what makes them anxious, they just get better at avoidance. And the person behind the defenses continues to suffer.

If Dr. A hadn't brushed aside my urge to tell him the story of my head pain, this would have been my watered-down story: "I had a headache for six years. Now, I feel better. The doctors told me I would still get headaches from time to time, so it's something that happens, something I'll have to deal with for the rest of my life. It's no big deal. The only thing that works for me are opioids. Thankfully, it's all behind me now."

And that would have been all I said and all I believed.

At the time, I didn't know that this version of my story was a lie told by my defenses. This story came from my dismissing, pleasing, avoidant, denying, minimizing, and self-neglecting defenses that didn't want me to know—or share—the truth. And I had no idea I had those defenses.

> Dismissing: *It's all behind me now.*
> Pleasing: *I'm easy.*
> Avoidant: *Nothing to see here!*
> Denying: *It's no big deal.*
> Minimizing: *I must take opioids forever. No big deal.*
> Self-neglecting: *Who, me?*
> Truth: *I have massive trauma.*

My defenses would have told the story because I didn't yet have the capacity to experience my emotional pain. These emotions made me anxious, thus I used defenses to fend off my anxiety about emotions. Defenses either wiped away my memories or labeled what happened to me as Not Important.

What I could have told Dr. A was that the headache began on November 3, 2007, at exactly 2:30 a.m. I was twenty-two years old. When the headache began, it felt like an enraged and invisible hand grabbed my skull and refused to let go.

What I couldn't tell Dr. A was that I was smack in the middle of an early life crisis when the headache began. I didn't know I was miserable. My first job out of college was chosen by one of my most common defenses, which was pleasing. Instead of looking for graduate schools to become a therapist, I took a detour. I planned to get two years of business experience, go to a dad-approved highbrow business school for two years, and then become a therapist. My dad thought I'd be a natural in business consulting. I loved seeing myself in his eyes. What's the harm in living his dream for a couple of years, especially if it made me feel special? So I accepted a consulting job outside of Washington, DC, near my boyfriend. But my new job was not that of an IT consultant, as advertised. And, after my boyfriend dumped his Chinese food in my bathtub during a drunken weeknight, I discovered he was also not as advertised. I sat in heavy traffic, did a job I despised, and wondered what was wrong with me because I hated every minute of it. I tried to make things better by breaking up with the bathtub boyfriend and beginning a new relationship. Then, on November 3 at 2:30 a.m. the headache began.

I couldn't have told Dr. A any of this because my dismissing, pleasing, avoidant, denying, minimizing, self-attacking, and self-neglecting defenses had tossed all these details away in the box labeled Not Important.

I also couldn't tell Dr. A how I related to my headache because I didn't notice. I didn't notice the impact of something like a brief conversation with my father after the pain hadn't stopped for a few days.

"This isn't going to affect work this week, is it?" my dad had asked three days into the headache.

I didn't know how to answer his question. Headaches were supposed to last only a few hours. This one hadn't stopped. I didn't realize then that he seemed more worried about how the headache would affect my work than how it affected me. That realization, along with many others, would come later. Instead of seeing reality, I joined my dad in his denial. I deployed a common type of defense called *self-attack*. If feeling anger toward the person we depended on makes them uncomfortable (anxious), we protect our caretaker by turning anger back to ourselves. Our anger gets redirected onto us. Thus, instead of the other person (my dad) being the problem, I was the problem. With self-attack, the problem was no longer how my dad responded to me. I could call myself the problem. Phew. I get to stay close to Dad.

Self-attack takes many forms. In this case, I flooded with shame at the thought of letting my headaches affect my work. I wouldn't be at my best, and for that, I felt like a failure, a suboptimal person who couldn't figure out how to be her best self while suffering from a severe headache. And my dad was there for me. I had no excuses. This was the story my self-attack and shame told me.

Since I didn't know the difference between my defenses and reality, I couldn't have told Dr. A about any of this. I still had the same defenses as I sat in front of Dr. A during our first session.

I still had the same defenses when I saw my first neurologist, who, after over two thousand hours of constant head pain (nearly three months), asked me, "How would you say you were feeling in general?" His eyes briefly left his paper to meet mine.

"Well, my job isn't stressful, and my personal life is great," I must have said because that's exactly what's written in my medical record. I wasn't lying to him. My job wasn't stressful, I thought. Boringly easy, in fact. My personal life was great, I thought. Nothing significant had happened, I thought. After all, I had a well-paying job, a car, and an apartment. People had it much worse than me.

While those facts were true, I wish I had the capacity to tell the doctor the other truths in my life. *Pain has turned my life upside down. I graduated from college and moved to a new city. My ex-boyfriend had a drinking problem, and I broke up with him in a cruel and insensitive way that I feel terrible about. My new boyfriend likes work more than me. I hate my job. I don't know if I care about business. I fear my dad will be devastated if I don't go to Harvard Business School. What should I do with my life? I don't know how to be reasonable with myself. I've had excruciating head pain for over 2,065 hours with no explanation or relief. Please help me.*

Instead, I said, "My job isn't stressful, and my personal life is great."

No big deal. I didn't realize I was in denial, ignoring myself.

I needed to be easy.

And I would have been trying to be easy if I told Dr. A the story of my headache from the perspective of my defenses, which would have been, "I had a headache for six years. Now, I feel better. The doctors told me I would still get headaches from time to time, so it's something that happens, something I'll have to deal with for the rest of my life. It's no big deal. The only thing that works for me are opioids. Thankfully, it's all behind me now."

This was far from the whole truth.

6

Emma: Wallflower

When there are no medical solutions to physical pain, people worry that they look hysterical or crazy or are making up their pain. This is far from reality. There's real pain, real effects, and the pain and suffering are really in the body. There is something wrong.

But there's a catch. Real physical pain sometimes has a psychological cause. For instance, Emma struggled with jaw pain, headaches, teeth grinding, and acid reflux. Jaw pain, tension headaches, and teeth grinding can be caused by anxiety in our voluntary muscles (meaning the muscles that we can move by choice). When someone looks visibly tense, they have tension in their voluntary muscles. While tension is an optimal level of anxiety for learning in therapy, if chronic, it can wreak havoc on the body. Emma also had acid reflux, which can be caused by anxiety in our involuntary muscles (the muscles we can't move by choice). Acid reflux is a higher level of anxiety than tension in our muscles. Tension meant Emma was below her threshold of anxiety. Acid reflux meant she was above her threshold of anxiety. I had to gather more evidence to find out if her physical pains were caused by anxiety and psychological processes.

Emma saw all the doctors she could think of. When she got to her dentist, she thought she had the answer. Her dentist said she had headaches because she grinds her teeth.

"Sure. But why do you grind?" I asked.

Emma looked at me as if she was waiting for me to give a magical answer.

There was more silence.

"Well, I don't know!" she snapped while looking straight into my eyes.

"Would you like to find out?"

"Well, I suppose maybe."

Suppose maybe was the defense of hypothetical speech, which is a way to hide our opinions from others. Two feet firmly planted on the fence. When hypothetical speech masquerades as definitiveness, we can't be known by another. But it was not the time to tell her about this defense. After all, I still didn't know the problem with which she wanted my help. Also, if I pointed out defenses that hurt her now, she wouldn't know why I was pointing them out. I might seem critical instead of helpful.

"I also pick my nails and heels!" Emma unexpectedly spit out as if she couldn't contain her words. Then, she disappeared by gazing out the window. She wanted to be seen, and yet by looking out the window, she also said, *Don't you dare see me! Don't come close. See me! Don't see me!*

"I'd like to stop picking. That would be good if you could help me with that. I mean, if you can help," she added.

Her recurring concern seemed to be *Can I be helped?* I was already hearing unconscious whispers of her problem, of her history. Her previous therapists didn't help her. Who else didn't help her? Apparently, history taught Emma not to depend on anyone. From Emma's point of view, why should this therapy be any different than her other failed attempts to get help?

"What's your understanding of what gets in the way of an intimate relationship?" I asked, trying to identify an internal emotional problem. Did Emma see her issues with dating as something outside of her control?

"I have no idea," she said with a scoff.

"What behaviors contribute to your issues with dating?"

Emma simply shrugged.

Aha! She put up a wall between us by being vague and dismissive, which answered my question about what behaviors contributed to her issues with dating.

"Nothing comes to mind?"

Emma scrunched up her nose and said, "It's like, I walk away and don't care."

If someone says they walk away and don't care, they'll likely walk away from me. If someone says they fake intimacy, they're likely to do this with me. What they do outside, they'll probably do in therapy, too, which is good news because we can study these relational processes as they occur between us.

Emma had difficulty describing her internal emotional problems. While some can describe their problems in words, others show their problems through actions. Emma belonged to the latter category. Instead of vocalizing her problems, she demonstrated them in her behavior, notably distancing herself not only from me but also from others.

"So besides walking away and not caring, your role in not being able to date is unclear?" I asked.

She said nothing, silently withdrawing from me again.

"You're not sure what you do to contribute to not having a meaningful relationship?" I asked again.

Emma shrugged and dove back into her cuticle exploits. She was constructing a wall between us.

"You pick at your nails," I noted. "Pause and look away."

She giggled, then became silent. I decided to become silent as well.

Therapy fails if people come, sit, and wait for the magic to happen. *Do unto me your magic, crazy wizard therapist! Wave your wand!* But I can't do therapy by myself. I must work with Emma, and we must work hard. In this moment of silence, I demonstrated that I wouldn't be the only one working hard.

The silence continued.

"I don't like being observed!" she finally blurted out. Tension rippled through her body, causing subtle twitches as she restlessly shifted on the couch. Emma had unveiled the crux of her dilemma: a deep desire to be seen, which had prompted her presence in my office. Paradoxically, though, being noticed felt unsafe to her, leading her to adopt various methods of concealment. In her hidden state, she became invisible, creating a barrier that prevented anyone from truly connecting with her.

"I'm usually a wallflower," she said. "I stay back, watch others. And now I'm here, and I can tell you're noticing everything."

"Yes, I'm noticing you. Would you like that connection and attention to feel safe so you don't have to hide? We're seeing more clearly that you don't feel comfortable being seen, and therefore you hide," I continued. "This would have a great impact on your ability to connect."

She crossed her arms over her stomach and spat out, "I don't know!"

A defiant position is when a client treats the therapist like someone who is barking orders. The defiant position says, *Make me! See if you have any power over me!* Emma came to me of her own volition because she wanted my help, yet she treated me like a powerful dictator with desires unlike her own. Whom do I represent in her past that makes her distance this way?

While it might seem that Emma was difficult, she was quite helpful. She was yelling about the very problem for which she sought my help.

She was saying, *I don't notice myself.*

When we don't notice ourselves, we neglect ourselves. When we neglect ourselves, we suffer massive pain. Imagine having a child you never looked at, spoke to, asked questions about, or interacted with. This would be neglect, and that child would be in a lot of pain.

I told her all this.

"Yes," she said with a sigh. "I see what you're saying. But neglect sounds so dramatic."

"And calling it dramatic is a way to dismiss the truth."

"I call things dramatic all the time. Or stupid. Or cheesy."

I nodded, waiting to see if she heard herself.

A profound silence lingered, unbroken. She couldn't hear herself. Her body trembled within its silent cocoon.

"You want to avoid the truth because it isn't what you hoped it would be," I said, breaking the stiffness of silence.

While some might focus on the intensity of my words, I must focus on the intensity of Emma's defenses. After all, they caused her loneliness, tension, body pain, and relationship problems. As her therapist, it's imperative that I don't overlook her. I must not confuse Emma's defenses for who she is, for who lies beneath. Instead, I must show compassion by attentively engaging with her and subsequently guiding her in recognizing the defenses that create her loneliness.

She exhaled sharply. "No, I get it," she said. Her mouth relaxed, and the trembling stopped. She still looked tense in her back and shoulders. "I don't pay attention to myself. And I don't like it when you do."

"It appears there's an internal mechanism within you that tends to overlook, dismiss, and neglect your own needs and experiences, resulting in a lack of closeness with yourself. This, in turn, hinders others from forming close connections with you." She nodded softly while looking into my eyes, letting out a small exhale between thinly parted lips. She was with me.

However, she soon started picking at her nails and gazing out of the window once more.

A genuine motivation led Emma to my office, yet another compelling force pushed her away. To give her healthy desire a chance, we needed to figure out how to reach her.

7

Michelle: Clawing Out

When Dr. A asked about my feelings toward him, I wanted to tell my story, look at the floor, rub away my tattoo, and laugh over my feelings. Yet I also wanted to face my feelings. This is therapy in a nutshell: help me, don't help me. See me, don't see me. Expose me to the truth, keep me away from reality. One side is our innate emotional immune system calling out for health and truth. The other side is our resistance, which kept us safe with our caregivers. Therapeutic work helps tip the scale in favor of the healing force.

While I wanted to distract Dr. A with a watered-down tale of my incessant headache, he was on the side of my healing force. He rejected my invitation to dismiss me and instead worked to radically accept whatever I was trying to avoid.

He was the first person to do so. I was pissed and grateful.

"What feelings are coming up toward me?" Dr. A asked again.

"I have anger toward you. And I also want to tell you about my head pain." (I had feelings I wanted to avoid by telling a watered-down story.)

"And in your claws?" (Dr. A rejected my invitation to ignore my feelings.)

I looked down at my hands, which had become powerful with curled and strong fingers.

I laughed.

He didn't.

I saw the impulse, the urge in my hands. *Is this what he wants me to do? Is this what I want to do?* Yes. It was. I wanted to scratch. As I slowly moved my hands in a scratching motion, a picture appeared in my mind of what would happen if I acted out my impulses. In the image, my nails scratched his face. This uprising of anger was not the same as freely acting out the impulse, which has little to no lasting therapeutic value. Instead, I was experiencing powerful urges, impulses, and wishes toward Dr. A without acting them out. My body was learning how to feel in connection with another person in a way where no one would have to get hurt.

I continued with my hands in claws. Recognizing the value of relinquishing control, I decided to embrace the surrender of my defenses. My wish was to uncover the depths hidden beneath the surface of my awareness. I let go of control over my facial expression and gritted my teeth. I felt a desire to go over to him and knock his head against the wall. From my comfort-refusing chair, I mimed and described the scene slowly: my hands coming around his head, grabbing and knocking it against the drywall behind him. I pictured the large dent left in the wall, his head cracked like an egg. Blood pooled out from the cracks in his skull. I was shocked at how easily the images came to me. These desires and images felt new to me. Typically, I didn't find myself harboring a desire to inflict harm on others by smashing their heads.

Then, the anger drained out of my body, and tears formed in my eyes.

"Can you see the eyes?" he asked, pointing to the floor beside me. He was referring to the eyes of the head I had mentally shattered, and I understood the intention behind his question. He wanted to help me uncover the emotions triggered by this brutal attack, guiding me to understand why I had built a defensive wall composed of head pain, storytelling, people pleasing, dismissal, distraction, and denial.

"Can you see the eyes?" he asked again.

Eyes serve as a gateway to the profound, unconscious connections within us, acting as an emotional power source. Try it: look into someone's eyes, and simply try to feel. And I mean try to *feel*, not think. A feeling is anything on the emotional spectrums of healthy anger, love, sexual desire, happiness, guilt, and sadness. Feelings are not thoughts. "I feel like you don't like me" or "I feel he is a nice person" are thoughts. If you wish, try it. Look into someone's eyes. Your reaction will either be a feeling, anxiety, or defense. Your reaction will tell you something about your invisible puppet strings.

What did I not want to see as Dr. A invited me to look into the eyes? What were all my defenses about?

"The eyes?" he asked again.

I looked away, re-creating the wall. I scanned the room for details. I looked at his diplomas and book titles. I felt the pain in my head. While I still wanted to tell him about my headache, something unexpected was emerging from a place inside me, somewhere I'd never been.

8

Walter: The Question No One Asks

"What feelings are coming up *toward me*?" I asked Walter after his body became tense and his nausea subsided. Walter was hovering around the threshold at which his anxiety was too high to explore his feelings, but in this moment, he was tense; therefore, we could help him face what he had always avoided.

I know feelings have a bad reputation. What's the point of being in touch with feelings? Don't they get in the way of reason? Aren't emotions for weak or needy people? Aren't we supposed to hide them? Can't we think them away? The positive feelings might be okay, but we should certainly avoid the bad ones, right?

Wrong. Devoid of emotions, our passage through life lacks a guiding compass. Feelings serve as our guide, leading us toward desires and away from aversions. Feelings are the glue that creates connection and intimacy. Bonding with others hinges on understanding and embracing our feelings. To nurture healthy attachments, it's crucial to be conscious of our emotions and urges, finding a balance between acknowledging them without impulsively acting on them or suppressing them. Feelings are an antidepressant. The belief that Walter could get rid of his feelings and be alive and well was a pipe dream. He was (barely) living proof.

"What feelings are coming up toward me?" I asked a second time.

Walter said nothing. He was still tense, so I asked again.

"What feelings are coming up toward me that make you tense right now and look out the window?" The third time.

"Oh, nothing. No feelings toward you," he said to the window. Walter emptied himself out of feelings.

A common question I get asked is "Do I always have to be feeling something?" I often respond, "Well, are you dead? Because the only time you don't feel is when you're dead or in a coma. Or on certain drugs." Or clients say, "But I don't want to feel!" I remind them, "That's what death is for." This wish for an emotional void is a form of emotional suicide. Now, I could see one reason Walter was depressed. He disconnected from everything, choosing to be emotionally dead while physically alive.

He was still tense, so I asked a fourth time. "What feelings are coming up toward me that make you tense right now? Look out the window?"

Some might also wonder if this question is a cliché. It can be. Television and movie therapists consistently ask this question. "And how does that make you feel?" That question is pointless and cliché. It's an incomplete, irrelevant question.

I was asking Walter a different question. My inquiry centered on our relationship, illuminating the links between unconscious feelings within it and the ensuing anxiety and defenses. I needed to ask about feelings toward me as they made him uneasy, leading him to unconsciously prefer connecting with a window instead of with me. If he continued this, it could make him feel lonely and depressed during our therapy. His defense is causing him distress in the moment. By asking this question, I can help him see that his suffering is caused by anxiety and defenses.

My question to Walter, "What feelings are coming up toward me?," implicitly says the following:

1. "I know you're in there, Walter. You can come out with whatever you feel."
2. "It's okay to have feelings toward *me*."
3. "You *do* have feelings toward me."
4. "You have things inside of you you're not aware of."
5. "Feelings make you anxious."
6. "Your anxiety about your feelings toward me makes you put up a wall."
7. "You can have more than one feeling at the same time."

When I ask this question, most are terrified they don't know the answer, and 99 percent of them won't. Walter doesn't know. I didn't know right away. I didn't expect him or anyone else to know. If they knew what they felt and could feel it, they probably wouldn't need therapy. The answers I can expect are the defenses and anxiety that cause their problems. The point of the question is to see Walter's response. How does Walter avoid his emotions? How do his defenses hurt him? How do his defenses create his presenting problems? Every response Walter offers shows me where he needs my help. Therefore, every response is perfect. Unconscious anxiety and defenses are never wrong answers.

I can't simply overlook or bypass Walter's defenses either, as doing so would allow these defenses to persist and inflict unnecessary suffering. Also, it would be a therapeutic betrayal if I saw his problem yet didn't point out or treat the cause. Imagine if a doctor prescribed pain medication for your back pain and you went home, looked in the mirror, and saw a knife sticking out of your back. You'd wonder why the doctor didn't address the cause of the pain and instead just threw a pill at it.

I could not send Walter home without pointing out the defenses that cause his suffering.

I asked Walter a fifth time. Someone was home. I had to keep knocking—especially since he had invited me over in the first place.

"What feelings are coming up toward me that are making you tense right now and look out the window?"

He responded by staring out the window.

Another common question I get asked is "Why are you asking about feelings toward you when you haven't done anything to cause them?" Well, I have—by existing as a potential helping other. The trigger for unconscious feelings is my mere existence as someone on which they need to depend. Depending on a person triggers unconscious processes. Wanting help triggers unconscious feelings based on past experiences in relationships. If you were let down, ignored, dismissed, betrayed, abandoned, stowed away, tortured, manipulated, disappointed, neglected, gaslit, or beaten in the past, relating to another human will often trigger unconscious feelings. If you have experienced any of these, forming new relationships can be terrifying. You might not even be aware of your terror. Walter certainly wasn't. His anxiety told me what his words couldn't: connection is frightening. His defenses told me how he deals with relational danger.

"What feelings are coming up toward me that are making you tense right now and look out the window?" I asked him a sixth time.

At this point, the desire to leave Walter alone and stop bothering him is also common. Yet why would I leave him alone with a knife in his back?

Walter kept looking away as if he didn't hear me.

"What feelings are coming up toward me that are making you anxious right now, looking away out the window?" I asked again. "Do you see how looking away functions as a barrier between us?"

"Feeling toward you?" Walter suddenly said, his eyes finally with mine. "I don't want to do something!" This statement was a negation, which meant feelings were moving toward the surface of his awareness. A negation is a display of the war between the defenses (*Don't feel! It wasn't good for you when we were growing up!*) and the will to live a truthful and fulfilling life of connection (*You feel! Share it! Please!*). At this specific point in therapy, I could translate his sentence "I don't want to do something!" to "I want to do something!" His reaction was a sign to keep going because the truth was trying to be heard, seen, and felt.

But suddenly, Walter stared at me vacantly. Something had changed. Before, he was tense and detached. Now, his eyes were empty, stuck, frozen on my face. His anxiety was now over the threshold. Rather than relating to his palm, the window, or the floor, he wasn't connected to anything. Nobody was home. This was not a bad thing. It would be bad only if I didn't notice it and kept on asking about his feelings. It was time to regulate his anxiety.

"What just happened there?" I asked, gently waving my hand over my face.

He wiggled his head as if to shake it from a dream. His eyes refocused.

"Ah . . . I don't know!" Walter said, now sounding thrilled. He looked back at me and repositioned himself, sitting upright. Since his anxiety was down again, below his threshold, I could continue to explore.

"And so, what feelings are coming up toward me that make you anxious and go away?"

His eyes looked at mine and stopped dead. Vacant. No one was home again. He was too anxious again. We were hovering right over his anxiety threshold, which had changed. Now, Walter was able to remain tense and distanced for many rounds of the question. Initially, he went over his anxiety threshold much faster. This was a promising sign.

"What happened?" he asked me.

"Well, when you go away like that, it's like no one's home, right? Your IQ crashes? Brain vanishes?"

Walter nodded vigorously.

"That's the highest kind of anxiety," I continued. "I know these are a lot of words, and I'll repeat them."

I explained that anxiety that takes out the senses is the other type of over-the-threshold anxiety, known as *cognitive-perceptual disruption*. Someone might hear a ringing in their ears, or their ears might feel like they're stuffed with cotton. Their balance might falter. The room might spin. Their vision might become blurry, or they can get tunnel vision. Their thoughts might start and then stop. It could be a dreamy feeling. Like smooth muscle anxiety, this form of anxiety means that their overall anxiety is too high. (See Examples of Anxiety and Resulting Issues in the appendix.)

"Oh, thank god you're going to repeat yourself!" he said, laughing. I felt another burst of energy inside my chest. It was wonderful to watch him learn and emerge. Maybe I could help him.

"This is another type of whoa-wait-we-must-slow-down anxiety. When I asked that question about feelings toward me, you kind of—"

"I kind of go away! Either out the window or out of my mind." Now, Walter was not only understanding it, he was also experiencing it, which would make the lesson stick.

"Exactly! Oh, I forgot to ask, have you ever had any accidents, traumatic brain injuries, or anything?"

"Oh! No, nothing like that . . . except for, you know, I guess smoking pot all the time!" With this statement he lifted his body about a foot off the couch and slammed it back down. "I always pushed through the anxiety, ignored it, I guess. I want to stop doing that because I'm drowning!"

We both sat in silence, his last word hanging in the air.

By always ignoring his anxiety, he always ignored himself. When we ignore ourselves, we can get depressed and drown in depression's deep, thick waters. Most people think ignoring or pushing through anxiety will make it go away, yet it rarely does. Instead, ignoring anxiety usually makes it worse. Furthermore, neglecting our anxiety communicates to our innermost selves that our discomfort holds little significance for us. Walter was now learning that depression is a normal response to someone constantly ignoring you, especially if that someone is you.

We worked like this until the end of the session, inviting him to relate to me, seeing how he avoided relating to me, regulating his anxiety when needed, and helping him observe himself without attacking himself. In doing this, we were already engaging in the healthiest relationship he had ever had: *You can feel toward me without hurting or hiding yourself. We will pay attention to you together. You can come out of hiding.*

At the end of the session, Walter stood up and clamped his hands together.

"This was exactly what I was hoping it would be," he said. "I really liked my past therapist, but, uh, this is much different. Incredibly challenging. Not just talking. It's very different. Thank you."

"My privilege," I replied.

9

Michelle: The Eyes

While I squirmed in his comfort-refusing, bullshit-rejecting chair, Dr. A looked calm and determined.

"And the eyes?" he asked again, trying to help me connect with the emotions that followed my rage. "What happens when you look in the eyes?"

Instead of looking into the eyes of the head I had smashed, I kept thinking about where my head pain fell on the pain scale. When you have chronic pain, you constantly evaluate your pain on a scale from 0 to 10. On the wall of most doctors' offices is a pain scale, from no pain to I-think-I'm-going-to-die pain. Little faces illustrate each number. The faces seem relatively unbothered until they reach a 6. This was absurd. If these scales were to be accurate for those in chronic pain, the 10 face should have an *X* over each eye. The 8 face should depict a person about to jump off a cliff. The 6 face should be the 10 because pain above a 6 slams your life into a wall. Pain above a 4 intrudes upon most thoughts.

With Dr. A, I was at a 6 before I smashed his head against the wall. Now, I was a 4.

"What happens when you look in the eyes?" Dr. A gestured toward my mental image of his body sprawled with a shattered skull on the ground between us.

He was relentless. And he had to be. The therapeutic partnership must be more relentless than the patient's defenses. If their defenses try to block emotions 1,285 times, the therapeutic partnership must block them 1,286 times. We must tip the scales to serve the patient's goals.

I knew if I connected with the eyes of the head I had smashed, I would discover more of what my defenses hid.

Though it might appear that I'd unraveled the revelation that my defenses concealed an urge for violence, this wasn't the sole truth lurking in the shadows of my unconscious. In numerous instances, anger is merely the starting point. Both Dr. A and I knew my defenses weren't there just to hide the anger. It was about what would come after the rage.

"What happens when you look in the eyes?" Dr. A asked again.

Suddenly, my mind darted from the projected image of his cracked skull to a memory of a photo taken of the back of my head after half my hair was shaved and my head sewn back up. It looked as though a six-inch zipper had been installed in the back of my head for instant access. I pictured what was underneath my thin, blond hair. My scalp looked like it had been mauled by Freddy Krueger.

"The eyes?"

I flashed to a piece of paper the doctor printed out and handed to me after an appointment.

Current outpatient prescriptions:

oxyCODONE-Acetaminophen 5-325 mg
morphine 30 mg
Memantine (NAMENDA) 10 mg
Onabotulinumtoxin (BOTOX) 100 unit IM Recon Soln
NorethindroneEthinyl Estradiol-Iron 1-20 mg-mcg

clonazePAM 0.5 mg

cloNIDine 0.1 mg

Propranolol 80 mg

BD INSULIN SYRINGE ULT-FINE II 1 mL 31 x 5/16"

Dihydroergotamine 1 mg/mL Inj Soln

METHERGINE 0.2 mg

Butalbital-Acetaminophen-Caff 50-325-40 mg

EFFEXOR XR 150 MG

TOPAMAX 25 MG

"Michelle," I heard Dr. A say. "What about the eyes? The eyes here? Do you want to see? Or do you not want to see?" He stretched out his hand and pointed to where I had imagined his body after I hit his head against the wall. Instead of looking, I examined the now-faded tattoo on my wrist. I remembered that when I had first put it on, the colors were vivid, beautiful even. I continued to escape the moment with Dr. A by thinking of my dad. How would he feel if he saw the tattoo and thought it was real? I loved my dad deeply. When I was young, I woke up before the sun to watch him get ready for work. It was our only time together. My dad worked one hundred hours a week, often traveling to multiple continents in the same week and was commonly gone on weekends. I would lift my tiny head after hearing him stir in his bedroom on the other side of the wall and quietly venture into my parents' bathroom. I watched him brush his teeth. I watched him run his hands over each tie before picking one out. And finally, I looked out the dining room window, watching him walk down the driveway to the train station and disappear. When he faded away, I pulled away too, feeling the weight of his absence.

"And what about the eyes?" Dr. A repeated, trying to block the routes I took to escape my feelings. My anxiety was in the form of tension. Thus, it was at the optimal level to head toward what I avoided. The metal detector was beeping, and Dr. A was trying to help me experience who I was. Yet I kept mentally escaping in other directions.

"Or do you not want to see?" Dr. A asked with strength in his voice.

"I want to see!" I exclaimed as I looked him in the eye.

Suddenly, the room became blurry. My anxiety was now too high.

Since defenses help anxiety diminish, anxiety increases when defenses are put aside. My heightened anxiety signaled that my defenses had just been pushed aside. High anxiety is helpful information that tells us where our capacities start and stop. When you find the threshold where anxiety goes above optimal levels, you have a benchmark to keep track of progress and capacity.

I looked at Dr. A and then back to the image of the cracked skull on the ground. I tried to look, to see the eyes in the bloody skull, the skull I had smashed against the wall.

A thought brought me away. Dr. A knew nothing about what had happened to me. How could I not tell him about my history?

Everything I was doing said, *Help me face what I avoid. Leave me alone with my defenses!*

We were watching my history unfold in front of us: *Feel, yet do not feel. Do not have rage. Entertain those around you. Do not be annoying. Avoid, think, don't make things a big deal, get physical pain instead of emotions, and run, run, run away as fast as you can from emotions toward others.*

Yet gradually, the healing force within me was gaining momentum, unlocking something deeper. We were going somewhere I had never been.

"Try. Try to see the eyes," Dr. A said gently.

Anger rose up in my body, and the projector in my brain cast an image of his body on the carpet with his head cracked open after I had smashed it against the wall behind him.

"I'm there, on the floor, like you said. And my head is cracked, yes?" Dr. A asked. He pointed to my imaginary picture on the ground between us. "If you look in the eyes." I looked down and tried to see the image of his head cracked open like a soft-boiled egg. I quickly looked away, scanning for carpet stains. "The eyes?" he repeated, bringing me back to myself.

"I don't want to be difficult!"

He said nothing.

"I don't see your eyes," I said.

"Try," he said firmly.

Slowly, I looked at the image in my mind of his face, and the eyes came to me.

But they weren't his. I tried to blink away the image and said nothing.

"What color are they?" he asked. Tears pushed through my eyes as I worried about whether my mascara would run. I didn't want to look ugly.

Then, I looked at the eyes, trying to focus.

"Blue. And gray," I said.

The gray-blue eyes sharpened into focus. Then, a nose, cheeks, and a complete face materialized, coalescing into the unmistakable image of my mother. There she was, from the projector in my mind, on the ground where Dr. A's body used to be. Her head was cracked, just as Dr. A's had been.

I burst into tears of shock and grief. With my defenses pushed aside, my unconscious had linked the anger toward Dr. A to its original source: my mom.

The patterns of our unconscious dynamics are like fractals—complex mathematical shapes that repeat themselves over and over for infinity. Like fractals, our unconscious patterns are the same no matter where you look. The relational pattern—the way I related with my parents—was now being played out with Dr. A.

When we are born, we have the human passions of love, anger, sadness, happiness, fear, a wish to bond, a need for comfort, and a need to bond for survival. Humans can be curious about sex, our bodies, violence, competition, and much more. And we are born with our own unique temperament. Each of us is a unique soup of human complexities and intricacies.

But what if our humanity wasn't acceptable to our caregivers? Relying on someone who would turn away when our vulnerable human aspects are revealed can lead to pain and fear after exposing our true selves. *Where did my person go? What do I do now?* We may feel angry that we were left alone, hurt and scared. *You didn't protect me! You scared me!* Our anger may come with violent urges, imagery, or even actual acting out of impulses. To a child, the urge or image of something violent may be as guilt inducing as acting on it. *Oh no! I can't think that! Especially not with the person I depend on for survival and comfort!* Consequently, we suppress these vulnerable aspects and devise strategies (defenses) to shield those we rely upon, ensuring their comfort and willingness to turn toward us once more. If we don't process and repair these emotions safely with another, the overall concept of humanness can become associated with rejection and pain. Best not to be human.

This pattern repeats whenever there is a new relationship. When we walk into therapy, the therapist's question "What can I help you with?" is really "How would you like to depend on me?" This new relationship triggers the invisible puppet strings to pull and tug, activating the unconscious process of feelings, which leads to our anxiety, which leads to defenses. And this all happens without our knowledge. If our conscious minds controlled this process, therapists would be out of a job. Only one session would be needed to point out the process, and then the conscious minds could go, "Oh, okay. I'll stop doing that." But this is not the case.

"This is so crazy to see," I said through tears after I saw my mom's head cracked open, her face scratched and bloody. I was experiencing the silent history stored in my body, the history that pulled at the strings of my defense mechanisms: *Do whatever you can to not be angry or make someone angry at you.* Dr. A was trying to help me break free of this impossible goal by accessing mixed emotions that lay dormant in my unconscious so I could be comfortable with what it meant to be me.

My defenses told a clear story: Emotions weren't tolerated. Stuff them down. Stuff them down with storytelling, head pain, avoidance, pleasing, minimizing, ignoring, doubting, denial, and self-attack. If I broke these unspoken rules, there were unspoken consequences (*You're no longer good*). My defense mechanisms pushed away rage toward my mom because I loved her, and because of this, I felt guilt about the rage.

A stirring began within me as I looked at the clear mental image of my mother's body on the floor. Like bees bursting from a knocked-over hive, memories with my mother exploded into my awareness. When defenses are ushered aside, memories, images, opinions, and feelings are free to come up. Picture a box containing the aspects of yourself that caregivers found unacceptable. To have the illusion of connection, we must get rid of the memories, opinions, and feelings that were unacceptable and put them in this box. Defenses sit on top of the box and make sure nothing escapes.

But then I entered therapy. Dr. A blocked my attempts to hide by inviting me to face what I avoided. He did not need me to protect him from what was inside me. He did not need me to put anything in the box. Slowly, my defenses moved aside, allowing the box to start to open. Memories flooded to the surface of my awareness, eager to be heard after decades of neglect.

I just wasn't sure if I was allowed to share them.

10

Emma: The Abused Body

"What feelings are coming up toward me that make you look away and not want to be seen? To hide behind this wall and not be known?" I finally asked Emma.

She could respond in three ways. She could respond with a defense, which would help me understand her. She could respond with anxiety, which would also help me understand her. Or she could respond with an emotion, which would help me understand her. Anything she did was helpful. I needed this information to help her understand her.

"What wall?" Emma asked with disgust on her face. This helped me understand how little she noticed about what was going on between her and another person.

"When you look away or don't answer me, this disconnects you from me. This puts a wall between us. Do you see this?"

Suddenly, her body stopped moving. Her body tension dropped as her anxiety increased.

"Did the tension just go away in your body?" I asked.

She drew her finger up and down her esophagus while making an ick face. "Yeah, my acid reflux," she said as if talking was painful. She swallowed hard.

It was time to regulate her anxiety, so I brought her through the series of events that led to her acid reflux, which also helped to observe her relational patterns with others.

"Let's see if we have this right. First, you had anxiety in the form of tension, and you put up a wall between us. The bricks of this wall were made of looking away, not responding to me, and picking at your nails instead of engaging with me."

Emma listened intently as I continued, looking directly at me.

"Then, when I pointed this out, when I saw *you*, unconscious feelings toward me became more intense, pushing your anxiety up. Anxiety increased, shifting from tension to acid reflux."

"But I don't have feelings toward you."

"Exactly. You either put up a wall and get tense or get acid reflux instead."

Emma said she hadn't noticed any of this. She didn't see any of this until I pointed it out. Of course she didn't notice. She ignored herself. What she couldn't tell me directly she demonstrated through signals in her body.

Emma still looked like she was in pain from her acid reflux, so I continued to draw connections between the events of the session so she could observe how her unconscious dynamics worked. By explaining the connection between feelings and anxiety, I was helping Emma *reflect* on her feelings rather than *feel* her feelings. This has the effect of increasing anxiety thresholds when someone is already over their anxiety threshold. Since Emma's body went over her anxiety threshold—she couldn't tolerate feeling, and her defenses weren't strong enough to regulate her anxiety—helping Emma to think again would regulate her anxiety back down to the optimal level. Thinking is also referred to as intellectualizing, which is a defense that helps regulate high anxiety. Some defenses are helpful in some cases and not helpful in others.

I repeated the observations over and over until she sighed and said, "I thought acid reflux was stress. My job is stressful. That's all it is."

"But right now, you're not at work. The tension is here in the room and increased as we spoke together. It increased as we worked to understand what you want my help with. It went up higher when I asked about your feelings toward me. It seems to increase because of what we're doing here together."

Emma nodded slowly, taking in my words.

"I don't know. I usually take my medicine, and it goes away. It's acid reflux, not anxiety."

"Acid reflux *is* anxiety, severe anxiety. And we can see what triggers the acid reflux. When I ask about feelings toward me, acid appears. Does the acid reflux follow how stressed or anxious you are?"

"Actually, yeah!" Her eyes briefly met mine, as if we had dug in the sand and found treasure together.

"There's a relationship between feelings and anxiety," I said, feeling hopeful. "Unconscious feelings can cause anxiety. We care about tension because tension causes you to grind or clench your teeth or get headaches. Oh, and your headaches, are they are tension headaches or migraines?"

"Right, tension headaches, definitely not migraines," she said, sitting up and reaching for her cuticles. Tension headaches are caused by muscle tension. While their effects are devastating, they're still a form of under-threshold anxiety. Migraine headaches, on the other hand, can be caused by the higher level of anxiety called smooth muscle anxiety.

"How often do these tension headaches happen?"

"They happen a lot. At work, sometimes other times."

"Do they happen on dates?" I asked, hoping for a piece of the puzzle.

"Yeah," she said through a tightening jaw. I waited for her to make the connection, to see that unconscious feelings were triggered by dates, causing anxiety, headaches, and harmful defenses that kept others away. I watched as tension crawled down her back, shoulders, and neck. Would she let herself see the life she hid inside her?

"Oh my god, I am such an idiot!" Emma blurted out. As soon as she did, the tension decreased in her body. "You must think I am such an idiot!" To reduce her anxiety, Emma shifted into the defense of self-attack: *I'm fat, dumb, ugly. I should have known that. What's wrong with me? I should be better. I'm such an idiot! Why can't I do this right? Will I ever get this? I should look better. I should be perfect. I can be perfect. Perfection is an achievable goal.* This is all self-attack.

"And now the acid reflux is gone!" she said as if we had performed a magic trick. But before we could share this moment of relief together, she shoved her excitement down and looked away. She couldn't have or share this positive feeling.

"Would it make sense to let me know every time you feel even a little bit of acid reflux? That way, we can see exactly what's causing it because whatever's causing it is right *here*." I pointed to her, to me, and then to both of us. She nodded slightly and began to pick her nails.

Emma's difficulty with intimate relationships was becoming clearer. She did everything she could to demolish any feelings within herself and between herself and another person. Without feelings, she was alone. Without feelings, she couldn't form connections. She used the defenses of self-dismissal (*My pain? Oh, it's nothing*), self-neglect (*I don't exist*), and self-attack (*I'm an idiot!*)—a killer trifecta—to avoid facing her feelings.

I had a hunch about what caused the internal mayhem in Emma because it was the same for almost everyone who came into my office. Anger came up when I pointed out her defenses and paid attention to her. *How dare you point out how I've protected myself?* At the same time, she was grateful when I pointed out her defenses and paid attention to her. *Thank you for finally seeing me and not buying into my barriers. Thank you for not confusing my walls with who I am as a person.*

Emma had unconscious mixed feelings toward me. Could she tell me this? Of course not. Her defenses kept her feelings and desires outside of her awareness. Yet I could see the anxiety and defenses, the signals of feelings rising closer to the surface.

It was probable that when Emma sought support and connection in the past, she experienced pain. The individuals who caused her distress likely dismissed her feelings and desires, prompting her to conceal her true self. A patient who exhibits self-neglect, self-dismissal, or self-attack may have acquired this behavior as a response to the way they were treated.

However, now it was Emma who treated herself this way. She was the only one who could do something about it. She didn't do it on purpose. It wasn't her fault. Yet once I helped her see those defenses, it would be her responsibility to do something about them.

"Ugh, this is all useless. Just, I don't know, being here. I don't think there is much we can do."

And there it was: Emma was now dismissing herself, me, and the therapy. The relational pattern making her lonely was in front of us. She was breaking up with me. And it was only our first date.

"That thought just came into your mind? What's the effect of that thought? Not the content, but the effect it has on you?"

"I feel like giving up!"

"Hopeless? Doomed? Even helpless? What's the point?"

She nodded aggressively.

"Like you do with dating?"

"That is . . . that is exactly what stops me from dating!" She put out her arms with her palms facing the ceiling as if to say, *So!?* She looked at me as if I were the dumbest person she'd ever met. I looked at her, waiting to see if she heard what she had said.

"I don't see the point!" she said.

As I temporarily lost hope that she would try to work with me, I realized I felt as Emma did. Hopeless! *Why connect with Emma if she won't work with me?* Her pattern emerged in me. My felt experience gave me more compassion for her.

The same pattern emerged in each of my patients. The pattern is this: If our feelings endangered an early bond we needed for our survival, those feelings will trigger anxiety—a signal of danger. And in response to that anxiety, defenses automatically rise to hide those feelings and protect those we love. Anxiety is the signal that feelings were dangerous in the past. Defenses are how we learned to protect others from our feelings to preserve the relationship we needed. How we ward off these unpleasant feelings is unique to each of us. Defenses silently tell the history of our suffering. Our defenses echo what others required of us.

My invitation for closeness ignited mixed unconscious feelings in Emma. These feelings caused her anxiety. Her defenses came in to stop the feelings and anxiety. And her hopelessness was a way to justify not connecting. The self-dismissal made her think that she didn't matter. Even worse, her self-attack made her feel like an idiot. This created an illusion: *Them, good. Emma, bad and alone.*

"Here with me," I said, "we can re-create the same symptoms and issues you have in dating. Like a pattern. There is a tendency to dismiss something you want. This dismissal and resulting lack of hope is here with me as it is with dating. Would you say this pattern hurts your dating life more than other elements of your life?"

She sighed. "Yes, it does. I see it." She tightened her mouth and pinched her lips together.

"Would you like to see what's causing these defenses of dismissal and self-neglect to come up? Because we know you're not choosing to do it consciously. Would you like to learn what is going on in there?" I pointed to her chest. "To finally do something about these defenses that get in your way of fulfillment?"

"Well, I can't say no to that, can I!"

"Of course you can. You don't have to look at a single thing. It's totally up to you."

She raised her eyebrows and looked at me like I was the biggest liar she'd ever come across.

"Really," I followed up. "I have no right to invite you to do anything you don't want to do. This is your therapy. Your life. Not mine. It doesn't make a difference to me what you do, other than the fact that I obviously want to help. Forcing people never helps, and we do know that if these defeating, dismissive thoughts continue, it will be very difficult, if not impossible, to find a safe, secure, and fulfilling connection. It's still completely up to you."

These reminders of reality weren't a trick to get her to open up. They were facts. I have no right to ask her to do something she doesn't want to do. It's a matter of human rights.

"No, I do. I want to figure this out," she said with a sigh. "I do. I do, I do, I do," she said, more to herself than to me. "But I don't have feelings!" In a way, she was right. She did not have *conscious* feelings because defenses and anxiety covered them. "I just really don't know how to answer your question! I don't like that I can't do it! I can't answer the simple question of what I feel toward you!"

This was self-attack again: *I should be perfect, able to answer everything.* Self-attack seemed to rule her life, punishing her to cover her feelings.

"Well, no one likes it when they can't answer questions. I know I don't. The question is, What's the atmosphere like in *there*?" I pointed to her. "Is it kind and patient about not being able to do something? Or super bitchy?"

"Super bitchy! I don't even know what the alternative is."

"Do you want my help to find out?"

Emma took a moment to think, looked into my eyes, and shook her head no.

11

Michelle: The Post-its

"I don't want to tell you this memory," I said, glancing at Dr. A, who was looking at me with curiosity.

My statement to Dr. A was a negation, which both conceals and reveals what we want. When I said, "I don't want to tell you this memory," I was really saying, "I want to tell you this memory." Yet to reveal my wish was too much of a betrayal to my mother, so my defense spoke through with "don't."

Dr. A was silent, letting me wrestle with my internal conflict.

Finally, I spoke.

I told him how my mom had moved nearby several years ago, around the time when a doctor suggested I get a procedure to look at the blood vessels in my brain. My mom had offered to come with me to the procedure. My boyfriend, Devon, had as well, but I told him the procedure was no big deal and I didn't need anything. More denial and self-dismissal. What's worse, I invited him to dismiss me and didn't realize it. He accepted the invitation. What's even worse: I was proud of how much I didn't need him. I was easy. Easy meant desirable. I begrudgingly agreed to have my mom there not because I wanted her to be there but because she would be hurt if I rejected her offer. When she asked, every muscle in my body clamped down, as if not to let her in. I gulped down my no and said yes to her. I betrayed myself to be loyal to her.

"When she asked to come to the procedure, I did not want my mom at the hospital," I told Dr. A with shame. The shame had a strong message: *You feel bad because you are bad.* Somehow, my mouth kept talking, despite the shame I felt.

"It felt too vulnerable to have her at the hospital. I don't know if this makes sense, and I'm sure I'm wrong or being cruel. It just felt like it was too late to accept her care."

I told Dr. A that when I was growing up, my mom was a stay-at-home mom while my dad worked. Live-in nannies helped raise my two sisters and me. The first nanny arrived when I was around eighteen months. My older sister was five, and my younger sister wouldn't be born for another six years. In total, I had eleven live-in nannies before the age of ten. (It might have been twelve or more. No one's memory was clear.) Each nanny was supposed to stay for a year, yet some quit after only a few months. One was fired for hitting me because I sharpened a pencil in an electric sharpener while she was on the phone. One forgot my younger sister on the changing table while my mom reportedly watched through a crack in the door. I don't remember most of them. Maria was my favorite. She once took me across the river by my house and up the hill, which was not allowed. I felt adventurous and free with a partner in the woods that were often only my own. I never said goodbye to any of the nannies. Once, I asked my mom whether she remembered us saying goodbye to the nannies. She responded, "Well, no. They weren't actually family."

Nannies rotated and left suddenly with no goodbye. I remember returning to Maria's empty room, vacuum cleaner marks already etched into the carpet. It was as if she had never been there. Only our last nanny stayed for over a decade, through my parents' divorce, and into my mom's heart.

"How old were you?" Dr. A asked.

"I was ten years old. She was our last nanny. All the others came before her, before I was ten."

I immediately liked her. Her boisterous, in-your-face personality clashed with my parents' quiet and buttoned-up lifestyle. One of her best qualities was unabashedly badmouthing my older sister to me. It was music to my ears. I often slept on the nanny's bedroom floor and went on any errand she ran.

As I shared with Dr. A, I became dizzy. I blinked, trying to reset my brain. It felt like I was committing a crime by opening my mouth. One part of me whispered, *Keep quiet.* But then, a force inside me pushed me forward and said, *Talk.*

"Me going to boarding school as well as her new connection with my mom created a distance between me and the nanny."

"How did you find out about their relationship?"

"During spring break of my sophomore year of boarding school."

I told Dr. A how I started to wonder if they were in a relationship because conversations between them had long become intimate whispers with soft, locked eyes. They would disappear and reappear without explanation or acknowledgment. Whatever they had, it didn't involve me.

"I had asked both my mom and the nanny the same exact question: 'Are you in a relationship?' I remember my words like they've been tattooed on the inside of my eyelids ever since. I said, 'Because if you are, I would understand. Because, as you know, I'm also in a relationship with a girl.'" I stopped and wondered if I should keep sharing with Dr. A. I was entering territory my mom would hate. But then the same force emerged, and I went on.

"My girlfriend at the time, mind you, was on a cruise with her best friend, which made me want to pull out my hair one strand at a time and eat my insides with a single chopstick. I was jealous and missed her horribly. Anyway," I said with a sigh, "I told my mom and nanny that I would want to know if they were in a relationship so I could understand their relationship." If I knew, maybe they'd stop ignoring me. I'd be in their club.

"What did they say?" Dr. A asked.

"They said, 'No, we're just very close.' They both said the exact same thing."

I told Dr. A how, the following day, I remembered my wet, long hair sticking to my back after coming out of the hotel shower. I began to look for a hair tie and unzipped my mom's small makeup bag, where I thought she might have one. I pulled out the first thing on top: four or five neon pink Post-it notes stuck together like a limp, sad book. I saw the nanny's large, circular writing on the front of the first Post-it.

"I can't remember what it said exactly. Something like 'To my love, something something, I love you.' Something highly romantic about kissing something. 'I cannot wait until something something.'"

Without turning to the next note, I dropped them on the floor. In my head, I said, *You will remember this forever. You will even remember that you dropped the Post-it notes because it's so dramatic.*

Outside the bathroom, the hotel landline blinked red. I listened to the voice message and heard my mom say that she and the nanny would be having dinner at a neighboring resort, and I was welcome to join them. My little sister would be in day care. It was six o'clock in the evening, and I hadn't seen them since breakfast.

With my heart pounding, I decided to join them.

"When I found the other resort, I saw them sitting in the middle of a restaurant."

"Wait, what?" Dr. A cut in.

"What?" I asked.

"How old were you?"

"Fifteen. Spring break sophomore year of boarding school."

"And you were out there on your own?"

I felt irritated, like, *Duh. Why wouldn't I be? Why is this an interesting part of the story to you, Dr. A?*

Instead, I said, "I don't understand."

"You were only fifteen and out on your own?"

"I had already been living away from home for a year and a half. This was normal. I don't understand why you're asking." Despite my annoyance with Dr. A, I heard his point. I ignored it and moved on.

"I sat down at the table with them and showed them the Post-it notes. My mind started swimming. I could not understand the questions coming out of my mouth or the words coming out of my mom's. The nanny was silent. All I could register was my mom's blurry figure turning to stone. It's hard to remember the details of this specific moment. I do remember what came next."

The hazy dinner ended, and the nanny picked up my little sister from day care while my mom and I sat outside the restaurant. Now she spoke more freely. She told me she and the nanny feared anyone finding out and "agreed, if anyone were to find out, the nanny would leave the family." My mom asked if I would go back to the nanny's room, with my little sister sleeping soundly in the bed next to her, and tell her she didn't need to leave, that I was fine, and to please, please stay.

She had another request for me: do not tell anyone. "You knowing is bad enough," she said. It seemed I had ruined my mother's life. I had to do something to make it up to her.

I told Dr. A that as I walked to the nanny's room, I imagined her having a hard time accepting my invitation. Maybe her suitcase was already filled with barely folded shirts with sleeves hanging outside a jammed zipper. Maybe I would interrupt sobs. Instead, when I opened the door, she was in bed, reading calmly with a book light setting her aglow. I sat on the edge of the bed and gave her my mom's speech. I told her she didn't need to go. I was fine. She accepted without words, as if she knew she wasn't going anywhere.

I don't think I ever found a hair tie that day. I learned that my long hair could double back in on itself. I didn't need my mom's tie anymore.

I looked at Dr. A and felt shame. I couldn't believe I shared this. Who was I to share this? How could I possibly tell the story my mom never wanted me to tell? It was more evidence of my badness, of being a horrible person and, even worse, a horrible daughter.

But then, another voice spoke up from inside me and said, *It happened to you, and you are allowed to have your feelings. This is your history.*

Instead of listening, I sneered at it and moved on.

12

Walter: Shame and Other Games

Instead of walking into my office with two bags of rocks over his shoulders, Walter bounced into our second session. While his face was still a deep red, his shoulders stood straight.

He's cured! I (half) jokingly said to myself.

He sat down on the couch and lightly squeezed his hands together. I smiled and continued to look at him.

"Oh! I go?" Walter asked. I nodded. "I'm not used to being the one who starts."

I rarely ask how people are doing. Unconsciously, the client is always telling me how they are doing through unconscious anxiety and defense. Do they arrive mainly with defenses? What type of defenses? Do those defenses keep me away or keep them away from themselves? Do they see the defenses? Or are they mainly anxious? What type of anxiety? Does it need to be regulated? Or are there feelings coming up immediately? Are they toward me? Someone else? And how does this all relate to their core problem? While I listen to conscious words, I also listen to unconscious anxiety and defenses. Our true voices speak in different tongues.

"Well," he continued, "I don't know." He sighed again. "Uh . . . I don't know." He looked out the window and said nothing more. He was constructing a wall between us. His tension was a good sign for a man who had just been a human puddle of depression the session before. Going from depressed-puddle-man to tense-attached-to-the-window-man was the direction we wanted. While neither man yields the type of connection and meaning Walter craved, a puddle man's defenses and anxiety would hurt him more than a detached man's defenses and anxiety.

Since Walter and I already had a conscious therapeutic alliance, I could dive right in.

"What feelings are coming up here toward me that make you tense and look away?"

"Um . . . that's a strange question." It was as if I hadn't asked him that eighty-seven times in the last session. Why the loss of memory? I decided to log it and continue.

"What feelings are coming up here toward me that make you tense and sigh and look out the window? That make you put up this wall between us?"

"Uh . . ." His eyes glazed over, and his neck flopped to the side. He had gone over his anxiety threshold.

"Did you just lose focus, lose tension in your body?"

"Yeah! Kind of like last time when you asked me that question."

Now he remembered. Unconscious defenses keep feelings and insights out of our awareness, making us sometimes appear less intelligent. Walter was a smart man, but his defenses kept him temporarily unaware of what we had done in the last session.

"We see a few things together. First, you were sighing and tense, right?" At my observation, Walter nodded, looking directly at me. "And then when I asked about your feelings toward me, your body slumped over and became more depressed. Does that follow your experience?" Making these types of connections regulates high anxiety.

"Yes!" He dragged out the *s* as a long sigh escaped his mouth. "Yes, that's right." Then he slumped back over like a broken sack of potatoes. I briefly wondered if he was saying "That's right" to please me or comply. The defense of *pleasing* is when people try to make others happy instead of relating to them as their true selves. Similarly, the defense of *compliance* is when people go along with whatever someone else is saying instead of relating to them as their true selves. Pleasing and compliance kill intimacy and growth. Therapy will fail if pleasing or compliance goes unnoticed.

Walter seemed to genuinely agree with what I observed. He suddenly looked uncomfortable.

"My stomach is upset."

"Your intestines are upset? Like diarrhea?"

He instantly flushed red at the mention of diarrhea. I thought of my own tomato face and couldn't help but smile at him, from one tomato face to another.

In response to my question about his bowels, Walter wiggled his hand back and forth to indicate something like *It's kind of a diarrhea feeling*.

Since his anxiety had gone above the threshold, I repeated what we knew, which was that his anxiety was tension when he came in. When I asked about feelings toward me, his anxiety shot up and went into his intestines and his body slumped, which meant his anxiety increased over his threshold. Understanding this sequence—feelings create anxiety, which creates defenses—is part of what helps people crawl out of a well. Recognizing patterns helps us make sense of what previously looked like chaotic randomness. The practice of understanding patterns is like a rope ladder being lowered down the well to the lost soul below.

"Yeah, how weird is that!" He popped up as enthusiasm and tension came back into his body. "I'm getting used to the fact that anxiety can be in my intestines."

We needed to help Walter see why these anxiety changes happened now. What was the source of this anxiety? One thing was certain: he had unconscious feelings toward me that made him anxious and detach from me. When I asked directly about the feelings toward me, his anxiety increased. When his anxiety increased, his defenses couldn't work well enough anymore to decrease his anxiety. He could no longer detach and instead became a limp noodle. One of our goals was to help his defenses work better so it was harder for his body to go limp.

"It doesn't make sense!" Walter continued. "I get that there are *feelings*. But they're not toward you. They're toward *me*!"

Bingo.

While I knew exactly what had just happened, I must also explain it to Walter. By sharing as much information as I can about his invisible puppet strings, Walter will hopefully become the driver of change, whether I'm there or not. For Walter, when I see it, I share it.

"Exactly. That's how you've learned to redirect your feelings. It's as if you're not allowed to have feelings outward toward another person. Instead, they all come back on you." I directed my hands to face me. "They hit you in the intestines, for example. They hit you with depression. Your frustration toward others hits you over and over." It was as if Walter was surrounded by a wall that bounced back all his anger toward others onto him. He got nailed by his anger and frustration every time he was frustrated with someone else. "You said you had feelings toward you, not me. What were the feelings toward *you* when I asked about feelings toward *me*?"

Tears began to collect in his eyes. "Oh, shame. Great shame." He suddenly looked like a man who had committed a terrible crime. As he wilted, I imagined a world where everyone felt safe to feel their feelings without suffering from punitive shame. Walter's shame was a *defensive affect*; it covered his anger toward me. A defensive affect blocks other feelings that produce anxiety and link to anxiety-laden content. For example, we can use sadness to block anger. *Weepiness* is one of the most common defenses. Instead of feeling anger, people become weepy. These tears do not help us feel better or bring about true empathy and connection. They just make us depressed. When we are weepy or crying over other feelings, something feels off. It can also be the other way around, where we use anger to cover deep grief. The point is we need to look at the *function* of the feeling. Does this serve as a defense? Or is this a core feeling that will help the person heal?

"Shame? Meaning feeling bad about yourself? Like you're terrible?" I asked.

Walter nodded.

"In this case, shame covers you with self-hate. Shuns you into the corner. Makes you want to disappear."

Walter said nothing, staring at me like I was nuts. Trying to comprehend that shame wasn't a feeling seemed to short-circuit his brain.

"Shame can be adaptive, but it's rare," I continued. "It's most often used as a punitive tool, like right now. All I did was ask you what feelings were coming up toward me. Why does this punitive I'm-so-terrible shame happen right now? When this punitive shame comes in to attack you, you feel depressed. It has the same outcome as if you were attacked."

The experience of punitive shame is like the aftermath of being bullied or having someone be mean to you repeatedly. Shame attacks. Shame is most often a defense against other feelings. It's rarely therapeutic. Anger, love, happiness, sadness, sexual desire, and guilt are therapeutic if felt (not necessarily acted out). The defense of shame says, *Stick your head in the sand, and never let anyone see your horrible self! You are bad! You should be ashamed of who you are as a person! Hide forever!*

Walter started to nod his head emphatically.

"The question is, what's causing the shame *now*? Would you like to find out?" I asked.

He nodded his head as if to say, *Yes, I would like two million dollars*. His fingers played with his shirt buttons, and his eyes widened.

"What feelings are coming up toward me now if you hold off that shame?"

He sighed. "Well, you know, a month ago—"

"That's a month ago. What feelings are coming up toward me now?" His attempt to change from now to a month ago functioned to avoid knowing and experiencing what he felt at this moment. If we kept looking at then, he wouldn't exist in the present. Not existing in the present leads to depression.

Walter took a breath, held it in, and slowly exhaled.

"I'm so bad at this!"

He was right. He was bad at identifying feelings toward others. However, he didn't state this as a fact, but rather as if it was shameful. He had rotated to another defense, self-attack. Part of the task of therapy is to smoke out the defenses people inadvertently use to avoid the experience of feeling and deep insight. Walter went from detaching to shaming himself to trying to go back in time and now to a classic self-attack. Another task of our therapy was to help Walter see this in action so he could make different choices. Therapists are not controllers, just describers and inviters.

"That attacking thought comes up, making you more depressed. That attacking thought starts when I ask about feelings toward *me*. And it drowns out any chance of you having feelings toward me. It's just shame and bullying toward you. It drowns everything else out." I used the word *drown* because it felt poignant when he used it at the end of our last session. It packed a punch.

His eyes suddenly widened, filling with energy. Had something clicked? "I wouldn't have believed it if you told me, but it's clearly what's happening!" His legs briefly lifted him off the couch. His anxiety was in the optimal state. I felt a jolt of warmth toward him.

"It seems the more you ask about feelings toward you, the more I feel toward *me*!"

"Exactly! It's like this mechanism inside of you immediately blocks feeling toward me and reroutes those feelings back to you."

"I don't want to be frustrated with you!" he exclaimed.

"Just because you don't want to be doesn't make your wish true. In fact, it seems that denying this feeling has cost you a lot in the form of depression and loneliness." I intentionally left out smoking because he didn't want to work on it. If he wants to in the future, he could make those connections when he was ready. "As I ask about feeling toward me, something inside you gets frustrated with *you*. As if I'm fine, and you're the problem."

"Exactly! I'm always the problem! It's me!" Walter's eyes began to glisten with tears.

Walter suddenly had tears in his eyes, yet this was the defense of weepiness. Weepiness was washing away his true feelings. His tears weren't sadness about the negative effects of this unwanted defense of self-attack. Instead, it seemed like Walter's tears were about how terrible he was. They drowned him out. They washed away any feelings trying to come out toward me. These tears contributed to his depression, not his freedom.

"Are these 'I'm so terrible!' tears?" I asked to make sure.

"Yes!" He popped a few inches off the couch again, excited to be understood once more. Then, Walter let out a long sigh. "I didn't realize there was a difference." He put his hand over his face, slumped down, and said, "If I let my frustration out, it will ruin everything."

Silence filled the room. His hand moved over his eyes, hiding him. "If I let myself have the frustration . . . toward . . . other people . . . that will make problems." He was probably right. Walter's life of avoidance would likely change if he could face the anger inside him. His life was built upon him being a guy with no anger.

"Instead of you facing the changes, all that frustration goes back on you in the form of depression or nausea. Anger doesn't just evaporate. Do you see how that operates?"

Walter looked at me and nodded.

"And these symptoms, the self-attack, the bullying, shame, and depression, did these begin recently?" It was a rhetorical question, and we both knew it.

"No, of course not. I've been dealing with this for as long as I can remember."

"But you weren't born with it."

He paused, chewing on the statement. Walter was born with all his feelings. Wanting. Connecting. Needing. Attaching. Asking. Yearning.

"I suppose you have a question to ask yourself, which is whether you want to face your feelings and stop this attack before it comes back onto you. We've identified a big part of what's causing your depression and anxiety, which is that your feelings are getting trapped inside of you. Feelings toward others make you anxious, and you protect others from your anger by keeping them inside. You protect them in ways that are painful to you. Yet at the same time, you're not sure if you want to be aware of your feelings because it might change parts of your life. It might cause too many problems. And it might. I don't know your life, so I couldn't say. You have some things to think about. If you wish, our task can be to help you face these feelings so they no longer trigger anxiety and this aggressive self-attack that causes depression. So you can be a free man. Or is it better to keep going this way? Only you can answer this."

"I can't keep doing this."

"You can. You've been doing it for decades."

Walter slowly leaned forward. His hands covered his forehead. Even more slowly, his body began to shake. A sob was attempting to emerge. Then, even more slowly, his body shook in multiple waves with his sobs emerging, and as they did, his body was free.

"It's been such a long time," he said.

"Such a long time," I echoed.

While sobbing, his muscles relaxed, and his self-attack disappeared. He felt no shame or anxiety. He was now free to grieve for the life he didn't get to live because his defenses stole his freedom.

"I don't feel anxious at all," Walter said as the sobs waned. He took a tissue from the box beside him and looked at the clock, which told him the session was almost over. "For all these years with these defenses *killing* me! I have ... stuff hiding underneath all this anxiety. I had to see that and move past my defenses. I needed to see them, and I didn't before."

After confirming our next appointment, I opened the door for Walter to leave. He put his hands together over his chest as if to pray and bowed in thanks. I put my hands together and bowed back. He placed his hand over his chest and silently mouthed, *Thank you.*

13

Michelle: Memory Boils and Other Betrayals

"My mom said it was one of the worst things that ever happened to her."

"What was?" Dr. A asked with a concerned look on his face. I wished I knew what he saw. I didn't trust my own opinions, my own eyes. I was used to seeing myself through my dad's or my mom's eyes. What did he see?

"Me finding out," I said. "My finding the Post-its was one of the worst moments of her life. I had 'pulled the rug out from underneath her,' she said. I made my mom's life very difficult. I told my girlfriend about a half year later, and I told each partner I've had since college. She knew I told, and she hated it. And she never wanted me to tell. I betrayed her."

When I stopped talking, Dr. A had a strange look on his face. I didn't know what it meant.

I started to look for more ways that I had hurt my mom. I figured if I could recognize how I'd been terrible to her, maybe Dr. A could help me figure out what was going on with me. Maybe he could make me into someone my mom would love.

Suddenly, a new memory came to mind, along with a feeling that I was bad for remembering it.

"A new thing is coming up," I told Dr. A. He raised his eyebrows, maybe in encouragement to share.

I told him how my mom and I were recently sitting around her dinner table. She had mentioned something about people who breathe with their mouth open. I wondered if she remembered telling me to breathe with my mouth shut. My mom would see me breathing with my mouth open and tell me not to breathe with my mouth open.

"How old were you?" Dr. A asked.

"Hard to say. Younger than eight because we hadn't moved out of our first house yet." I paused. "My mom would kill me if she knew I was telling you this. I shouldn't. Maybe I didn't understand what happened. Or maybe I'm complaining. Or maybe I'm making it up!"

Whenever I opened up and shared, a sense of liberation coursed through my body, but the freedom was quickly restrained by shame and its companions of self-criticism, self-doubt, and self-neglect. It was the war: *Please, free yourself! Don't you dare share!*

My defenses were ferocious. Yet these defenses did not get in the way of therapeutic work. They *were* the work. Dr. A and I needed to learn what my defenses were (shame, self-attack, self-doubt, self-dismissal), what caused them (anxiety about the emotions associated with my memories), how they functioned (to keep me from my deepest feelings), and their cost (they will turn me into a bloody pulp of suffering to shut me up and protect my mom).

"Are you making it up?" Dr. A asked.

I sighed. "That's the thing. I don't know why I said that because I know I'm not. I hate this feeling inside, like I'm not to be trusted. Like I'm twisted up. Something's not right inside me."

I was adopting someone else's voice. Something wasn't right inside me.

"What is the rest of this story with the mouth breathing?"

I sighed again. "I would close my mouth but I'd have difficulty breathing. And I'd try to close it, but it wouldn't last long. When I tried, I'd panic. When I couldn't do it, my mom said something like, 'Well, let's try this,' and she went and got some tape and put it over my mouth and sent me to bed. Later that night, I couldn't breathe."

"What did you do?"

"I rushed into her bedroom, pointed to my mouth and made sounds until she woke up and removed the tape." I stopped again. "I feel like a complainer. As I look at this memory, I realize I could have taken the tape off myself. But I didn't. I didn't want to get in trouble. Here!" I said, throwing my arms into the air. "Here's an example of where something's wrong with me. At the dinner table where she recently mentioned people who breathe with their mouth open, I asked her, 'Do you remember asking me to breathe with my mouth closed? And the tape?' My mom sat for a few seconds, slowly shook her head, and said, 'I don't think that ever happened.'"

"And what did you say?"

"I said something like, 'Oh, I wonder where I got that from.'"

"Did you really wonder?" He sounded warm and curious, not accusing as I would have assumed him to be. My assumption came from my projection onto Dr. A of my own judgment of myself as a liar. And this judgment of myself came from my mom's reaction to me bringing up this memory about mouth breathing—"I don't think that ever happened." I thought, *My mom can't be wrong, so I must be.* To not be in conflict with her, I adopted her voice instead of mine.

"Yeah, I guess I did wonder. I still do! I knew it had happened, but I also questioned it. How could she not remember that? It must be something wrong with me. And why would I even bring that up? I think I brought it up to see if she was in the place to remember and acknowledge it. I'm sure I also brought it up to hurt her."

Dr. A's eyes met mine. They were kind. He looked as if he saw something within me that I craved to see. *I want his eyes*, I thought to myself. *What does he see?*

Grief rose up my body, and I burst into tears. I cried and cried, feeling an ache deep in my chest. Briefly, I experienced a sense of liberation within my body, only to have it disrupted by the concern of mascara streaking down my face. I grabbed a tissue.

"I might not wear mascara to these sessions," I said, wiping away black.

He smiled.

Suddenly, an image of my childhood pet bird formed in my mind, another memory demanding to be heard. How much remembering was I allowed to do?

"I, uh, this sounds like a crazy change of subject, but I had a bird once. Her name was Tilly. I don't know if I should share this now," I said through tears and the defense of pleasing. Part of me still related to him as someone I needed to please.

He nodded for me to continue.

I began to tell him about the bird my mom purchased for me when I was eleven. I was grateful and excited. Tilly was a good bird. She let me pet her and scratch her neck. And she sat on my shoulder without pooping—sometimes. I was even allowed to take her into the shower. Tilly would spread out her wings and enjoy the mist of the shower. I had a buddy.

About two years later, I came home from school and walked into the kitchen. My mom had placed a long yellow measuring tape around Tilly's cage.

"What are you doing?" My voice was quiet.

"Measuring the dimensions." I waited for her to continue. She didn't.

"Why?"

"Two weeks ago, I put an ad in the paper for someone to come and get her, and someone finally responded. They're picking her up soon."

Something didn't make sense. Did I miss something? My mom seemed normal. Is this normal? If this is normal, what's wrong with me? My mother continued to measure the cage, slowly double-checking each side.

"Moments later," I said to Dr. A, "my mom and I were lifting Tilly and her cage into a stranger's hunter-green Suburban. We placed her in a trunk that closed like a hungry mouth. I never saw her again."

My body began heaving massive sobs of grief.

It felt like coming home. There was a physical pleasure in sobbing, in completely losing control. Dr. A sat quietly, his presence a comfort.

"I still have dreams about Tilly," I continued. "I find her somewhere, in a cage. No one has cleaned it, and she's emaciated. Her seed's all gone. She doesn't have her feathers. She's nearly dead. And in the dream, it was my fault she'd been abandoned. All the years since I left her, no one had cared for her. It's always too late when I find her." I cleared the tears from my eyes with mascara-stained tissues. "I really can't get past this feeling like everything I'm saying is stupid. I'm complaining about a bird! I had a lot of privilege! I mean, come on! How dare I complain when I had so much?"

We sat in silence. I didn't notice my defense of minimization, where I told myself it was no big deal. I didn't see my defense of self-attack, where I criticized and judged myself. I believed every word of it. And worse, I felt the sting of shame as I spoke through each defense.

"I had a great childhood. Genuinely. My parents gave us fantastic things. My mom went through a lot of effort to take us places, like taking me to piano lessons in the city. She set up Easter egg hunts, gave us fantastic Christmases. And I know there are more good things I can't remember." I stopped, trying to search my memories for something that could show Dr. A that, despite the recollections piling up now, my mom was a good person. "My childhood was great. Things did change, maybe when I was thirteen. I had a falling out with a close friend. I went to boarding school. My parents got divorced. My mom had a relationship with the nanny, and, this might sound mean, it's like she went nuts."

"Went nuts? *Nuts* is vague." Vagueness is a defense that shrouds specifics in darkness. Specific information triggers more feeling than vagueness. To experience the difference, think of someone who hurt you. Now think of their name. The specific name packs a punch, as opposed to *someone*.

"I don't want to bash her."

"Talking about what happened is bashing her?"

"Well, to her it is. And I know I haven't been the most pleasant daughter." I paused. "I can't think of a specific example of her going nuts."

"You can't think of *one*?"

Examples bubbled up.

Keep her secrets. Don't hurt her.

"I can't think of any more examples."

I lied.

Lying, by either giving false information or hiding truthful information, is a therapy death sentence. It is one of the only defenses that can kill a therapy's progress. Therapists are not mind readers. Usually, a therapist has no idea the client is lying and can't do a thing about it. You're on your own.

"Again, I wasn't around much. I was at boarding school. Before that, it was great. Everything we needed was covered. I could go to boarding school. I got to go on trips."

"You had things, but that doesn't mean you had a lot."

"Uh-huh," I said, looking down at his chair and picking at a stud that held the chair together. I looked at the clock, which told me we were close to the end of our time.

"Can I try to put it all together?" I asked.

"Of course."

I described how I came in with anxiety in the form of tension in my body. I resisted connection with him by looking away and projecting my father's judgment onto Dr. A. I resisted connection because connection triggered painful mixed feelings. Together, we pushed past my defenses of looking away from him and projecting onto him and tried to push past my self-dismissal, neglect, and minimization, with moderate success. As he persisted, I felt gratitude and anger toward Dr. A. We worked to help me feel the anger since the anger made me anxious. We helped my body feel anger toward Dr. A and the urges behind it. Next, my healing life force put forward an image of my mom, directing us to where the real issue was. Then and only then could I face and process some of my feelings without defenses. Giving these feelings attention created a frenzy of memories I hadn't thought of for years. Being able to share the memories allowed me to start to grieve.

I didn't tell Dr. A that I withheld many of these memories. I didn't mention the head pain or anything about the pills. I didn't tell Dr. A about the shame because I didn't consider it something I deserved to live without. It was my proper punishment.

On the drive home, I thought about what Dr. A had said: "You had things, but that doesn't mean you had a lot." I knew what he meant. He was talking about the life advantages that can come from having unconditional love, acceptance, and care. You were safe to feel without being rejected and therefore may have less anxiety and defenses as an adult. That unconditional love can sound like this:

"You are angry with me. I love you. You are lovable. Tell me more."

"You are sad. I love you. You are lovable. Tell me more."

"You have sexual feelings inside of you. I love you. You are lovable. Tell me more."

"You don't understand something. I love you. You are lovable. Tell me more."

"You feel something different from me. I love you. You are lovable. Tell me more."

"You feel guilt, made a mistake. I love you. You are lovable. Tell me more."

Dr. A's words echoed as I drove away. "You had things, but that doesn't mean you had a lot." As my mind repeated his words, I began to imagine dancing with Dr. A like the children in Charlie Brown cartoons. They each moved freely, alone yet together, with no one worrying about their mascara.

14

Emma: Whose Fault Is It Anyway?

Even though Emma wasn't sure if she wanted to discover an alternative to her harmful defenses, she came back for her second session. I was relieved. Wanting to help a client when you've chosen to be a therapist is obviously normal, yet my desire felt more like a wish to show her I could help. *See! There is help! I can save you!*

"I realized after my last session that I don't want to talk about my family," Emma said after she sat down on the couch.

"Thanks for telling me. We certainly won't if you don't want to."

Emma took a deep breath. "Okay."

A few beats of silence passed before I asked, "Question though: why not?"

"I don't know. I think you . . . I feel like you'll blame them and put everything back on them." She put her arms out in front of her, her palms facing me. "And I have a great, *great* family."

Emma was unintentionally using the defense of projection. Like we breathe without thinking, Emma unconsciously projected. Projection is a multifaceted defense that can take many forms. In this case, she took something within her that she couldn't consciously tolerate—wanting to talk about her family—and projected it onto me. Supposedly, I was now the not-so-proud owner of something that belonged to her.

I told her I didn't want to blame either. As fun as blame can be, it wouldn't do any good. Blame simply says, *It's your fault! You do this to me! It's because of you I am suffering!* That would be inaccurate and wholly untherapeutic.

"Right." She nodded her head, looking pleased and relieved.

"But, uh, where did that thought come from? About the fear of me blaming your family?"

"I just, I know you're going to ask about my family."

"Did I do anything last time that made you feel like I would blame or judge them? If so, it would be helpful for me to know."

She thought for a few moments and started shaking her head back and forth. "No, you didn't."

"However, there is causality, which is different from blame," I cautiously added.

Emma raised her eyebrows and looked mildly disgusted. Her patience was dwindling.

"Blame says, 'It's your fault. Period.' There's no therapeutic exploration or ownership of behaviors. And if we blame your parents for what you're doing now, who is to blame for your parents' behavior? And then who is to blame for your grandparents' behavior? And so on. It also leaves out the fact that your family is not at fault for what you are doing today. You're responsible for it."

Emma nodded her head.

"However, there is causality," I carefully continued. "Causality is X leads to Y, which leads to Z. It's true that our family environment causes certain defenses to form. However, they aren't sitting here making you attack or dismiss yourself. That's you."

"Even if I don't mean to," she added.

"Exactly."

It's not fair. We learn how to survive by using these defense mechanisms. It's not our fault we learned them, but it is our responsibility to change them. If we wait for someone else to change us, we will go to the grave the same person we are now.

"We shouldn't blame your family," I added to seal the point.

"No, that's clear now," she said with a genuine closed-mouth smile. She folded her hands neatly on her lap.

I wondered what would happen to Emma's anxiety since we had dismantled the projection of therapist-as-family-crucifier. Defenses, like projection, decrease anxiety; therefore, I watched to see if her anxiety would spike, a new defense would emerge, or a feeling would come up.

"I have some acid coming up again, and my head is *killing* me," she answered as if I had spoken my thoughts out loud.

Suddenly, my head did too. Empathy has its pros and cons.

"The headache was here before I walked in, but the acid reflux is, like, right now."

"Right before you mentioned not wanting to look at family?" When Emma projected, she disowned a wish or feeling inside herself that she couldn't yet tolerate. I had suspected she projected her judgment or wish to talk about her family. With the projection no longer active, the arrival of anxiety supported this hypothesis.

Emma added that the acid reflux came right when she realized I didn't want to blame her family. Her response supported that she was no longer projecting her wish to talk about her family onto me. Her acid reflux (anxiety) shot up because the projection (defense) vanished. This defense (projection—*my therapist wants to talk about my family*) helped her not get acid reflux (anxiety). She wanted to talk about her family (trigger), which caused her feelings (likely anger, guilt about the anger, love, grief) that made her anxious (acid reflux).

"The acid reflux came when you realized I didn't want to blame your family," I repeated.

"Yes. And now we have some information," Emma responded helpfully.

"Exactly. You want my help with this acid reflux and the headache. What you're unsure of is whether you want my help with how you get in your way with dating—for example, the self-attack *'Super Bitch,'* as you put it, and giving up if you don't think something will easily work out."

Sighing, she said, "Yes, I do want to see if you can help me with those, and I don't know about the others. I mean, no . . . of course I do, but I don't know what the alternative is."

"And how is your acid now?"

Emma held her breath, and on the exhalation she said, "Uh, it's gone. That's super weird."

Since Emma needed to see what caused her anxiety, I explained that the anxiety went down because we were paying attention to her without attacking or being mean to herself. We had also stepped away from talking about her family.

She smiled. "Yes, it's super weird how it works like that."

"You don't want me to blame your family for all your problems," I said, flailing my arms dramatically in the air like an unwieldy puppet. Kermit the Frog came to mind.

Emma laughed. "I guess that does sound kind of ridiculous."

"Any reason you had this thought come up? This worry of looking at your family?"

"Well, my family and I are really close." She smiled and looked wistfully at the carpet. "I see them all the time. My sisters are probably my best friends. Twins. Younger than me by a few years."

I had learned a lot about Emma. She had many pain symptoms originating from psychological processes and therefore had a psychophysiological disorder. Many personality traits are often linked to psychophysiological disorders:[1]

Having low self-esteem	Often feeling responsible for others
Being a perfectionist	
Having high expectations of yourself	Having rage or resentment
	Often worrying
Wanting to be good or liked	Being sad
Frequently acting hostile or aggressive	Having difficulty making decisions
Frequently feeling guilt	Being a rule follower
Feeling dependent on others	Having difficulty letting go
Being conscientious	Being cautious, shy, or reserved
Being hard on yourself	Often holding thoughts and feelings in
Being overly responsible for yourself	Having difficulty standing up for yourself

Emma had many of these traits.

Emma sat quietly. "My head is better now too," she said. "I swear this is so weird. I never realized I changed so much or so quickly." She was observing herself. The former wallflower was engaging with me. A wave of goosebumps flooded my skin.

"I want to tell you something that happened that reminded me of what we've been focusing on with all this body stuff," she continued. "I never thought there was a connection before, but then something happened with my sister. My sister has a new boyfriend, and when she told me, my stomach went nuts."

She wanted to talk about her family.

She shared that she had always felt like the third wheel next to her twin sisters, the fifth wheel among her whole family. When one of her sisters got married, she and the other twin sister now had something in common: they were alone together. It felt good to be a pair.

"I remember them being born and realizing I would have to do everything on my own. I was certainly not going to be the center of attention. I mean, my parents would have their hands full."

"Wow," I said. "You remember being that young and that thought going through your mind?"

"Oh yeah. Standing right by the hospital bed with two new babies in my mother's arms." Her mother didn't have enough arms to hold her too.

Emma went on to explain that as the twins got older, she was often left alone to do things for herself since "she was capable and the good one, a rule follower." Her mom and dad went to the twins' basketball games, leaving Emma to hitch rides without her family to her swim meets.

I was marveling at her ability to share more about herself when a familiar defense crashed the party.

"I can't believe I'm bitching about all this!" Emma suddenly blurted. "Nothing big happened to me! I wasn't, like, sexually abused or, like, you know. I'm being ridiculous! A big, spoiled baby!"

Ah yes, the I'm-a-big-spoiled-baby-if-someone-had-it-worse defense. I hear this at least once a day. Through loving attempts to quell discomfort, parents, friends, caretakers, social media, or even our communities often say something like, "At least you don't have it as bad as so-and-so" or "Others have it way worse than you." While these statements are often true, they dismiss and avoid the person's pain. The person hearing them has nothing to argue with and is left with a sense of shame at having such pain. *If others have it worse, what right do I have to feel pain?*

"Yeah, I get that a lot," I said. "A lot of people say that to me. All the time. And we should all knock it off," I said, laughing. Emma laughed too. "You or anyone saying that doesn't help anyone. You're not serving anyone. It doesn't put a halo on your head."

"I guess not, but it's still true!"

"It *is* still true. You could've had it worse. Much worse. However, you're using a fact to cover up other facts, which means it's not the truth. It's like a type of fake news. The other part of the picture is you went through what you went through, and it was painful."

Emma let out a long sigh. "That's true. It's not that they wouldn't come to my swim meets. They did. It's just that, well, they *never* missed my sisters' games." Once the defense of shut-up-you-complainer was gone, she was free to speak again. "If it were between me or them, both of my parents would go to watch my sisters play, or one would come to see me. *Both* never came to see me. You know what, though, we did have a family dog, and I really loved that dog. In fact, I love animals."

My chest tightened as I imagined a loyal dog sitting and watching Emma swim from the bleachers. I had no idea if this specific image was true, but it created tension in me. Since I was young, I craved a buddy. I wanted a dog. Too dirty, my parents said. No, no, no. With each of my repeated inquiries, my mom's disdain crystallized more and more until it was like an iceberg between us.

I listened as Emma described how the dog would come to swim meets and sit with one of her parents. I kept waiting for her to stop since she was hesitant to speak about her family, yet she continued.

She told me about how her father would videotape each of her sisters' basketball games. When they got home, the whole family would watch them, and her sisters would get critiques. While Emma knew it was probably annoying for her sisters, she envied the attention they received. She'd watch the tapes until she couldn't stand it, at which point she would leave and play her violin.

"I have a complicated relationship with the violin," she added.

I felt another push of tension in my body.

"What do you mean, a complicated relationship with the violin?"

"Well, my mom really wanted me to play, so I would. But if I made a mistake, she would yell at me from the kitchen."

"Like, actually yell?" People often said "yell" yet rarely meant it.

"Yeah, like an actual yell. And if I didn't practice, she would point it out. And even as an adult, she'll make comments about how I don't play, how the violin has gone to waste."

Emma said she didn't get to play the pieces she wanted to play. She played what her mom or violin teacher wanted her to play. And boy, did she play. She said it was her thing. Her relationship with the violin culminated when she was nineteen, when she had a huge performance that she practiced for "like, all the time."

"You must have been really good," I said.

"I honestly have no idea." She either wasn't paying attention to herself or dismissing her skill.

"Do you have a recording or something? What pieces did you play?"

"I don't remember."

Bull, I thought.

"I think my dad recorded my final performance," she continued. "But this isn't what I wanted to talk about."

I could have brought her back to the violin, as this was bringing up valuable emotional content; however, I was learning that Emma needed a therapist who didn't yell at her that she wasn't practicing her feelings. I didn't want to scream at her from the kitchen or hiss when she made a mistake.

"Anyway, my sister, who's not married, started dating this guy." *Ah, your partner was taken away!* "And she brought him over for dinner, and, uh, my stomach was upset, and I began to spiral. And I got completely depressed. The spiral was thinking

I would never find anyone. I would be the odd one out again. I got depressed after the spiral. And I see that was an attack on me, like you said."

It was now clear that she had a wish to talk about her family. She was aware of the anxiety and defenses resulting from her hidden feelings.

I decided to say nothing to see where her desires would lead us.

She looked at me as if she was waiting for me to speak.

I didn't.

More silence.

Suddenly, she let out a long guttural groan, as if to say, *Goddammit, this stuff is hard!*

"Indeed," I replied.

"I do want to talk about my family, and I don't think they're to blame for what I'm doing to myself."

"We know you weren't born ignoring, dismissing, and attacking yourself. We also know that this is how you treat yourself. Would it be helpful to know the cause? How this type of self-treatment was learned?"

She nodded and added, "I hate that . . . that causation might be true."

"And either way, it's your responsibility to do something about it. It could be that your family dynamics caused you to learn how to treat yourself in a way that's no longer helpful."

"Never helpful!"

"Well, it must have been at some earlier point. Otherwise, you wouldn't have learned these defenses. You didn't learn to dismiss, attack, and ignore yourself and your feelings because you were weak and stupid. You learned this way of relating to yourself because you were strong and adaptive. And now, it seems you're ready to adapt again."

It's critical we honor the defenses. Every defense, no matter how harmful, was once the answer to the question, *How can I stay close to my tribe? How can I get my needs met?*

"Oh, my fucking ... sorry ... god." Emma waved her arms in the air. "I don't think I can do this."

"You certainly don't have to."

"Yeah, I, uh, really don't think I want to."

Her jaw tightened.

I sat, my body tightening, waiting to see what she would do next.

"I don't," she said again.

15

Michelle: The Insertion

The moments after therapy are often rich experiences filled with insight as our defenses have just been challenged while anxiety was regulated. Often, feelings and memories become clear, opinions and decisions form easily.

On my drive home from Dr. A's office, I kept thinking about my mother. Why did she show up in my unconscious? Could I really have that much rage? *Should* I?

Suddenly, my mom's voice popped in my head.

"I can come to the hospital. That's what moms do!"

That was my mom's reply after I told her about one of my upcoming hospital stays. I had experienced over eleven thousand hours of continuous pain. My doctor had recommended a days-long medication infusion to break my headache. I loved the idea of attentive hospital staff and receiving intravenous medication to take away my pain. But when I heard my mom say, "I can come to the hospital. That's what moms do!" I felt my insides buckle and my muscles turn to iron. I did not want her there.

My mom added something like, "I would just have to let my boss know and do a few other things. It's been a madhouse at work. I'll have to move a bunch of things around. And hopefully, the traffic will be okay. It was terrible the last time I drove that way!"

Talking to her felt like being in a bumper car. She wanted to help, yet it also seemed like helping was a burden to her. She described such hardship. Even when she loved me, it seemed I was making her suffer. I told myself that she was trying.

"I'm sorry you have to do all that," I made my mouth say.

I couldn't tell her that I didn't want her there. I couldn't. I couldn't tell her that it was too late to "do what moms do." I feared that if I told her how I felt, she would show up anyway and call it "what moms do." My mom was not one for boundaries. I once caught her with binoculars crouching down by our window and spying on my sister's date with a boy. Another time, she crawled through the mulch by our basement window to spy on fourteen-year-old me while I watched a movie with a boy, at which point she allegedly told my dad that she couldn't trust me, and I had betrayed her.

"Oh, it's fine," my mom responded in a chipper tone after I told her I was sorry for her troubles getting to the hospital. Her mood suddenly shifted to suggest there was no hardship at all. *Did I misunderstand her? Am I mishearing things?*

"Thanks, Mom. I appreciate that," I made my mouth say again. I figured I felt appreciation somewhere inside me, so I'd better say it. I might regret not saying thank you to my own mother. Who doesn't say thank you to their own mother?

"Oh, of course, sweetie," she said with the sentimental sweetness of a caramel-coated candy apple. She often had a smile that didn't move her eyes. I imagined it on the other end of the line and shut my eyes hard.

I couldn't tell her it was too late.

"That's what moms do!" echoed in my mind on my drive home from Dr. A's office just as it had as I looked at her from my hospital bed.

And what about not being there before? I felt a twinge of shame and self-blame arrive with this thought, a shrinking despite the energy rising in my body. *How dare you think about before! Look, she's trying to be nice. You're going to hurt her feelings.*

As I drove home, I tried to remember positive memories; however, I remembered very little about my mom's role in my life. I remembered even less before boarding school. I could call up some positive memories, like when she told me I looked beautiful in an outfit she bought me or when she helped me write my first English paper. I knew there had been more positive experiences, many good things she had done for me. Yet I couldn't remember as much as I thought I should. Simply remembering the negative experiences made me feel cruel, as if I hurt her. I frantically wished I could fill my gaping void of memory. Searching for positive recollections turned up only vague, sketchy wonderings. Piecing together a memory from fuzzy data felt like lying or making something up. I was aware of the perils of memory—that memory can reform, degrade, and re-create itself with new themes that suit our fears. Was I to be trusted?

I once told her I wished I remembered more positive experiences with her. She brought up the corners of her mouth and exposed her teeth.

"Oh! I remember so many great moments!" she said wistfully. "I remember turning around and seeing you sitting in the back of the car, collecting things for My World."

My World was my self-created afterlife. Whenever I saw something I liked, I'd pick up my hand as if to claim it for my own heaven. If we drove by a dirty dog or a cherry tree, I would pick up my hand and scan them with my palm. Now, that dog and that cherry tree would be waiting for me when I died. I never took people.

I couldn't tell my mom that my heaven did not include her.

Instead of positive memories of a mother-daughter connection, my memories had sharp, painful edges, like from when I was around five or six years old one hot summer day. I had discovered some slugs on the shaded rock steps of our back porch. Looking closely, I saw they had adorable, independently moving eyes. They could be dogs. Tiny, small, probably-not-as-messy dogs! This would please my mom, who rejected dogs as dirty and unruly. I took a slug in the palm of my hand and, excited, brought it inside to the kitchen. I outstretched five tiny fingers before my mom.

"Look, Mom! A pet!" I felt glee in my tummy.

Horrified, my mom looked at the shiny trail on my palm from the slug's foot. She immediately took me to the sink, washed my hands, and flushed the slug down the drain. I don't remember how I felt watching the slug disappear down the drain. I do remember the pressure of her hands against my palms.

"Where did you find it?" she asked.

I took her outside to the shaded rock steps.

Suddenly, she produced a white plastic salt shaker from our dining room table, which seemed to come out of thin air.

"Why do you have salt?"

"Here, look at this. This is what I want you to do. You're going to pour this on each of them, okay? Here, look."

As soon as she poured the salt, it struck the back of a slug that immediately disintegrated. Then, she handed me the white plastic salt shaker and walked back inside the house. I poured salt over each of the slugs, watching them shrivel up. I told myself that they were morphing, like a caterpillar changing into a butterfly. I hoped this would please her. My throat ached.

I didn't want to remember moments like this, but I did.

During and after the divorce, my mom seemed to disappear even more. When she was physically in front of me, her attention was often elsewhere. Attempts at closeness were painfully unsuccessful, like when I was in college, and we were talking on the phone about my new boyfriend (the bathtub boyfriend, in fact). I enjoyed telling her where we went when he visited, what we had spoken about, and how much I liked him. It felt good to talk to a mom, to have her listen.

"Did you sleep with him?" she suddenly asked. Her voice attempted to sound innocent. I knew better.

"Uh..."

Her voice hardened. "Did you sleep with him?"

"Uh..." *Just tell the truth. It's the right thing to do.* "Yes, I did."

Suddenly, I heard a crash, and the phone went dead. After hearing the crash and silence, I stood still, staring at my apartment's brick wall as my vision blurred. A few seconds later, my phone rang again.

"Sorry, I threw the phone," she said, exasperated. I could only guess what was going on in her mind, but it felt like I had been lured into an intimacy trap and then judged for being a whore and thrown away. My mom didn't feel safe.

It felt like she was there when I didn't want her to be and gone when I needed her. Because of this, her presence didn't feel like it had to do with what I wanted.

From a young age, I didn't seem to mind hard conversations. In fact, they seemed fascinating, liberating, and real. I'm guessing this was one of my many aspects that made me an outlier in my family—and one that made me seem scary. I had attempted to talk with my mom about our strained relationship many times in the hope of change and the elusive feeling of mother-daughter safety. It would start and end the same way.

"I want to understand what gets in the way of our relationship so we can move on and try to repair it," I would say after bringing up that I wanted to talk. "I don't want to keep bringing up the past, but this past is still in the present. Something isn't quite right. I want a good relationship, but patterns and issues still block our ability to be close." I spoke like this even before becoming a therapist.

"When am I going to stop paying for what happened?" she'd reply, clearly defensive. We both had different ideas about "what happened." Maybe I needed to be clearer?

"Mom, it's not that you had a relationship with the nanny. I understand that. I really do. I hope you remember that I've told you that, and I mean it. My issue isn't with your relationship, it's with all that has happened around that. It's with what's happened since then. It's with what's still happening now."

Something shifted. "We don't need to dwell in the past." She said this with an eerie sweetness that made me feel like I was either being callous or living in a fun house.

"Well, I don't think it's about dwelling on the past. It's about how understanding what we've been through can help us now."

She shook her head slowly and clicked her tongue. Tears and a description of her pain often followed. Once again, my wish to talk had caused her pain.

One thing was clear: I was cruel.

It was my fault that she wasn't happier with me. I was the victimizer. She was the victim. Me having my memories made her suffer. Me being myself made her suffer. To speak was to hurt her. To remember the past was to betray her. To talk about it was mean.

I needed to protect my mother. I was the problem when I didn't.

After the Post-its, I fell into a deep depression. After six months, I burst and told my girlfriend, thus betraying my mom's secret and feeling like an even worse daughter and human being. I had committed a horrible sin worthy of my mom's hatred. Couldn't I have stayed silent so she would be comfortable? I felt torn between being loyal to myself or to her denial. Her denial became my denial. Her denial became my reality. My reality became meaningless.

I remembered back to how I felt as I lay in the hospital bed with my mom sitting in the room with me. Why couldn't I forget everything now that she wanted to be at my medical appointment? What if she was different this time? Sometimes she could do nice things. What if I was unforgiving? *Am I a monster?*

Suddenly, I felt some relief in my hospital bed. *I am the problem.*

If I believed that, then at least we would finally agree, and I wouldn't have to want her to change. I could have my mom if I agreed to her terms and conditions. I could have a mom if I protected her and ignored my thoughts, feelings, history, and ultimately myself. I could have my mom if I saw myself as she saw me.

Yet I could never figure out the right thing to do when it came to my mom, like when I was fourteen, and my mom finally gave me permission to use tampons. Standing over the toilet, I tried to insert my first tampon, but I couldn't get it in. My mom stood outside the bathroom door.

I heard a light knocking.

"I . . . I can't," I said. I felt humiliated.

"Huh?"

"I . . . don't know why but I . . . I can't get it in . . ." I had never had anything inside of me before and was panicking on the other side of the door. I wanted it to go in and be done.

Then, she said, "Do you want me to do it?"

I froze. It felt both horrifically wrong and kind. How can those two things be true at the same time? Without answering her, I began to try again with no success.

"Um . . ." I responded. "Um . . ."

"Do you want me to try?" she asked again. While part of me was warm to the idea that she would help me with such an intimate act, much more of me was screaming *NO*.

"Okay," I said, opening the bathroom door.

She told me to lie down on my back in my bedroom. With a humiliation that burned my chest, I pulled down my underwear and lay down. She unwrapped a new tampon and slowly inserted it between my legs.

We did not speak.

After she inserted the tampon, I stood up and thanked her. I couldn't help but think that my mom was the first person to put something inside me. I later wished she had stayed on the other side of the door and explained how to insert the tampon. I wished she would have heard my panic and helped me gain the confidence to manage my body. I wished she had stayed out. Yet the tampon was in. I felt repulsive yet grateful, angry yet relieved.

We never spoke about it again.

16

Walter: The Suicide

"I felt like the last session was very good. I got to see all these ways, or defenses as you call them, that get in the way of my emotions. The shame, the weepiness tears, the . . ." Walter stopped. "It's hard to remember them all. But it's still amazing how different this is from my past therapies. It's not like I'm all better, but I can tell something good is happening. These past few days, I noticed when I got nauseated or felt that shame. I don't want to say I feel better, but I feel . . . less bad."

These were his words, yet he said them to the window.

I was elated with both his hope for our therapy and his new solid defense: pushing me away and relating to the window. While some clients welcome a therapist into their emotional world, others use defenses to keep therapists out. Here are a few examples:[1]

- Using vagueness and generalization such as "I was feeling bad kind of."
- Going off on tangents.
- Using hypothetical speech such as "Maybe" and "I guess."
- Saying cover words such as "Well, I thought it was *weird* she said that."
- Exhibiting distancing body language such as turning away or looking out a window.

- Going into a thought cave and keeping one's thoughts to oneself.
- Not wanting to be certain, such as "I don't want to say I feel better, but I feel ... less bad."

For these individuals, anxiety rarely gets too high because the defenses effectively reduce it. Unfortunately, these defenses effectively keep other people away. These patients often come to therapy with issues surrounding intimacy and closeness.

Walter started therapy with defenses that weren't yet strong enough to regulate his anxiety. He initially crumbled under the weight of his anxiety. Now, things were different. After only two sessions, he could put up a wall between us. This might sound like a step in the wrong direction, but it wasn't. When clients make this shift, they report feeling more able to navigate life's challenges. Imagine going from brain fog, lack of energy, debilitating shame, or nausea to muscle tension and detachment. I'd take the latter.

"Do you notice you're looking out the window, away from me?" I asked.

"Oh! I didn't!" He laughed and looked at the wall behind me while thoughts ran through his mind. I waited for him to share them.

He didn't, staying in his thought cave.

"Are there thoughts going through your mind?"

He nodded. Silence. He was keeping me out.

Finally, he said, "Oh! Yes, I guess it would be good if I shared them with you."

He guesses. I felt a heat rise in my stomach and stop in my chest. I was annoyed. Walter wanted me to help him, and I wanted to help him. However, I couldn't help him if these barriers continued. Feeling my anger alerted me to his barrier. Feeling is a key clinical tool that alerts the therapist, *The patient is rejecting you.*

"Looking away, being in your thought cave, being a guessing man puts up a wall between us. What feelings are coming up toward me?"

"Thought cave! Yes, that's how it feels!" He tensed up his jaw around the word *feels*. He sighed. "I don't know what feelings. I don't know if I have any. Can't I not have feelings?"

"That's what being dead or high is for. A part of you wants to relate to me like a dead man."

"I'm not dead yet."

"No, you're not dead yet. So what feelings are coming up toward me?"

"You're saying . . . I'm looking away and saying . . . being in my thought cave because there are feelings toward you?" Walter's eyes bugged out. "But I don't have any!"

"Right. Instead, you avoid your feelings by a deadening, an emptying out. Why end the life inside you before you're dead?"

At this, Walter buckled forward and started to sob. It came on quickly, as if it had been waiting to burst out for decades.

"Let it through," I said. "Let it through."

He sobbed and sobbed and finally said, "My brother . . . he hung himself. He did that to himself. Many years ago." He reached toward the tissue box and yanked one out. It was the most power I had ever seen in his arms. He buckled again and sobbed.

"And my father basically drank his life away. He deadened himself too," Walter added.

Walter described a family history of men who killed themselves through alcohol or suicide. Numbing his senses with pot, he became a living ghost, much like the beloved brother and father he cherished.

"And I sometimes think it's my fault. My brother was going through a hard time. He was depressed. He came to stay with me because he was having a hard time. And I let him stay, but then it got too hard. And I thought ... I honestly thought that having him get back out there would be good for him."

There was silence.

"And so, I told him," he continued, "kind of like, tough love, I guess, that it might be best for him to get back out there, to his home, resume his life. And he left. And he seemed okay. But then ..." He took a moment to take another tissue and began to sob. "But then ... my other brother found him hanging in the basement. It wasn't even twenty-four hours after he left."

He silently sobbed, his body lurching forward and his hand cupping his nose, his face flushed, wrinkles deepened with pain.

"Do you feel like you killed your brother?" I asked.

"No, I don't think so. I shouldn't have told him to leave!"

"Do you feel like you were responsible for your brother's suicide?" I repeated after hearing his conflicting answers. Walter looked at me. "Who put the rope around your brother's neck?" I asked.

"My brother, my poor brother," Walter said as he began to sob again. "I wish I told him to stay! But I couldn't have known!" Walter said, coming to his own defense.

Walter's brother killed himself. Walter didn't kill his brother. Walter's self-blame was common. Many suffer from what I call the manic butterfly effect: if we did anything in a long line of causation that led to something terrible, we believe we are at fault. Often, this is not true.

"He didn't tell me he was going to do it." Walter inhaled and gulped down a sob.

On the one hand, blaming himself could be a defense against his rage toward his brother for killing himself and guilt about his rage. On the other hand, he could feel guilty for not providing more for his brother. No wonder he had wanted to die. I wasn't sure which direction to go, and I wouldn't until I received signals from Walter.

"I do have guilt that I didn't do more for him," Walter added.

"What happens if you just focus on that, that you did not provide your brother more support, yet disconnect it from the idea that you caused his suicide?" I was trying to help Walter feel the difference between punitive guilt and healthy guilt. Punitive guilt chases us everywhere. It can't get enough of making us feel horrible. We don't feel it usually. Instead, we repeat guilt-laden words to ourselves. Healthy guilt is a feeling, and it ends. While it's painful, it also releases us from suffering. In contrast, punitive guilt makes us suffer forever.

Walter put his elbows on his knees and his head in his hands. "I don't know if I know how to do that."

"What is it like to separate this guilt from you being the one who is responsible for his suicide? Just and only that you wish you gave him more support and didn't."

"Why did he do that?" Walter began to cry while he made small fists and gritted his teeth. Anger was emerging. Walter had protected his brother from his anger by blaming himself. He felt guilty about his anger. He loved his brother. He protected the memory of his brother from his anger, yet he had not protected himself.

He needed to learn to protect himself from his self-attack.

"He ended his own life," I said.

"He did." Walter leaned forward as another wave of grief overtook him. "And there was nothing I could do in that moment! I wish I supported him more . . . but . . ."

"You weren't down there with him in his basement, putting the rope around his neck."

"No! I wasn't. Oh god." Walter wrenched forward with another wave of anguish and grief.

Defenses can stay forever, like a thick fog with no break in sight. Anxiety can stay forever, like the feeling of being caught in an electric fence with no one to free you. Yet feelings are temporary waves.

Some days the water is calm, with waves barely lapping onto the sand. Other days, a storm pushes up large, powerful swells. Walter had been trying to avoid emotional storm after emotional storm, which pushed back the normal ebb and flow of his humanity. Now he was letting his emotions move through his body and out of his mouth.

"Why . . . why did he leave me?"

"I don't know. But he did."

17

Michelle: The Only Savior

I told myself I wouldn't take opioids on the days I saw Dr. A. I wanted to get what I called "a raw read."

"I take the pills for any breakthrough head pain," I told Dr. A when we started the next session. "I've mentioned I have a history of head pain. In short, I had a headache that wouldn't go away, and now it comes and goes. Opioids are the only thing that helps. I still take them whenever my head hurts. But not on session days. I thought you should know."

"What happened with your head?" Dr. A finally asked.

"Well, I woke up one night with a headache when I was twenty-two and it wouldn't stop. I couldn't figure out why my head wouldn't stop hurting. I darted from one possible cause of my headache to the next. I had my eyes checked. I went to see if my wisdom teeth had something to do with it. Was my diet weird? Was my infatuation with candy finally catching up with me? Did I need more protein? Was it changes in air pressure? Was Mercury in retrograde?!"

I laughed. This time, so did he.

"I'm kidding about that last part," I said as we smiled at each other. "I couldn't figure out what was causing it. It was a long journey."

A "long journey" was a vague understatement. I remembered my first visit to the doctor after the first night of the headache. Typos and all, this was the first description written by a doctor:

Michelle M. May is a 22 yr old female for eval fo headache- sudden onset on Nov 3, early AM, awakened her at about 2 AM. Worst headache eve- global, also had sweats, no nausea and vomiting. She used Tylenol, has been taking it since then but still has the HA . . . Neck feels stiff to her.

After that doctor's visit, I had a scan that showed the lower back part of my brain extended slightly below the opening of my skull, tiny veins in unusual clusters, enlarged lymph nodes in the brain, mild disk degeneration, and bulging disks. So many things were wrong that I assumed we had found the answer. I didn't know that the likelihood of finding these issues is incredibly high: 37 percent of people in their twenties have disk degeneration and 30 percent have a disk bulge. This increases to 52 percent and 40 percent in their thirties.[1] My results were all labeled as normal abnormal findings.

"I kept thinking we had found the answer, but we didn't," I said, turning my mind back to Dr. A. I told him how my neurologist, unable to help, referred me to a specialist after 7,440 hours of pain, or just over three hundred days.

"The doctor mentioned something about a Chiari [pronounced 'key-AR-ee'] malformation. I had never heard of a Chiari malformation. In this condition, the lower part of the brain, the cerebellum, flows out from the bottom of the skull. The doctor said it probably wasn't my issue, so we moved on."

"I haven't heard of a Chiari malformation either," Dr. A said.

"Yeah, the pain was bad, constant. It never stopped. About a year after the headache started, I discovered that opioids could help me live my life or at least live more than I was."

"That is torture," Dr. A said, shifting in his seat.

I thought back to when I discovered opioids. It all started when I began wondering when I should give up and pretend my never-ending headache wasn't there. To attempt denial as a treatment plan,

I played tennis on a blistering hot day. During the match, my head pain grew from a 5 to a 6 to a 9. Pain seared my body like a flame against bare skin.

"I went to the ER after particularly bad pain, and they gave me Vicodin," I said to Dr. A.

There was more to the story, yet most of the details were in the Not Important box and shoved into the darkness.

Clients have various reasons for not sharing important information. One reason is that they don't have access to material because they put it in the Not Important box. Another reason is that they know something is there, yet they don't share it because it appears normal or justified, like my shame when talking about my mom. Another reason is the defense of withholding (or lying), which is when we know what we don't want to say, and we choose not to say it. In this moment, I didn't share because I had put most of what happened with my head into the Not Important box. My Not Important box was underneath layers of defenses. It was still untouched. At this point, Dr. A and I were only at the outermost layer of my protective crust. This is why therapy is not a fast process. It takes time and drive to find, retrieve, and pry open our hidden boxes.

What I didn't share with Dr. A were the details of the visit to the emergency room after the tennis match. The physician and nurse flirted with each other as they laid me on a table on wheels to do a lumbar puncture.

"Should this table be moving?" I asked, my voice shivering. They waved me off, telling me it was fine. While the nurse and doctor continually laughed and teased each other, my boyfriend, Devon, and I looked on in disbelief. Neither of us said a word. I was silent. I didn't want to cause a scene.

"Don't move," the doctor said.

After I lay on the unstable table, he stuck a needle in my back. As I braced, the table moved. Then, everything vanished. I fainted. It was a mercy killing of sorts, a gift from my body. I awoke after the lumbar puncture was finished. They found nothing abnormal. The doctor did offer one thing: an opioid for acute pain.

"What did they find at the ER?" Dr. A asked after I told him I went to the emergency room and they gave me Vicodin.

"They didn't find anything wrong that night. I thought, *How could there be nothing wrong?* I didn't understand. Was I completely crazy? I didn't want to sound crazy or, even worse, be inventing something. I was accused of that once. When I was maybe eight years old, I went to the emergency room because I had a pain shooting from under my nail up to my chest. The doctor told my mom there was nothing wrong with me and I was there for attention."

"How do you know?" Dr. A asked.

"Because the doctor pulled my mother only a few feet away to say it. People don't realize how much children hear." I sighed. "But a day later, my middle fingernail began to separate from my finger because of fungus under the nail bed."

Dr. A winced.

"I know. I did end up eventually taking the Vicodin for my head pain, even though I didn't want to at first."

My hesitation to take opioids stemmed from a series of knee surgeries when I was eighteen. Doctors prescribed an opioid. I took one, fell asleep, and accidentally farted (or "putted" as my mom had us say. Not even "pooted," which is more common, but "putted." No saying "fart!") in front of my oh-so-attentive boyfriend at the time. How could I produce such a thing! I blamed the opioid. I was mortified and took the remaining offenders to the sink and happily washed them down the drain (which I now recognize is not the proper way to dispose of medication).

"The next day after the lumbar puncture, my then-boyfriend, Devon, and I went to New York for the US Open. I ended up getting a bad, very bad headache and taking the Vicodin there. That's where I discovered it helped me."

At least, that's how I wrapped it up for Dr. A. I couldn't tell him what really happened because—you guessed it—I had labeled it as Not Important. What happened was that instead of asking myself, I asked Devon if we were still planning on going to New York City the very next morning after the lumbar puncture and the flirting medical staff. I wasn't supposed to do more than mild physical activity for twenty-four hours after the lumbar puncture, which meant no lugging a suitcase onto a bus, sitting in an uncomfortable seat for over four hours, lugging a suitcase to an apartment, and walking all over New York City.

"I feel fine. It's not like we'll be doing much," I told Devon when he asked me if I'd feel good enough to do it. More denial and self-dismissal again. And I didn't see it. Instead, I told myself I had already been such a burden. How much of this could any reasonable boyfriend stand? I was reaching Incredibly Difficult Girlfriend levels. I had to minimize the problem (me) as much as I could.

When I woke up on the day of the Open, I was in too much pain to go. My body said no.

"Do you want to get the Vicodin filled and just see what it does?" Devon asked. I could barely muster a yes. Once we arrived at the pharmacy, I blacked out on the floor. When I woke up, Devon gave me the new bottle of Vicodin. I grabbed the cap, twisted hard, took out a pill, put it in my mouth, and swallowed.

We walked home, Devon bracing to hold up my body. I vaguely remember the dappled sunlight, entering the apartment, my body on a sofa, like a dream. Then, the Vicodin took hold.

Comfort entered my bloodstream, bringing relief to every corner of my body. The tension I wasn't even aware of around my eyes, spine, legs, and shoulders all disappeared. I could think, move, and see. I was even a little happy. I felt safe. The pain plummeted from a 9 to a 2.

Maybe I can live, I thought. I'm not going to bother anyone anymore. I had my solution.

All I could tell Dr. A was that opioids allowed me to go on. They helped me so I didn't have to leave as early each day from the job I hated, I wasn't as annoying to my boyfriend, and I had less pain. The details of my self-dismissal, self-neglect, self-attack, and denial didn't matter because I didn't know they were defenses. They were just who I was.

Part of a therapist's job is identifying defenses, outlining the function of the defense, and showing the cost of the defense—how it hurts the patient. Then and only then can a person decide if they want to turn against the defense and face their feelings. Yet my mind had taken all the details out, so Dr. A couldn't observe how my defenses functioned in these memories. He could work with only what was in front of him, the defenses I enacted right in the room.

"Appointment after appointment, scan after scan, medication after medication, the doctors still found nothing," I said to Dr. A with a long exhale. "Only the opioids helped. I did try to go to a therapist for support with chronic pain. She handed me a two-disc CD set on meditation and told me to try it. I stopped going after three sessions."

"Not helpful," Dr. A said behind a fist that covered his mouth.

"No, not helpful. And also," I said with a long sigh, "lurking behind the pills' helpfulness was a hard truth. Over time, I had to take more to achieve the same level of pain relief. Sure enough, one Vicodin started to feel like an Advil, as effective as a breeze trying to stop a plane crash. One Vicodin became two, two became three, and three became four. Slowly, I stopped feeling the high, and yet pain relief still followed."

I completely empathized with those who choose drugs or suicide to deal with a life of constant pain. The risk of suicide nearly doubles for those with chronic pain, and almost 20 percent suffer from suicidal thinking.[2] Death often sounded better than a life of constant pain with no way out. Taking away the opioids with no other solution felt like the end. Having the opioids lose their effectiveness over time also felt like an impending end.

"You still take them, the pills?"

"I do, but much less. I take only half of a pill or one full one if the pain is bad." Suddenly, I began to worry that Dr. A thought I had a problem. This was another example of the defense of projection, which is where we take something we can't handle within us and project it onto someone else. In this case, I was the one who thought I might have a problem. I couldn't tolerate owning that opinion since I loved my pills, my little saviors. Thus, I gave my opinion to Dr. A. *He* was the one who might think I have a problem. Not me. I also had supporting facts that I didn't have a problem. I wasn't abusing the medication. I took them as my doctor ordered. I took them only if I had a headache. Nothing else worked for my headaches. I didn't get high. It helped me. These were true statements. Yet there were other factors I didn't see.

After worrying that Dr. A thought I had a problem, I waited to see if he'd say anything. He didn't.

"I take a half or whole pill if have a headache," I continued, "which is maybe four or five days a week. I take one only if my head hurts. I made sure not to get caught up in abusing them. I told my doctors I was worried I would keep having to take more of this stuff, so I asked my doctor if she'd mind changing from one type of opioid to another. I hoped my tolerance would go back down because I wasn't using the same opioid over and over. My doctor was willing to try my plan, even though I knew that plan also had an expiration date."

This was before the opioid epidemic was on every news feed. Even though I had no clue about the epidemic, each time I asked for a refill or a different type of opioid, I feared my doctor would pull the plug. I had chronic pain and no solution. I used opioids responsibly. How could they take away the only source of relief I had? There was no effective solution except death or drugs for a hell that seemed to come from nowhere.

Pills continued to provide a temporary answer, giving me warmth and comfort. Pills had always given me comfort. When I was young, I was always offered an over-the-counter solution. When I had growing pains, or at least that's what my mom called them, she handed me acetaminophen. When my tummy hurt, it was an antacid. Physical issues received attention. Emotional issues did not.

"Opioids changed everything," I told Dr. A. "I'm where I am because of opioids." And that was the truth.

18

Emma: The Cool Girl

Each time I see a patient, I try to relate to them as they are in the current moment. The British psychoanalyst Wilfred Bion wrote that therapists should aim to approach each session "without memory or desire."[1] Roughly, this means therapists should try to relate to the client in front of them and not get mixed up with their own drives and wishes. I took a kindergarten-level understanding of this concept and tried it for about six months before I began to resent Bion, or at least the Bion that existed in my head. Without memory or desire? What am I, a dry erase board? No. I didn't think I could pull it off, so I aimed for something different: being aware of my memories and desires. I would see how and when they are pulled on and use this information to inform my sessions and my own development.

Emma pulled on all my memories and desires.

"I found a recording," she said as she sat down for the next session. "The one of me playing the violin at that big concert."

Emma was the human embodiment of an internal tug of war. She wasn't sure I could help her, yet she kept showing up. She wasn't sure she wanted to explore herself, yet she kept looking. She consistently changed the subject yet circled back. Every person in therapy wants to change and resists change. Emma displayed both sides beautifully.

Come here.

Go away.

Emma forced a smile through the emerging pain on her face. She said she saw "a really unhappy girl" when she watched the recording. Water collected in her eyes, but as soon as her tears appeared, she wiped them away with the back of her hand. The tissue box next to her was untouched.

"I had to see it to realize how miserable I was," she continued. "I didn't remember, but it was pretty clear when I saw it." She picked at her nails, her head down as she examined them. "I was very good. I practiced so much for that concert, so I better have been!" Her sentence began with a compliment and ended with a slap, which was an example of how positive feelings about herself created anxiety that was taken care of by the defense of self-attack.

"Whose voice was that? 'You better have been?' It didn't sound like you."

Emma sat and thought, looking down at her beaten nail beds. "Actually, maybe my mom's? Maybe?"

I noticed how she avoided my eyes, a defense against emotional closeness with me, and said, "maybe," which was another defense against emotional closeness with me. I was about to comment on these defenses until I remembered that her self-attack, self-dismissiveness, and self-neglect were more important. *Don't be like her mother—or Emma!—picking at everything.*

"What about *your* voice when you see this really unhappy girl?"

She began to tear up again. "I was proud. And sad." Emma's sadness and pride were finally seeping out, entering her body in a way that would help her.

"Oh my god," she said, her head suddenly popping up. "You know the acid reflux? I haven't had to take my medicine at all. I hadn't realized it until now because I wondered if you were going to ask me about how I felt."

While I knew we had a lot of work ahead of us, this was a promising sign. We were blocking her self-neglect and self-dismissal by paying attention to and labeling her feelings as important. She was a little more able to feel. Simply noticing her anxiety and defenses and allowing a small amount of emotion through her body allowed her acid reflux to vanish within only a few sessions.

"I don't want to focus on this because I want to talk about dating. But I don't want to talk about dating!"

"Whatever you like!"

"I want to find someone: at least, I think I do," she said. I was already confused. "I have had relationships before, nothing too serious or too . . ." She looked at her cuticles and searched for the right word until it came to her. "Good," she said. She picked a piece of her cuticle off and then told me about a few dates where "nothing significant happened." There were no deep bonds, no intimacy. She described her relationships like she was describing a lack of ripe melons in the grocery store. "None of them were really . . . that great."

Then, her healing forces delivered us another gift.

"You know, this is randomly coming to mind right now." I'm always excited when someone says "randomly coming to mind right now" because it means her unconscious is trying to give us a present, something from deep within pointing to the wound that needs attention.

Emma went on to tell me how when she was in high school, she had a guy friend, Tom, whom she really liked.

"He ended up asking me to prom, which, like, was a huge deal." She had been waiting for prom for years, anticipating how it would be for her. Who would she go with? What would she wear? How would it feel? She said yes to Tom with no excitement. She didn't want to let him know how she felt. She said she really liked him, and he had no idea.

"He didn't ask me because he *liked* me either," she added as she flipped her hair out of her eyes.

"How do you know?"

She didn't know for sure. She figured he didn't like her because when it came close to prom, he ended up telling her that he found another girl to go with. He asked Emma if she minded, and she said she didn't. She didn't mind at all. She was a no muss, no fuss kind of girl. Easy-breezy.

"I remember being like, 'Nope! Not a problem!' and really trying to not look devastated." But she was.

She tossed her hand to the side before she resumed playing with her nails. "I wanted to be . . . this sounds stupid. I can't believe I'm saying this. I wanted to be, you know, the Cool Girl."

I looked at her, my head tilted and bottom lip out as if to say, *Who?*

"You know, the girl who . . . well, it's like the Gillian Flynn book, *Gone Girl*. Have you read it?"

I shook my head. *I've seen the movie.*

"The Cool Girl doesn't care. She's easygoing. She loves beer and football and can have sex for days or something. And she doesn't get angry. Don't be difficult! That's another feature of the Cool Girl."

Emma looked up at me and smirked.

"Don't be difficult," I added. "Anger makes you too difficult. It sounds like what you did was a way to sand off your edges and get rid of any part of you that didn't fit that Cool Girl definition. What's the cost of this Cool Girl facade?"

"I don't know."

"You don't know, or you don't want to think about it?"

Emma threw up her hands. "It costs me a lot!"

"Do you want to make it difficult for a cruel defense like this to operate inside of you? It's the defense that—"

"Ruins everything!" Emma blurted.

"You were pretending to be the Cool Girl instead of you, which means your life isn't your own."

"Yes, that's right," she said with a sigh.

"If we put aside the Cool Girl façade, what do *you* feel when you think of Tom wanting to take another girl to the prom? Let's help you feel what wasn't allowed to be felt to get comfortable with feeling it now."

"I don't think I realized this until right now. I was devastated. I really wanted to go with him."

"And your feelings toward him for devastating you?" She was confusing a trigger—his action—for her feeling. This misattribution is a common cause of psychological confusion and suffering. People hear they should feel their feelings, yet they don't know what the feelings are. Devastated, disappointed, hurt, manipulated, gaslighted, abandoned. These are not feelings. These are triggers. Sure, she felt hurt because he hurt her. But if we stayed in the hurt, she would not be able to see her anger toward him for hurting her. Focusing on the hurt navigates us inward and away from the feelings toward the other. The feelings toward the person who hurt us move out and through. I needed to help Emma identify the trigger (he hurt her) and invite the feelings so she could live the life she wanted to live. Yet—with Emma as my witness!—this was a difficult task.

When Tom chose to take another girl to prom, Emma was devastated. Instead of feeling the emotions triggered by the devastation, she turned to the Cool Girl defense. To add insult to injury, she thought the rejection meant she was unlikable. Without realizing it, this was how she turned her anger toward him back onto herself.

The Cool Girl defense is a culturally sanctioned façade that is a pile of bull. The internal transformation into the façade of the Cool Girl (or Guy or Person) is a harrowing process that forces us to suppress our emotions and undermine our authenticity to avoid expressing genuine feelings.

After I asked how Emma felt toward Tom, her eyelids reddened. We sat in silence for a few moments before I added, "I know you're not sure what it looks like to *not* be cruel to yourself, to *not* dismiss, attack, or neglect yourself, and, of course, you wouldn't know. You can't know until you know. Also, you have shared with me that you're not sure if you want to find out. You want my help with the acid reflux, headaches, TMJ . . ."

"Nail and heel picking," she added.

"Right. And you're not sure if you want my help with these cruel defense mechanisms that have cost you and could cost you more."

She clamped her teeth down hard around her bottom lip.

"Emma?"

She looked up at me. I bit my lip to show her the connection between her jaw tension and biting herself, a transparent form of self-attack. She instantly released the bite and burst into tears.

It was a privilege to be in the presence of her tears, of her real pain. And as I sat with her, I wondered, *How many have sanded themselves down in the hopes of being accepted and not bothering a single soul? How many have allowed themselves to disappear?*

I had sanded myself down. From ten years old until I went to boarding school, I went to a beloved piano camp during the summer. At the end of one summer, both my mom and dad came to pick me up and bring me home. As I sat in the back seat, I felt an empty car around me. No one spoke. As we drove away, I felt like I was drowning in grief. I didn't want to leave camp. I said little and didn't have my usual vigor upon seeing my dad.

"How long is she going to do this for?" my dad barely whispered to my mom.

My dad was referring to my silence and sadness, my failure to perform for him. When I heard him, a heat inside me rose and quickly died. My honest reaction—me—was buried by a thought:

How long was *I going to do this for?* I had to end this sadness immediately. It displeased my dad. The cost was too high. I didn't want him to go away and like me less for my sadness. I choked it down and pretended I was fine. I knew how to perform the role of a good, easy daughter. The outer conflict disappeared while the inner conflict became worse inside myself, alone in the back seat.

"Let it go through," I said to Emma while she cried. "As much as you want."

19

Michelle: Too Much

"You barely mention your older sister," Dr. A said at our next session.

"My older sister and I didn't get along. There's too much to tell you about."

"Too much?"

A therapy session—life, really—is a push and pull between wanting to reveal ourselves and wanting to conceal ourselves. The first wish—to reveal ourselves—is the part of ourselves with a healthy emotional immune system geared toward truth and connection. The second wish—to conceal ourselves—is the part of ourselves created to fit in with our family, community, and culture. While both sides want connection, the concealing one is confused about what real connection feels like.

"Sorry, I mean *not* too much. There's *not* too much to tell you about. We had normal fights."

My original statement, "too much to tell," was a product of the war between my two sides. When I said "too much" instead of "not too much," I was both concealing and revealing the truth at the same time. In intensive therapy, we are trained to listen to these signals from the underground that hold the truth.

After a few sessions with Dr. A, I had shared only a small amount of history about my head pain and told him almost nothing about the surgeries. While Dr. A knew about the opioids, we rarely talked about them. I was relieved. I didn't regard my opioid use as a problem. It was a solution. And I wasn't wrong, but I wasn't completely right either.

My history was not a big deal (minimization, denial). What happened was minor (denial). People had it worse (rationalization, dismissal). I felt stupid even saying anything about it (self-attack). I was ridiculous (self-attack). I should keep my mouth shut (self-attack).

"You said, 'too much,'" Dr. A pointed out. "Too much to tell."

Dr. A's persistence sent a message to my defenses: the therapeutic team is not giving up or being defeated by your defenses. The defenses that hurt you are no good here.

"Well, uh, because, um . . ." My head became dense with fog. My anxiety spiked over my threshold because my defenses were challenged by Dr. A's persistence against them. An increase of anxiety is often the result of defenses collapsing. This is a good sign if the defenses that are failing are the ones that hurt the most. Many incorrectly assume this spike of anxiety is a sign that something has been done wrong. This is incorrect. Instead, an increase in anxiety signals that harmful defenses are less active in that moment. At this point, the therapeutic team can regulate the anxiety with a helpful defense instead of a harmful defense.

"Because, um . . . honestly, my family . . . they can exaggerate, or walk, I mean . . . dance around something, or . . . I don't trust that they're being honest," I stammered. I noticed how difficult it was for me to speak or think. Then, a familiar and harmful defense came in to regulate my anxiety. "And then I begin to wonder about myself. What about me? Am I like that?" I inadvertently started to use a common harmful defense: *Wait, maybe I'm the problem!*

It is a developmental achievement to look at ourselves and wonder if we are contributing to a problem. This is part of being mature.

However, if our wondering shifts the focus away from other facts or brutalizes us, then this self-analysis becomes harmful.

"You switch and begin to wonder about yourself," Dr. A observed. "But your family, they were dishonest?" Dr. A was blocking my defense of I'm-the-problem by keeping the focus on them.

"Honestly, I feel stupid telling you about my upbringing." I was still attacking myself. "I had common sibling issues like everyone else." I was minimizing. "I wasn't beaten or sexually abused by my parents." I was lying to myself. "I'm serious, Dr. A. I mean, come on, I'm from Connecticut!" I turned to humor as a defense against reality.

"What you are saying, this is defense, no?"

"Defense? It's true what I'm saying."

"Of course, it is true that people had it worse. But when you say this comment, it, uh . . . it . . ." Dr. A couldn't find his words.

"It pushes my pain down."

Dr. A nodded.

I paused. I didn't know what to do. Forces were pulling on me from all sides. There was a force that said, *Share, be free*, and another force that said, *Don't you dare open your mouth, young lady.*

"I don't think my sister liked that I was there. There was love between us. We played in the sand dunes in the summer. She told me she was a cat, and I was an owl in a past life, and I became obsessed with owls because of her words. Sometimes, when we'd go into a store, I'd say I liked something, like a small wood carving of an owl, and then she'd secretly buy it for me and give it to me in the car. But she was also very . . . uh . . . and . . ." The room danced around me as my anxiety stole my next thoughts. "That's how . . . a lot of older siblings can be. It was a real mix. My mom told me several times that she didn't react well when I was born."

"Problems between siblings are about feelings toward parents, problems with the parents. Siblings can take out their unprocessed feelings toward their parents on each other. It's easier to act out feelings with a sibling if parents are unable to offer a stable connection. Problems between siblings are often about the feelings toward the parents. Sibling bullying is a way of managing feelings toward the parents."

"And you know what?" I said, continuing as if I didn't hear him, "I remember her picking her cuticles like crazy. It was the first time I'd ever seen something like that. We were young, and she would pick the skin on her thumb and peel her skin from her thumbnail to down here." I pointed to the second knuckle of my thumb, the one closest to my palm. Dr. A winced. "I know." Grief started to push up in my throat. "A little girl pulling and picking her skin off like that? My problems are small." The last statement stopped my grief dead in its tracks.

Dr. A stared at me with concern in his eyes.

"Connecticut, Dr. A!" I said, laughing.

Dr. A didn't laugh. Instead, he sat quietly, which gave me a moment to realize I had turned a moment of empathy for my sister into a lack of empathy for myself. I was using the defense that said I can feel something about my problem only if it's the worst problem or is bad enough in someone else's eyes. The trouble was there was always going to be someone who had it worse or thought my problems weren't a big deal.

I began to wonder how I could get out of the loop I had created. *What if I stopped dismissing myself like this? What if I valued my feelings, thoughts, and memories? What if I could feel better? Could I take better care of me? If I stop devaluing my experiences, how would that impact my life?*

What if remembering these experiences was my body's way of begging for the attention it needs to feel better?

Am I not horrible for remembering?

Am I allowed to remember? To tell my story?

Am I not bad?

I suddenly reeled forward, grief overflowing my body. In that moment, I was free.

Yet the freedom didn't last. I felt a headache come on, followed by a thought about a conversation with my mom.

"Is it okay if I tell you what's coming up?" I asked Dr. A, relating to him as my commander instead of relating to myself as the commander of my own life. He nodded.

"During sophomore year of boarding school, I would get this pain in the left side of my chest. After a while, I told my mom, who drove to my boarding school to take me to the doctor. The doctor sent me home with a heart monitor. By home, I mean boarding school. The next time I felt the pain, I was to push the record button on the monitor and the data would go to the doctor. My mom asked me if I had used the heart monitor, and I must have shared that one time I pushed it to see what would happen even though I didn't have any pain. Now, flash-forward to a recent conversation where my mom and I were talking about anger. I was trying to help her see the benefits of getting in touch with it, and she goes, 'You know when you made me angry? When you said you pushed the heart monitor just to see what it did back when you were in boarding school.' I didn't know what to do or say, so I said, 'That's sad that I did that. I must have wanted to see if anyone was paying attention.' It just popped out of my mouth."

While I didn't realize it, I was telling Dr. A a story about how physical pain can be a way to reach out for care and connection when emotional pain is ignored.

"Anyway, now my head hurts. Nothing ended up being wrong with my heart anyway. That was a long story, sorry," I said with a grimace. "I loved boarding school. It saved me. I don't know what I would be like if I stayed home. I also think I was in a lot of pain."

"And your head hurts right now?" Dr. A asked with raised eyebrows.

"I know that pain can happen because of repressed emotions. I had an actual brain problem. This is probably residual pain. The doctor said this would happen. It's common with what I had."

"It hurts now?" he asked again.

I put my head in my hands. I didn't want to look at my headaches. I was tired of looking at my headaches. I just wanted to dive as deeply into myself as possible to be a better therapist and person. I tried to keep my head pain entirely separate.

20

Walter: My Juice and Other Breakthroughs

Walter sat down and cleared his throat.

"I want to talk about the ten-thousand-pound gorilla in the room." I had no idea to which gorilla he was referring. There were many. A zoo, in fact.

"Which is my juice. My pot smoking! My all-the-time pot smoking! I don't think I've been entirely honest with you about how much I actually smoke." He paused. "And I want to be."

Why was Walter ready to explore this problem now? Gradually, we alleviated Walter's emotional anxiety by creating awareness. As he learned to tell the difference between his true self and the inadvertent strategies he employed to evade his feelings, he became more attuned to them. Recognizing the self-directed attacks, he gained insight into the repression of his anger toward others, understanding the reciprocal impact of that repressed anger on his well-being and its role in fueling his depression. He could see his defenses, and he could do something about them. Similarly, his relationship with anxiety underwent a transformation. Now equipped with the ability to recognize and acknowledge his anxiety, he found new avenues for self-soothing. Unlike before, he could now comfort himself by embracing his feelings rather than instinctively pushing them away. With diminished anxiety, the need for defenses diminished as well. Consequently, his symptoms abated, paving the way for a less daunting prospect of addressing his pot usage.

We cannot do anything about anything if we don't know it exists.

I asked Walter why now was the time to work on his smoking. He looked directly into my eyes and told me that pot was getting in the way of his feelings.

"Like you said, I'm a dead man before I'm dead."

He went on to describe how much he smoked. He was right—I had no idea how much he actually smoked. He said he smoked all the time, from when the sun came up to when he went to bed. Previously, the only thing I knew for sure was that he smoked a lot and had agreed not to smoke on the days he came to therapy. Being high or influenced by any substance, such as drugs or alcohol, in a session is not helpful. Some say it would help them open up, yet that is the problem. It's a fake opening up. The substance protects you. And part of therapy is helping someone see what they inadvertently do to keep up a wall or hurt themselves. Active substances in the body make this impossible.

"I smoke and smoke and smoke and smoke," Walter added to drive the point home.

"And you now want my help to . . .?" I wanted him to lead me. He was in charge.

"Well, I'm about eighty-twenty on this. The bigger part of me wants to look at this, to change it. The smaller part of me doesn't. Well, maybe it's the other way around." He paused and frowned. Then, he bounced up on the couch and said, "But I've tried many times! I've already tried not to smoke! And there were a few times I did stop, but I went back to it. I can't do it! So why try? Something's wrong with me. I know I'm going to fail." Then, he slumped over, his wrists floppy. It was clear he couldn't think about changing for very long before the defenses of doubt and attack came down hard upon him. No wonder he hadn't been successful before.

I flopped my wrists to show Walter the shift. He laughed, and his body became tense again.

"Do you notice how when you talk about trying to change your smoking habits, the idea of instant failure slams into you?"

Walter nodded emphatically. "I want to work on changing it. But I don't think I can!"

"There's that doubting and attacking thought again, huh? No wonder you haven't been successful in the past. Those thoughts don't allow you to think about success." These thoughts were defenses against his power. Something about him having power triggered unconscious feelings, which set off anxiety, causing the need for doubting thoughts to obliterate his power. If his power were to continue provoking his anxiety, it would be hard for him to evolve.

"But I know I will fail!"

I stayed quiet, giving him time to hear himself.

"I did fail a lot before I succeeded in quitting cigarettes," he continued. "I knew I would fail, so I built that into my success plan."

I slapped my legs with both hands. "That's a brilliant plan! You build failure into your success plan with pot." In the middle of Walter's *I can't*, a message came through from the deep: *But I could before*. He had made quite a U-turn. One second, he was beating himself down, and the next, he was providing himself with a powerful solution. Therapy is a dance between our powerful and honest human selves and our resistance to it. Walter and I were in a waltz.

"You know what, that really takes the pressure off," he said after I repeated his words.

"Whatever plan you come up with, you will falter. We'll have a plan around those failures. We keep going. Like you managed to do with cigarettes."

"Right. I guess I want to talk more about it, but I'm not ready."

"About your relationship with pot?"

"Well, I don't know if I would call it a relationship!"

"Of course it's a relationship. Pot has been your best bud since you were nine. Just a little boy. What happened when you were nine?"

"Not much. Nothing really." He shrugged as if to say, *Nothing to see here! Move along!*

I waited. There was no chance this was true.

"I would walk my dad to work," Walter continued as if he was reporting the weather. "I would go down to the end of the driveway with him. I would wait for him to come home." His words could have been my own. I imagined saying goodbye to my dad as he walked down the driveway to the train station.

Don't go. Come back. Be with me.

"You wanted to be with him," I said.

Walter silently nodded his head.

"It broke me," he added. "Why didn't he want to be around me? And this is about the time I started to smoke."

"You say it like there was something wrong with you," I said. "That attack comes back on you now, huh?"

He nodded through emerging tears.

"These attacking thoughts are cruel to you."

"They make the depression. I hate them." He didn't hate himself anymore, he hated the thoughts that came up to hurt him. He had successfully differentiated himself from his attacking thoughts. The relationship we have to our defenses determines our success in triumphing over them. If we view our defenses as "just who we are" or don't see them, we won't do anything about them. If we are proud of them and identify with them as necessary parts of ourselves, we won't do anything about them. Why should we?

When people say, "The defense is just who I am! I am my defenses!" I respond by comparing our defenses to a smoking habit. A smoker is certainly the one who bought the cigarette, lit the tip, stuck it in their mouth, and inhaled, but they aren't the cigarette itself. In fact, they can flick that cigarette in the trash if they'd like. This flicking is nearly impossible, however, if the reason for which they use the cigarette is never dealt with. That's where therapy comes in. Asking someone to flick away a cigarette without dealing with the reason for the nicotine is cruel.

"If you put aside the attacking thoughts about you, what feelings come up toward your father for leaving?" Walter attacked himself due to the discomfort of his anger toward a man he loved.

He looked out the window and then to the wall behind me. I waited for his eyes to snap back to me. They didn't. Walter was building a wall between us, avoiding me.

"What just happened? Did you see that?" I asked.

"Yeah, I looked away again. I don't want to look at my father." To avoid his feelings toward his father, he avoided me.

"And you don't have to. And we also see that this wall comes up here with me. We were connected, and then you went away. What feelings are coming up toward me?" If Walter retreated every time mixed feelings occurred, he would take his loneliness to the grave.

"Anger!"

"And how do you feel that anger in your body physically?"

"But you didn't do anything," Walter said trying to rationalize away his anger.

"How do you experience this anger in your body toward me?" I asked, blocking his defense.

"You didn't do a thing," he repeated.

"How do you physically feel the anger toward me?" To get to the person underneath, to help the drowning person out of the water, we cannot be deterred by the waves trying to smack us away.

"I feel it in my, in my . . ." He looked down at his outstretched hands. "In my hands. And my arms! I feel it in my arms."

"And what's the sensation like in your arms and hands?"

"Energy! Uh, it feels good! This is different!"

"And what happens when you stay with that feeling? This anger toward me physically in your body?"

"It feels good! It feels powerful! I feel powerful. I also feel in control."

Now, Walter could feel his anger without getting depressed or disconnecting from me. He was experiencing his freedom and a connection. He could have his anger with me and stay with me. Anger didn't threaten the relationship. In fact, it bolstered it. He was angry with me, and he wasn't doing anything to hurt me.

As anger moved through his body, his anxiety was at an all-time low. Regulating anxiety is the key to therapeutic emotional exposure, empowerment, and control.

We smiled at each other.

"And what do those arms and hands want to do to me, in the safety of your mind? What does your body want if the anger can come out toward me?"

"It would slap you across the face."

After the words came out of his mouth, Walter's shoulders and face lost tension. He had hit the limit of his body's capacity to feel. He couldn't hold the remaining anger in his body. Instead, Walter turned the slap on himself.

"What just happened?" I asked.

"I shouldn't have that aggression in me."

"You do. We all do. See, you do have a problem: instead of feeling your emotions, you become aggressive with yourself. You don't have an impulse problem. You have the opposite. You don't explode, you implode. You're in control of your anger hurting others; however, you're not in control of your anger hurting you. You take the hit to protect others. This is the core of your problem. You've been denying your humanity. Denying your anger. You've been mixing up the desire to hurt with the act of hurting. Burying your anger. Hoping it will either go away or not exist. Pretending to be dead. And yet the anger is in there. And instead of facing it, it goes back on you. There is a hypocritical tyrant in there covering you, isn't there? And it's not innate in you. It's a learned mechanism. You weren't born with it. Let's let you have your birthright. Your life."

"I want my life back!" Walter sat up.

If we went to jail for these thoughts or urges, there'd be no one left to run society. In fact, if feelings were actions, we'd all be dead or covered in semen! And maybe, if we were shown that feelings and urges were okay, we wouldn't be anxious when they came up, and we'd be in control of those urges.

"And here you had an angry feeling toward me in you, which made your body feel energy, powerful," I continued. "The urge behind it was a slap. It was just an urge. You didn't do anything. Is it your belief that your true feelings are wrong? Is this why you play a dead man?"

"I think it is!"

"And are you willing to do something about it with me right now? Because you don't have to. You have a right to keep this belief system about what is right and wrong. It's up to you to weigh the costs and benefits. I'm here only to help you see the causes of your suffering. Only then can you make informed choices about your life."

He turned his head to me. "I can't live like this. The anger, it did feel great." He straightened up again and let out a sigh.

"And if you didn't cover yourself with punishment, how would you feel after looking at my face after you slap me?"

"Oh god . . . I feel terrible. I would feel guilty." And with healthy guilt instead of his shame, Walter began to cry tears that could lead to his freedom. Except for the sound of sobs, there was silence as Walter felt a previously amputated part of himself—the anger toward someone he cared about and the resulting guilt.

"It feels different. Bad still, but different from shame. And depression," Walter said through tears.

"Guilt doesn't feel good."

"No, it doesn't. It *is* different."

Another wave of guilt moved through his body, with currents of movement that looked like howls emerging from his throat. I sat with him in silence. His body shook freely as emotion moved up and through his body. He could sit with me and himself, with the anger and gratitude about our work. He could have all his feelings toward me and be with me. He could be him and be with another.

Walter sighed and repositioned himself on the couch. "I want a relationship like that with my wife, where I can have my anger and my love. But I don't know if she wants that with me. I surely wasn't allowed to be angry with my mother. Oh god, certainly not my father."

Walter's body never got to experience these feelings as safe. They would threaten his most important relationships. His parents didn't know what to do with his feelings. When we're kids, not having our parents around can feel like life or death. Thus, we do everything we can to remain in their favor, including pushing back our anger toward them. As kids, we wonder, without consciously doing so, how much of ourselves we have to give up to be loved.

"My father never said he loved me," Walter added.

No wonder he turned to pot. It provided the comfort his father didn't give.

"Never," Walter said again. "That's something I would've remembered. He was always drinking, drinking as soon as he got home. I think this was around the time he told me he was moving away." Walter's eyes filled with tears again. He reached for the tissue box and ripped one out. "My dad, he was moving away. He was going to live by himself, far away."

He paused.

"I was nine," he said with a sigh. The year he started smoking. "My father never told me he loved me. Never. And now he's dead." Walter's limp hands became fists.

"He never told you," I echoed.

"Never."

Walter felt anger toward a father he loved. Anger is easy if we don't have warm feelings toward someone. Love is easy if we feel only love. Yet only love or only anger is never the case when we relate to a real person. To help Walter, we had to help him feel both together.

"I want to kill him, like actually kill him."

"And how do you feel that murderous rage in your body? Toward this man you love?" I had to help him face his deepest feelings so he didn't fear them. Then, he could free himself from solitary confinement because he could realize that his only murder attempt was the violence his depression did to his soul.

Walter sighed and stretched out his strong arms. "I want to grab him by the throat." His hands reached out and grabbed the air. His face held the expression of a man seeing what he described. Walter began to sob. Large waves of grief and guilt passed through him.

"Let it through as much as you can. It's painful to see what's been locked inside."

Since Walter's brother died from a rope around his neck, seeing his hands around his father's neck must have been especially painful. I wondered if these same aggressive urges were toward his beloved brother as well.

"Let the guilt go through," I said.

"I loved him."

Now a free man, he broke into sobs.

21

Michelle: Out of the Box

As I put my head in my hands, Dr. A sat silent. The evidence was mounting: my headaches increased when I blocked emotions in the session. This was a completely new discovery. I thought my headaches were due only to structural problems in my brain and the aftermath of surgeries. Doctors even told me occasional headaches would be normal after the procedures. My therapy sessions revealed a more complex picture.

"I can't count how many times my head was cut into," I said, lifting my head out of my hands. "How can we tell the difference between headaches caused by psychological processes and headaches caused by what I went through and what was wrong with my brain?"

Dr. A crossed his legs and sat back in his chair. "We can watch what it does in here, as we have been. You can tell me what your head pain is doing as we sit and learn from it. You know the drill." He was referring to the fact that I had also treated headache patients.

There are myriad causes of headaches. There is neuroplastic pain, which is pain caused by our brain mistaking safe signals from the body as dangerous signals from the body.[1] There are tension headaches caused by striated muscle anxiety, sympathy pains, unconscious dynamics, structural issues (such as Chiari malformations), other brain abnormalities, tumors, brain injuries, dehydration, and on and on.

I was worried Dr. A would oversimplify the cause of my headaches. Too often, I found doctors saw only what they could treat. I needed someone who would try to see the whole picture.

In fact, I needed to see the whole picture.

I decided it was time to take my surgeries more seriously. If we were going to look at my head pain together, he needed to know.

"I need to tell you more about what my head has been through," I said, making "my head" the recipient of trauma instead of me.

It is a myth that therapy cleanses us of all anxiety and defenses. Even as I became healthier, taking my surgeries out of the Not Important box, I still used a defense that made the subject of my pain my head rather than me. The conflict of *see me, don't see me* was still raging inside me, yet the part of me that wanted to be seen was gaining strength.

"It's important to me that you have a bigger picture." I sighed, feeling relief as I made myself clear. I looked at Dr. A, who was looking back at me, waiting. "It was hard to not know the cause of the pain, to go through so many doctors. And the fact that I didn't understand insurance made it more complicated." I looked down at my wrist, where the temporary tattoo had been during our first session. "I was haunted by surprise medical bills," I continued, "and I lost a lot of my savings. Thank goodness I had some financial help from my dad."

As I spoke, I noticed a growing desire to pull away from the surgeries, to change the subject to something else. I didn't want to tell him because saying it out loud would make them matter. I wanted those years gone, erased, eviscerated, because every single moment of them hurt. When in chronic pain, every moment aches. Because emotionally, chronic pain is not just the pain itself. Sure, there's constant physical pain, and there's also the anguish of not having an answer, the torment of thinking you have an answer when you don't, the wondering if you're nuts, the strain on relationships, the anticipation of the next thing that will help, one failure after another, and then, finally, true hope. And then disappointment. And then, hope. And then, *learned helplessness*. Learned helplessness is a term that comes from a study in 1968.[2] Researchers found that when dogs were repeatedly zapped with electric shocks the dogs couldn't control, the dogs eventually stopped taking action to protect themselves. For example, after a while, the researchers opened the cages to allow these dogs to escape, but they wouldn't. They had learned action was useless. This is common in chronic, unexplained pain patients.

"By the end of the first year of the headache, I was heading toward learned helplessness, if I wasn't there already. The first time I felt hope for true change was three years after the headache began, when I met Dr. B. He was a specialist in treating headache patients and was highly recommended. At first, I barely cared because years had gone by, and only opioids had helped me. So why would he?"

I flashed back to my first meeting with Dr. B. Even though I was with Dr. A, I felt Dr. B's presence as if he was still leaning over me, his hands applying light pressure around my scalp. His manner was humble, unassuming, and gentle. When he pushed, I winced, and he apologized with sincerity and a gentle pet to my head. He told me I had peripheral neuropathy of the nerves surrounding my head, and he would do a procedure to give the nerves around my head more room to breathe as they may be squished or cut into by a bone or something else. If that didn't work, he would cut them, one group of nerves at a time.

Devon and I were left speechless.

"While driving home, Devon began to cry," I said to Dr. A. "It was the first time I saw the impact my pain had on his life. We had never talked about it. Through a squeaky voice, he said, 'It has just been so long.' I had never heard Devon say anything like that."

"Your pain was a burden to him."

Dr. A's words stung. He was right. Chronic pain impacts everyone who has a relationship with the pain sufferer. I felt a pang of guilt for not having thought about Devon's feelings until that drive home from Dr. B's office.

"For the first surgery, my dad and his wife flew in the night before. My father had married a lovely and quirky woman when I was eighteen. If he was all business, she was all art and spirit." I threw up my hands to illustrate my stepmother's free spirit. Dr. A smiled. "We drove to the hospital, where we would meet up with my mom. The thought of my mom and dad together in the same room calcified my body. Now that I reflect on it, I realize I ignored the tension."

"You didn't notice you," Dr. A added.

"I didn't notice me." I paused, allowing the silence to give room to the echo of our last sentence.

"I'll always remember the entrance to the operating room. It felt like the door to heaven. While the room was white, clean, and cold, I was warm underneath heated blankets. Once I was under anesthesia, Dr. B cut four incisions into the back of my head. He separated the blood vessels from my nerves, giving them more room to breathe. And he found something: one of my blood vessels had grown right through a nerve. I thought this could be my answer. Yet, of course, it wasn't. What I remember is when I woke up, my dad was frequently peering out of this speckled blue curtain that separates the rooms. He was looking for the discharge nurse." I could see my dad, peering out and away, with tightness all over his body, as he asked about the nurses.

"Where are the nurses? When do you leave?" he asked, his face red.

"They'll be here," I said, trying to reassure him in the haze of anesthesia. Soon, my dad was up on his feet, looking for a nurse to discharge me. My body stiffened. I didn't want to leave. While I wanted to stay in the hospital forever, I needed to leave faster than my body was ready so my dad could be comfortable.

"After the anesthesia left my system, my pain returned," I told Dr. A. "To my delight, we scheduled the next surgery. For this one, the doctor made four incisions, two above each ear, creating room around the nerves under my temples. This time, he found nothing abnormal."

"Two surgeries?" Dr. A asked.

"No. More. After the anesthesia left my system, my pain returned. We scheduled the next surgery for a few days before Christmas. Before cutting into my head for the third time," I said with a laugh, "Dr. B leaned toward me and said, 'We are going to cut the nerves that make you frown. You won't be able to frown after this.' He leaned back and gave me a wide closed-mouth smile, as if he was gifting me a Lamborghini. I frowned, apparently for the last time, and nodded back." Dr. A frowned and then raised his eyebrows. "Are you showing off?" I asked with a smile. This time, Dr. A laughed out loud.

"Go on," he said after he laughed.

"He sliced into my eyelids to sever the nerves running from my eye sockets up through my forehead. This time, he found nerves growing directly into my skull. He said they would have more space now. Again, I was excited. Yet after the anesthesia left my system, my pain returned. For the fourth surgery—" I heard Dr. A sigh. "Are you okay?" I asked him without thinking.

"Yes, go on."

Now, I sighed. I told him how Dr. B went into the same incisions on the side of my head. This time, he cut the nerves so that they no longer fired signals to communicate pain. Yet the pain continued. I was surely crazy. For the fifth surgery, Dr. B cut the nerves that ran up the back of my head. After all five surgeries, I felt only a little better. The changes after each procedure were nearly imperceptible. It wasn't enough, not enough for the rest of my life. There was only one surgery left, where Dr. B would cut the last remaining nerves surrounding my skull. If that didn't work, there wasn't any more he could do.

"What was going on in your life at this point?" Dr. A asked.

"By this point? I had quit my consulting job, waited tables, and walked dogs, which didn't cover the costs of living and medical bills. All thanks to opioids, I then applied to graduate schools, went to school, graduated, and began my residency. By the fifth surgery, I was planning to start my private practice. With chronic pain and the waning power of opioids, I wasn't sure if I could."

"You did a lot during this."

"I did. With chronic pain, something in me snapped. Like, I can't just lay down and die. And opioids, my precious little round pills, helped me do all of this. All I did was think about the pain and how to decrease it or distract myself from it."

As I sat in front of Dr. A, I could feel my old self in my current body: my future terrified me, my present hurt me, and my past felt like it never existed because the pain of the present erased it. I didn't think the past mattered. And until this moment, all of it had been labeled Not Important.

"We can try to look at this together; however, I'm not sure if we can do anything about it. There is a lot going on in there," I said, pointing to my head.

"Now you have another headache doctor," Dr. A said with a closed-mouth smile.

Confused, I attempted to furrow my inert brow.

"Me," Dr. A responded.

The idea of Dr. A helping me with headaches after all I had been through seemed not only silly but also impossible. I didn't tell him.

22

Emma: Ghosting

When Emma came in for her next session, she shared that she had been on a date. I was in the middle of throwing a secret party for her between me and myself when she interrupted it by telling me not to get excited.

She didn't like him.

She noticed that she told herself she wouldn't like him, he wasn't tall enough, he wasn't very good at talking, and he was weird all before she met him. The whole time she was sitting with him, she was looking for problems. How is he eating? What does he order? How much does he drink? After a while, she realized she didn't want to be there. She wasn't having any fun.

"It doesn't sound like anyone in their right mind would be having fun," I said once she was done telling me about her date. "You noticed a devaluation process. The guy didn't stand a chance."

"No, he didn't. But you know what? Whatever!" she said, throwing her hands up into the air. "A couple of weeks ago, a guy just ghosted me. We had this date set up. It was even a second date, and I kind of liked him. He was supposed to pick me up for a game, and he . . ." She stuck her arms out with her palms facing each other. "He. Just. Didn't. Show. Up!" She clapped between each word. "And that's happened to me, like, three other times."

Instead of facing the reality of goodbye, her date had disappeared.

"That really is horrible," I said, shaking my head.

"How are we supposed to date with people doing that!" Emma said, throwing up her hands in a helpless *What can I do?* posture. She paused and looked down. "I did that last week," she confessed to her nails. Her hair fell in front of her face, hiding her expression.

I looked at her, both confused and seeing stars from emotional whiplash.

"I ghosted this guy," she said, flipping her hair up and facing me.

"*This* guy? The one you were just telling me about?"

"I don't know what's wrong with me!"

It was a valid question. "Well, first, let's make sure the environment in *there*," I said, pointing to her, "is safe enough to answer that question honestly. There's an attack coming on you when you ask, 'What's wrong with me?' The question is coming from the Bitch. I don't know about you, but I don't like learning about myself from a bitch."

She nodded and moved her butt back and forth on the couch as if to settle in. I was surprised at her immediate willingness. She let out a loud sigh.

"You want to figure out what you're doing to sabotage connecting. And to not dismiss someone through criticism or ghosting."

She tensed her jaw and began to pick at her nails. "Yes, that's what I want." As she spoke, she dug into her cuticle and ripped off a piece of her skin. "Ouch," she whispered, looking down at the damage. What probably seemed like nothing to Emma was painful to see: She had declared she wanted something good for herself, which was a big deal for Emma. At the same time, she ripped off a piece of her skin. She drew blood.

"As soon as you say you want to do a good thing for yourself, a piece of you got ripped off." I mimed the assault with my own hands and threw in the "Ouch" for good measure.

"Oh my god, I didn't even notice."

Inviting her to do something good for herself triggered unconscious mixed feelings (a warm one and a not-so-warm one) toward me. These mixed feelings caused Emma anxiety. Her body fixed the problem (anger toward a person she cared for) by rerouting the anger onto her. If she felt only good things toward me, she wouldn't be anxious. Something about our interaction—our relationship—triggered mixed feelings toward me. Emma learned that she needed to remove parts of herself to attach to her caregivers and belong in our culture. She created pseudoattachments not as herself but as her defenses. The Cool Girl, the easy one. Her raw feelings, thoughts, wishes, and opinions were not acceptable as they made her too needy, too difficult. To solve the problem, she put all her feelings, thoughts, wishes, and opinions into her Not Important box, dug a hole deep within her, and buried the box deep within the hole.

Emma's relationship with me was different from her early environment. Our relationship was not about accepting her harmful defenses as her true self. Our relationship was about being open to her feelings, thoughts, wishes, and opinions, *no matter what they were*. This shift in relational patterns stirred up unconscious mixed feelings toward me that linked to feelings toward those who did not offer her a secure and open bond. When I offered a secure bond in which she could be herself, this triggered feelings and her history of dealing with them—her defenses. When I was not like others, the box in which she had buried her feelings reopened, which triggered her anxiety and defenses that had helped her stay within her original tribe. "Don't look at me! I don't have needs! I don't have feelings! I'm easy! I'm the Cool Girl! Don't pay attention to me!" These defenses and her anxiety about her emotions caused her current struggles: loneliness.

When I pushed the feelings button, the defenses "Don't look at me! I don't have needs! I don't have feelings! I'm easy! I'm the Cool Girl! Don't pay attention to me!" poured out.

When I pushed the let's-do-something-good-for-you button, aggression toward herself popped out.

"Yeah, I didn't see that I did that," she repeated after I pointed out that she ripped off a piece of herself after declaring a wish for herself. She didn't notice herself. With this self-neglect, she couldn't pay attention to herself enough to give her the care she needed. Since she couldn't see her self-punishment, she couldn't stop it. No wonder she was uncomfortable.

"I only had a hangnail," she added dismissively. "It's no big deal." And now she was minimizing. *Nothing to see here!*

We both looked down at her fingertip, where a small dot of blood had emerged from the wound. She immediately put her thumb over it to hide the evidence of violence.

"When you say, 'It's no big deal,' this is a way to dismiss yourself. And your wounds."

"My sisters speak like that to me all the time. And I do too. We all do. All the time, someone tells me to suck it up. Or that it will be fine. Or to not be negative."

Self-dismissal, self-neglect, and self-attack were her mother tongue she had to speak to survive and belong.

"I could be wrong, but it looks like you're starting to understand something in your heart." When I said, "in your heart," I worried Emma would call it cheesy. Calling something cheesy often means it's uncomfortable (anxiety producing). If I'm saying something meaningful and someone calls it cheesy, I label it the *cheesification defense*, which is a way to devalue meaningful content.

But Emma didn't call it cheesy. Instead, she started squirming around.

"It's really hard not to pick! The urge is coming up right now!"

"What happens as you refrain and just feel the urge to pick? What comes up in your body?"

Emma turned her face to the window and grimaced.

"I don't know!" she wailed, like a six-year-old.

"You have developed a habit," I said to Emma as she wormed around. "You discharge your anxiety by picking your nails. What's under this urge to pick at yourself? When you stated that you wanted something good for yourself, this created anxiety that you discharged by drawing your own blood."

Emma's legs straightened out in front of her. Her arms went out, and her fingers collected into two fists. Her jaw clamped down hard.

"What feelings are coming up inside of your body?" I glanced down at her fists.

"What? These?" She picked up her fists and let them go, showing me loose, empty hands. *Nothing to see here!* The defenses begged us to ignore her.

"They were fists, and now you show me empty hands, playing as if the feeling was never there," I said, rejecting the defense's invitation to ignore her. "This is another way to dismiss and neglect yourself. This is an invitation to neglect and ignore you."

Her hands went back into fists.

"It's anger!" Emma said with a tense, closed-mouth smile.

"And who is this anger toward?"

"Me!"

"This is how you *reroute* it. It comes out on you."

"I can't be angry with myself?"

"Of course you can, but how is that working for you? Anger toward you is a defense against something else. Do you want to take the anger away from you? To see what happens? To see what this picking covers up?"

"Yeah, because it sucks," she said, letting out a sigh.

"If you put your anger toward you aside, and you don't pick at yourself, dismiss yourself, or attack yourself, what happens? What feelings come up toward me? If you let them come out toward me?" I was challenging her to put aside all defenses to see what would emerge.

"I don't want to be angry with you!"

"Exactly. You don't want to be angry with me, and yet you are. Instead of facing the anger toward me, your anger reroutes onto you. Not wanting to be angry doesn't mean you suddenly aren't. In fact, *you* get attacked with your anger."

Emma stared at me, the wheels in her mind turning. Her jaw moved back and forth as if chewing on the idea.

"This is ridiculous!" she said flippantly. "Why would I have anger toward the person trying to help me?"

"Or is it ridiculous that there are mechanisms that attack, neglect, and dismiss you when you have feelings? Anxiety comes up and hurts your esophagus, head, jaw, and teeth. Mechanisms prevent you from being a free woman. And you're not meaning to do these things. Either way, it's happening, and it's up to you to do something about them." Her anxiety was still in the ideal zone, but that didn't mean she wanted to continue.

She began to pick her nails again and then stopped, which led to her straightening out her legs in front of her. She balled up her fists.

"Oh my god, this is too weird! I think there *is* anger in there toward you! I don't want it toward you!"

"What are you going to do about that? Now you know what's causing your pain, yet a part of you refuses to be kind to you. What have you done to deserve this treatment?" I was speaking directly to her unconscious belief that she deserved to be punished *and* her wish to become free.

Emma didn't speak. She was becoming even more resistant. Her defenses were forming a thick, seemingly impenetrable wall that could sabotage Emma's wish to recover. The presence of many defenses meant that feelings were trying to break through. The war was on. Feelings were close to the surface. If her anxiety was in the optimal levels and she wanted to, we could proceed. Most bail at this point, yet this is when a true breakthrough can happen.

"We know you also have a positive feeling toward me for trying to help," I said, holding up my left hand. "And there's also anger toward me. This anger gets rerouted onto you." I held up my right hand. "On the one hand, you have this positive feeling toward me, and on the other hand, you have this anger toward me." Emma nodded, still tense with tight fists, looking directly at me. "What is it like to have this positive feeling with this other feeling, this anger, *toward me* at the *same time*?" I moved both my hands together, interlacing my fingers. A positive feeling and anger together.

Emma burst into tears. "This is too weird! As soon as your hands started moving toward each other, my body freaked out! Something about acknowledging *both* these feelings together. It was like, whoa. It's a totally novel idea! My body is not used to that! It's not okay with that!" Emma was accustomed to taking anger toward someone else and putting it back on her. "I don't know," Emma said with a sharp, loud sigh. "I don't know about any of this. I don't want to be angry. If therapy means getting in touch with that, I don't know if I want this. I don't want to be angry."

Emma's brief breakthrough allowed her to experience that her body was not accustomed to anger and warmth being together. No one ever taught her she could be angry with a person she loved, and *the relationship could survive*. No one ever taught her she could be angry with a person she loved, and *no one had to get hurt*. No one ever taught her she could be angry with a person she loved, and *she wasn't bad*. No one ever taught her she could be angry with a person she loved, and *this anger could bring them closer*. Her unwillingness to face the feelings she avoided meant she could not have a new experience that led to change.

While Emma had a choice about whether she wanted to work together, she didn't realize that she had no choice about whether she was angry. None of us do. We can work only on what we do with our anger.

23

Michelle: Set Changes

Often, we can't tell our histories because our defenses obscure the truth. Instead, therapists must learn to understand the language of defense and anxiety, for they are often the only visible truths. If we withhold, however, usually therapists cannot tell. When we withhold, we are on our own.

I had withheld from Dr. A in our last session. I left out what happened right after the first five surgeries when Dr. A asked what was going on in my life. I realized my overediting on my drive home from our last session and vowed to share what I was aware of the next time I saw him. I needed to face what I avoided to find freedom from the suffering caused by my defenses. We cannot learn about ourselves solely by exploring what we're comfortable with.

"I saw last time that my head pain changed in our session," I said to Dr. A after a long exhale at the beginning of our next session. "And I'm open to talking to you about how the pain changes. I don't think it has anything to do with my emotions, even though it looks like it does a little. I still think it might be coincidence. I mean, a lot happened during those years of head pain." I paused as an image of Devon splashed across my mind. Dr. A must have seen my expression change because he asked me what was going on.

"Well, a lot happened in those years," I repeated with a sigh. The sigh told us that I had conflict within me, unresolved experiences

I avoided because of painful emotions. A sigh is one of the most common types of metal detector beeps. Where there's a sigh, there's often buried treasure.

"Those years were also the years I was with Devon, my ex-boyfriend. My whole life changed," I said, being vague.

"You seem to get tense," Dr. A said. "What feelings are coming up as you mention him?"

Dr. A was right. I felt tension in my shoulders and back. I immediately felt like I wanted to brush over the whole thing, using my defense of minimization and dismissal.

"Oh, it probably has to do with how the relationship ended," I said, not answering his question. "I'm glad it did end, but it was a weird ending." *Weird* was a defense called a *cover word*. A cover word is a vague word that covers the truth. *Strange, weird, awkward, odd, fine, okay*—all these words are covers for something more specific and revealing. The person using these words can't be known because they shroud themselves in vague concepts rather than specific details.

"Weird?" Dr. A said, looking at me skeptically. I had started to get used to this look. It often said to me, *I see you hiding something!* I had no idea if that was what he was actually thinking. I may have been projecting, thinking that Dr. A thought I was hiding something when I knew I was obscuring the truth.

"We were together for six years, all during the headache. Then, he met a girl in Germany. Our relationship had been good, but it was really a threesome: me, Devon, and my head pain." While those statements held true, they constituted the extent of the truth I consciously recognized. My defenses withheld the rest from me. I didn't tell Dr. A that the breakup was the most painful breakup I had ever experienced. I didn't because I hadn't let myself know it yet either. The knowledge was stored in the tension around my lungs that caused my sigh.

I thought back to Devon's text, which he sent only a few weeks after he left for a language course in Germany.

"I think I am starting to get feelings for her," the text read.

"What do you mean?" I had asked Devon over video chat. My face was numb. Devon said he didn't know what it meant. He didn't want our relationship to end, but he had feelings for her.

I turned my attention back to Dr. A and told him that Devon had met a girl.

"Him meeting this girl in Germany revealed that while our relationship was a good one, we were also struggling," I said to Dr. A. I paused, feeling as though my words didn't capture what I meant to say. "Basically, when he told me he had feelings for this other girl and went back and forth on what he wanted, I realized the relationship wasn't right for me."

I flashed back to what it felt like to face his indecision, which sparked my desire to make clear decisions. I needed to be more honest with myself. My healthy emotional immune system kicked into gear. I didn't want to wait for him to make up his mind. While our relationship was loving, something was missing, and not just because I was in pain and on medication. Many things were unsaid. To say them, we needed to speak a language both of us had yet to learn. He felt controlling, and I was stubborn. "Don't eat so many Oreos" versus "But they make me happy." "Why don't you like what I like?" versus "Why can't I like what I like?" "Don't say that because it makes that person uncomfortable" versus "But why is it always about someone else's comfort?" We were affectionate. He was critical and barely ever complimented me. I didn't notice. He could be cruel, never knowing it, and kind. I could be cruel, never knowing it, and kind. I had little to no access to sexual desire since pain and opioids infested my body. Basic tastes were different: many joys couldn't be shared.

I turned my attention back to Dr. A.

"Devon had lived six years with a woman in pain, someone who couldn't be herself or do the things she loved," I told Dr. A. "My life wasn't enough for him. After a week of heart-wrenching struggle within myself, after sobbing together over video chat, I decided that I, too, needed more. His indecision would cripple me if I also used it as an excuse to be indecisive."

I thought about the moment I ended our six-year-long relationship. Both of us were devastated. I wanted to be with someone for whom I was enough. We sobbed and sobbed, a world away and a screen apart. We spoke of how great our relationship was, how damaged it was. He was the man who had been by my side for six years, longer than anyone ever had. He sat in a strange new world in Germany in a room far away. I sat in our home, surrounded by the life we had made for each other.

"After the breakup, I went into hyperdrive."

"Hyperdrive?" Dr. A asked.

"Yeah, I guess my experience with rotating nannies and no goodbyes came in handy because I felt very little pain," I said proudly with a smile. Dr. A did not smile back. "I separated our stuff, signed a lease on a new studio apartment, packed, set up movers, bought new furniture, and completely unpacked and settled in within one week."

"Literally one week?"

"Literally one week," I said again proudly. "It was like the frenzied set change between a quick intermission of an elaborate Broadway play, except this was real."

Pride over defenses is common, especially if society admires them and your family is grateful for them—*Oh, you're strong to not shed a tear and move on quickly!* Goodbyes were always easy for me. I seemed to walk away from relationships with no problem. I had ended every relationship I had ever been in, except a two-week relationship with a boy in the seventh grade. My ability to move on was something I adored. I was immune from what the other humans (whom I considered weak) felt after a breakup. I was awesome.

Yet this wasn't the truth.

Strength is in facing pain, not burying or denying it.

I was only vaguely aware of the grief from this goodbye with Devon. I was also exhilarated about beginning anew. I wanted to design my apartment, see friends, and date. I single-mindedly rode the high of my new life instead of giving room for my loss. Because of my inexperience with facing and feeling grief, I didn't know that a goodbye could be a gain and a loss. Thus, I made goodbyes binary—they were either good or bad. In doing this, I both saved and lost parts of myself. I did goodbyes without *feeling* goodbyes.

"After Devon and I broke up, I had the sixth surgery."

"Sixth?"

I nodded. "I began dating before the bruising healed above my eyes. I created an online dating profile with barely any information about me. I wrote something like, 'Due to my job, the information I'm putting on my profile is limited.'" I went on a slew of first dates. I tried speed dating and even went on one blind date with a man who declared that he wouldn't allow a dog into his bedroom because it was "only an animal" and "dirty." His disdain made him an instant no. I met a man who showed me much of what I had been missing. He complimented me, recognized me for who I am, and made me feel special. He was visiting from another country and had to go home. I knew I had been special to Devon, yet he struggled to show it.

"Many men, upon hearing I was a therapist, recoiled and asked, 'Are you analyzing me right now?'" At this, Dr. A smiled. I wondered if he had experienced the same thing. I feared asking and went on. "A few insincere wordsmiths were obviously liars. I kept looking. I wanted to fulfill another life dream besides becoming a therapist, which was to hold the wrinkled hand of my husband until the day one of us died."

"This is your dream?"

"Yes, this is my dream. One of them. And then, I met Ben."

Ben was different. I didn't think he was interested in me, yet on our second date, late in the evening under a willow tree by the Potomac, I realized he was nervous. As he spoke, I slowly raised a finger, brought it to his lips, and leaned in. Kissing under the willow tree, peanut butter and jelly sandwich still in the corners of our mouths, we fell in love.

When I used vague words to explain to Dr. A that those were "hard years," my words obscured the truth while my body told the honest story in its tension, sighing, and defenses. The honest story was that I couldn't handle the reality of what happened. Instead, my genuine feelings made me anxious. The tension held back the urges of rage, the sobs of grief, and the pangs of guilt. The tension, sighing, and cover words were the signals that told us to dig. Apparently, my defenses overpowered us both because what I said to Dr. A next was "So I broke up with Devon after he met a girl in Germany. It was hard. The relationship was good, and it was also hard. Thank goodness this happened, though, because I got to meet Ben."

And we moved on.

If a therapeutic partnership (the therapist and client) misses an opportunity, another will present itself. My problem with facing grief and pain would present itself again and again. Like a train on a circular track with only one stop, the opportunity to look past my dismissing, minimizing, and self-neglecting defenses would come again and again.

24

Walter: The Pot Plan

Walter had a conversation with his wife. He told her he wanted to go to couples therapy, and she agreed. Shortly after, he had a dream of being surrounded by people who wanted to know and deeply understand him.

"It felt good," he said, concluding his story. He stopped and looked out the window. "How deeply can I know myself with the pot though?"

"That's a great question to ask yourself."

"And I realize," he continued, "I don't know the difference between my ability to think and what the pot does to me."

I didn't either.

"Pot Brain versus Walter Brain," I said.

"Exactly. And when I try to take the stairs, I can't. My lungs are killing me. It's taking away . . ." Walter stopped his sentence. I sat in silence, waiting. "You know, I used to have a real job."

Walter told me about when he used to be a software developer. He was good at it, yet he felt like he was outdated compared to "kids these days." He didn't think he could work anymore because of how much pot he smoked. What Walter said was true. A two-generation age gap can feel like sixteen in the technology world. He was behind. He was too high to learn.

"I want to think of a plan to stop smoking. I want to start talking about this." Tears formed in his eyes as he spoke.

"You're going to miss it," I said. "Your buddy. This grief comes up in you now."

"Yeah, I know. But I want to make this plan now!"

Walter was using the defense of let's-make-a-plan-to-stop-doing-constant-drugs to avoid his sadness. As his therapist, I couldn't complain.

I reminded him of the first step, which was to build failure into his success plan.

"Right. I love that. I think that's truly going to help me."

"What's it like to feel that hope?"

"Like a lifting!" He brought his arms up above his head. We paused to help him luxuriate in that feeling of hope. It was a foreign experience. Only a few moments went by before tears of grief formed in his eyes.

Feeling better often leads to a rude awakening. When we feel better, we feel the disparity between what we feel now and our past suffering. Grief is a natural response to the loss of time in which we could have been free yet instead suffered. When we see what we've missed, grief flows. However, if grief makes us anxious, we might avoid feeling better to deny there is something better. To avoid grief, we may avoid relief. This is why it was crucial that Walter and I worked to help him face his grief rather than deny it. Thankfully, Walter had worked hard enough to let himself experience his grief. Thus, he could move within grief, allowing it to carry his heart where he needed, rather than see it as a wall from which he had to turn away.

"I want to use that hope for my Pot Plan. I was hoping you'd throw out a few more ideas," he said.

To give advice or not? Sometimes, it can help. Sometimes, it can't. It's impossible to know beforehand. I will know only when I see Walter's reaction.

Since Walter said he smoked from the morning until bedtime, I suggested not smoking before noon for the next two weeks and seeing how that felt. "Meaning what feelings come up, how your anxiety is, and what defenses you notice coming up when you don't use the pot."

Walter nodded, liking the idea. He then looked out the window, deep in thought.

"Can I ask you a question?" he asked, turning his eyes back to me. I nodded. "Is it okay if I ask you how you got into this type of therapy?" It was the first time Walter asked me a question about myself. I decided to answer.

"Sure. When I first started working with clients, I felt the tools I had weren't enough for most people. After graduate school, it felt as if I had gone to medical school and learned only to dole out Advil." I stopped and wondered how much detail I should share. I thought back to my first placement, which was with a mental health team in a jail. My very first client was a woman who had killed her mother by smashing her in the head. The first time I sat across from her, I wondered if I was competent enough to help her. I felt this with most clients—the man missing parts of his body due to massive trauma, the man brought in by a slew of armed guards, the man who flooded his cell by plugging his toilet and smearing feces all over the walls. After the jail, I worked at a private group practice. Despite the difference in setting, I found myself asking the same questions. Am I qualified to help this person? Will they need only an Advil? Some of my clients found my skills helpful; however, most didn't. To my horror, one client even laughed at my interventions and said, "This feels like putting a Band-Aid on my chest after a heart attack." All I could say was "I hear you."

"I had a true lack of knowledge," I said, turning my mind back to Walter. "While we became familiar with a few approaches and techniques in graduate school, we didn't learn *how* or *when* to apply certain skills, nor what to do if they didn't work. I knew that most people desperately needed more than an Advil for their pain."

"Fascinating. And frustrating," Walter said.

"It was frustrating. I was also frustrated with the futility of diagnostic labels. Major depressive disorder, generalized anxiety disorder. We know what symptoms we have, but what we don't know—and need to know—is *why* we're suffering and *how* to make it stop. Anyway, I finally learned about the Triangle of Conflict, and the rest is history."

I reached for my yellow paper pad and drew the Triangle of Conflict.[1]

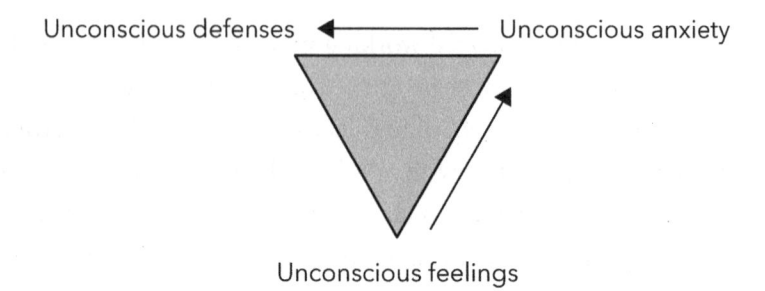

Unconscious defenses ← Unconscious anxiety

Unconscious feelings

"There are unconscious feelings, which can lead to unconscious anxiety, which can lead to unconscious defenses," I said, handing him the pad. "It's called the Triangle of Conflict. There's also the Triangle of Persons, which shows the three areas in which this pattern of feeling, anxiety, and defense plays out. Here, let me have that back for a second." Walter handed back the pad. I drew the Triangle of Persons and handed it back to him.

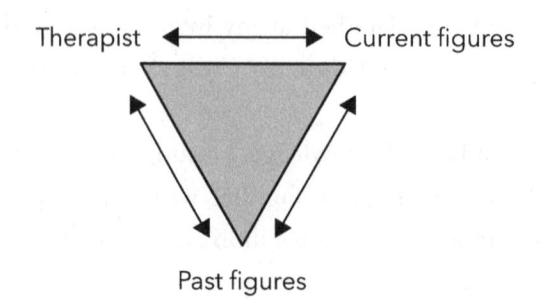

Therapist ↔ Current figures

Past figures

I described how these patterns can be learned in our early relationships with past figures, as well as how they can be played out in current relationships and with the therapist. We can study these patterns in all three relationship categories: our past, our present, and with the therapist in the immediate now. We come to therapy because the defenses we learned in childhood no longer work in adulthood. Or we come to therapy because our anxiety about our emotions is too intense. We don't know this is going on, hence the word *unconscious*. We work with this process in the session as it's happening with us in the therapeutic relationship.

"Is all anxiety caused by unconscious emotions?"

"No, we're much more complex than that. Often, there are multiple causes of our suffering."

"Well, this pattern, this is definitely what's happening within me," Walter said.

"Indeed. And I sometimes like drawing it this way. Here, let me have the pad again." He handed it back. "Here's the other way to look at it." I drew another diagram and handed it back to him.

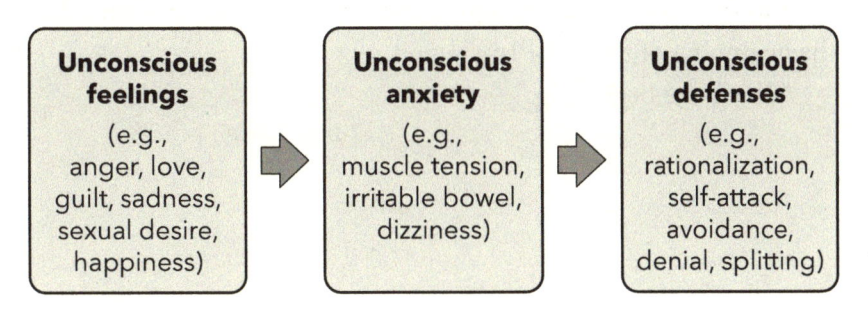

Unconscious feelings	Unconscious anxiety	Unconscious defenses
(e.g., anger, love, guilt, sadness, sexual desire, happiness)	(e.g., muscle tension, irritable bowel, dizziness)	(e.g., rationalization, self-attack, avoidance, denial, splitting)

"If we can help people face their emotions safely, we can cut this process off between unconscious feelings and unconscious anxiety. If emotions no longer trigger anxiety, everything else falls apart. And again," I continued, "there can be multiple causes. We're complex. This is one way our symptoms are caused."

Walter took a deep sigh, and I did as well.

"When I learned about how our unconscious systems worked, I realized therapy wouldn't just be an Advil. It could be more for many people."

We both paused, soaking in the moment.

Walter turned to the window and then back to me. "I needed more than an Advil."

I did too, Walter.

Suddenly, I felt a yearning for opioids. I looked at Walter and decided to test out the hypothesis that my personal experience was a communication about his.

"Are you going to miss it?"

"I'm going to miss it. It *was—is—*my buddy. It is. It still is. And I don't have a brother—I mean buddy."

Walter and I looked at each other. We both heard him.

"You miss your brother," I repeated.

"I do. Pot has been with me the whole time," Walter said, sniffling. He wiped his nose with the back of his hand and then took a tissue to wipe the back of his hand.

I looked at the clock to signal the end of our time. "Then that's the beginning of the Pot Plan," I said.

"That's the beginning."

25

Michelle: The New Name

I returned from a week-long Zen meditation retreat for therapists, during which we could not speak, look at, or interact with each other. We were to turn inward, sit deeply with ourselves, and be with whatever our unconscious gave us during this sacred silence and time together.[1] During meditation, we could not move. I decided not to take any opioids. While my back and shoulders felt immense pain from meditating for hours without moving, my headaches were minimal. A few days after the retreat, I realized I hadn't had head pain and therefore hadn't taken opioids. After a week without headaches, I was stunned. After two weeks without headaches, I was convinced.

"I know I haven't seen you in a bit because I went on that silent Zen retreat," I said to Dr. A at our next session. "I have some new data for us. I am now willing to look at and work on this postsurgical head pain."

"Really?" Dr. A asked with curiosity in his voice.

"Yes. I ended up not needing opioids for two whole weeks after the retreat. It doesn't make sense that the retreat would make my head hurt less if it were all just after-surgery pain."

Dr. A nodded silently and smiled. His eyes were soft and kind.

"By the way," I added, "I know you can't talk about it, but I heard you were able to see my friend! And you might not have realized she was my friend because she doesn't call me Michelle. She calls me Nia, which is my nickname from high school."

I let out a huge sigh.

"You sigh," Dr. A said, commenting on the beep of my metal detector.

"I'm sure this brings up a lot of feelings," I said, nodding.

I saw myself at fourteen, standing in front of my dorm room door. I told Dr. A that I got the nickname on the very first day of boarding school. When I arrived at my dorm room, there were two names on my door. Neither was mine, so I knocked on my dorm parent's door and explained I was Michelle and wasn't sure where my room was.

"My dorm parent pulled out a form and showed it to me, and under 'Nickname,' my dad had quickly scribbled 'n/a.' She thought it said 'Nia' and put it on my door."

Dr. A smiled.

"After we loaded my stuff into my room," I continued, "it was time for my parents to leave. My parents and I were standing in the driveway of my dorm. I don't remember hugging them, but I must have. What I remember is walking away and feeling like my dad had changed. He felt steely, like his soft cushiness was gone." I paused, looked down at the skin on my arm, and wondered how it would age.

"What feelings are coming up as you remember this?" Dr. A asked.

"It's hard to say," I said due to the defense of bullshitting. "Halfway back to my dorm, I turned back to look at my parents. My mom was in my dad's arms, crying. I was shocked. To see her tears, to see them touch. I remember thinking, *Is this a cause for touching?* I had no earthly idea that my mom had any feelings about me leaving. My mom's tears stunned me."

"And the feelings?" Dr. A persisted.

"Something inside of me was, well, I think I was angry, even though I had no idea I felt that way until now. My dad's arms were stiff around her. My mom wiped her eyes with these snow-white tissues she always kept in her purse. When I arrived back at my door, or Nia's door, I felt the name was mine. Nia was me." I stopped again to study the skin on my arm. "And you know, for the next four years, and to this day with anyone who knows me through high school, my name is Nia. The name spread. I could have corrected people and stopped them from saying it, but I didn't."

"What feelings are coming up now?"

"I think I'm sad. And I don't want to be."

Suddenly, my head pain shot up like a rocket. I winced.

"It's my head," I said as I felt my body tense. "It just went to a 6 on the pain scale." A surge of heat flew up my spine and into the muscles of my back. "I hate this pain! I hate this! Why can't it go away? What's wrong with me?"

"You have a sadness about this experience, about Nia."

I felt anger toward Dr. A for not understanding. I used it to clarify.

"Well, no, Nia saved me. Obviously not the name, but something about boarding school. Going to boarding school was one of the best things I did, and it was also painful."

I paused to allow a long sigh.

"How is it that my parents not wanting to be with me was the cause and solution to much of my pain?"

The words left my mouth before I had the chance to hear them.

"I'm not sad about Nia. I'm sad about . . . something else."

While I had just said what I was sad about, I didn't hear it. I didn't grasp that my parents not wanting to be with me was the cause and solution to much of my pain.

Dr. A asked about boarding school. They were the usual questions. Did you choose to go? What about public school? Going to private schools and boarding schools was what people did where I lived. At least, that's what I assumed and told myself. When I've asked my dad, he said he wanted me to have the best education. I had looked at a bunch of schools. Only one was a day school. No one was friendly there.

"I ended up choosing my school because, and I remember this vividly, I had visited on Prospective Students Day. I was out on this lawn and saw two Old Girls—meaning two current students—run toward each other. One of the girls jumped into the other's arms, and they fell down laughing. I wanted that kind of..." I searched for the word while I looked back at the skin on my arm. "I wanted that kind of bond. That kind of openness of affection."

"And there is also a buried sadness in you. And your head has pain."

My body tensed at his mention of sadness and head pain.

"Yes, but I don't want there to be." My head pain crept up. "I'm happy I went to boarding school. I don't know where I'd be if I didn't."

Tears began to fill my eyes. When I pushed them back, pain seared my temples.

"My head pain just went up again. I cannot believe this is happening! I've never noticed it this much, how it comes and goes. I felt sadness, and then I pushed it back, and then bam! Head pain! I know there must be sadness, but I also don't want there to be. It seems like pushing it back makes my head hurt!" I began to tear up again. "Why would I be sad? Why would I be sad about boarding school when it was good for me?"

Images flashed through my mind—my parents standing in the driveway, my dad's tense posture, my mom's white tissues, opening the door to my dorm, the darkness of my dorm room, a bottle of NyQuil.

I began to cry heavy sobs. As each wave pushed up and out of my throat, my head pain decreased. And as I cried, my awareness grew. My home with my parents wasn't where I found my emotional nourishment.

Often, sadness is thwarted by thinking. We put our sadness through trial before we're allowed to give in to it. *Why are you here, sadness? The reason better be good!* Yet needing a clear reason to feel grief often eviscerates grief. Sometimes, we must feel grief to give birth to its reason.

As I let grief fill my body, my headache vanished.

26

Emma: A Horse to Water

My heart pounded as I sat in my office before Emma's next session. What was going on?

I wanted to help her. I wanted to be the person who showed her a different way of life.

I want to prove to her that I can help.

Prove, I caught myself thinking. *Oh god, I totally want to save her.*

I flagged this wish inside of me. I wasn't sure what it meant. Wanting to help each client was normal, but why did I need to save Emma? I knew change was up to her. You can only lead a horse to water and can't force it to drink and whatnot.

I was now tense in my back. *Why won't she listen?* I heard my thought. I was angry with her. While it now seemed obvious after I spoke with myself, it was previously hidden in the tension of my muscles. *I want her to feel like she can rely on me for help.* I felt a warmth and an ache. I was angry with her, and I cared for her. *Okay, try to feel those together.* As I did, my back relaxed, my chest loosened, and my heart rate slowed.

It was vital to explore these questions about my reaction to Emma. For example, why did I become dizzy during our first session? All she had done was tell me that her prior therapist couldn't help. Why such high anxiety? I looked at the clock. The seconds clicked toward the moment I had to go out and get Emma. I decided to let my mind freely associate.

Emma's relationship with the violin. My relationship to the piano. I began playing piano when I was nine, which was late if you wanted to be a "serious pianist." I heard "not a serious pianist" in my dad's voice. He reminded me repeatedly that my piano teacher said I was "not a serious pianist." He also listened to me play the piano as he lay on the couch, his hands tucked underneath his chin like a contented, cute squirrel.

"I will always remember," I heard my dad say, "lying on the couch after dinner, listening to you play. It was one of the greatest things in my life." I saw a happy daddy falling asleep on the couch, hands balled up underneath his chin. However, this memory was not simple because when my fingers slipped and I played a wrong note, he would hiss between his teeth. Each time I sat down to play, I tensed up, desperately hoping I wouldn't make a mistake. I didn't want to ruin it for him. Shame sat next to me on the piano bench. Both images, the happy daddy and the hissing daddy, were true and existed side by side. I thought of Emma's mom yelling at her from the kitchen. I wondered if Emma had a similar image locked inside.

My mind came back to the present, and I looked at the clock. Only a minute had passed. I continued to let myself think freely about Emma. I thought of my dizziness during that first session, and then my mind went back to the memory of the first time I went back to my parent's house from boarding school at fourteen, which was only a few months after they dropped me off at boarding school. I sat on a barstool in the kitchen, looking at the *USA Today*'s colorful weather map. Slowly, my parents sat down to my left. One of my parents, I can't remember which, told me they were getting a divorce. I don't remember what words they used. I do remember looking at the colors on the *USA Today* map and replying, "That makes sense. I totally understand." I sounded like an adult who didn't need anything. I thought of Emma standing next to her mother's bed, her arms filled with two new babies. There was no more room for Emma.

My mind followed the memory of coming home to boarding school. Home was boarding school, not where either of my parents lived. While I didn't know it, I was severely depressed during my first two years of boarding school. Almost every night after lights out, I sat at the bottom of my bed, looking out the window into the darkness. Yellowed street lamps lit the browning leaves of the fall trees. My roommate slept only a few feet away from me. I could feel something wanting to come out of me, yet whatever it was, it stayed inside. And so I sat, my arms resting on the white windowsill, looking out at the dry fountain. Then, I reached for the NyQuil bottle next to me and chugged.

Suddenly, I thought of Walter. I thought of my opioids. What did this have to do with Emma? I wasn't sure. I looked at the clock in my office. It was 4:59 p.m. I waited for it to turn to five o'clock, stood up, and retrieved Emma from the waiting room.

She sat across from me, and our eyes met.

"It's nice to be here, actually," she said. I smiled back at her. Then, Emma began to cry. I sat with her, feeling relief all over my body.

"I don't even know why I'm crying."

"That's not a problem."

"You'll see me," she said, taking a tissue and wiping away tears from her cheeks. "I'll see me."

"If you're willing."

She nodded her head, looked at me, and smiled.

27

Michelle: Milkboarding and Other Forms of Torture

While I was preparing to embark on another Zen meditation retreat, something didn't feel right. When I thought of the meditation and how we couldn't move, anxiety swallowed me whole. My brain became a mess of fog and terror.

I still went.

Once I began to meditate, I broke out in a cold sweat, and my vision began to fade. I had to move. The impulse was too much to ignore. I slinked out the door, went to the bathroom, put the toilet seat up, heaved, wiped the sweat off my face, and returned to my motionless meditation position. I was terrified I was in trouble. As I stared at the wall meditating, I thought of my childhood dinner table. I had to eat everything on my plate and drink all the 2 percent milk that sat thick and heavy in a twelve-ounce glass cup, which felt like a gallon in my tiny hands. When I worked to drink all the milk, I felt as though I was drowning, forcing the milk into a little body that felt like it would explode. I couldn't leave until I ate all the food. It hurt to push it all in. I tried to solve the problem by putting less on my plate, but my mom's eyes guided my hand back to the serving spoon to get more.

Ignore your body. Do as you're told. Don't move.

When I returned from the retreat, my head pain came back. I told Dr. A when I saw him next.

"I don't know why my head pain came back quickly after the meditation retreat this time," I said to Dr. A. I was disappointed. I told him about what had happened on the retreat, how it was harder, that something was wrong.

As I spoke, I started to bounce in his comfort-refusing, bullshit-rejecting chair.

"This chair. Thank god it has *some* padding." I sounded like a teenager. Dr. A said nothing. I kept wiggling around, trying to get comfortable.

"And this is how I felt at the retreat!" An energy formed in my arms. "I didn't want to just sit there!" I gritted my teeth and grabbed the arms of the chair.

"How do you feel the anger in your body?" Dr. A asked.

"Strong, in my hands, in my arms," I said with confidence. As soon as I proclaimed my strength, resistance pushed the anger down. Pain seared my skull. "Fucking head pain is back!"

Dr. A didn't speak.

"Honestly, I still can't believe how much I now notice how this ridiculous emotional suppression, repression, whatever, causes this pain. I know holding back sadness does it, and now it seems like holding back anger does too!"

He nodded.

"This retreat was very difficult, having to sit and not move," I said with the tone of an indignant child. I paused to gather my strength, to corral my maturity. "Okay, let me see what I can do. Let me see if I can get to the anger and push past my head pain."

I see what you're doing, pain! I thought to myself.

Suddenly, rageful energy shot down my arms and into my hands. My head pain plummeted to zero. I looked up at Dr. A in shock.

"My head pain just went to nothing."

"What do those hands want to do?" Dr. A asked firmly. We were gearing up for battle together, fighting against defenses that hurt me.

Yet my cognitive defense mechanisms swiftly engaged, diverting my attention away from the rising tide of anger. *Why was the pain happening? Could it be real? How is it that tension creates head pain? What muscles are activated?*

My thinking pushed the anger aside, and my pain came back.

Thinking is one of the most common defenses against emotion. We can puzzle, analyze, and think, think, think about our emotions. This has nothing to do with *feeling* our emotions.

"Dr. A, the pain—it went way down when I felt the anger and then went back up when the anger hid. This is incredible."

I could administer the treatment now. I was the painkiller.

"What does the rage want to do?" Dr. A asked.

"I don't know! God, why am I being whiny? I know sometimes we truly are helpless. I am helpless to grow wings and fly away! However, I'm not helpless to feel!"

Helplessness is another common defense. It covers our power and fills us with lies about our incapacity. It puts up barriers to intimacy as we are not our true selves in relation to another person. When the defense of helplessness is active, we wait, expecting someone else to do what we can only do ourselves.

Suddenly, I saw my mother standing in the gorgeous floral skirt I helped her pick out for my younger sister's wedding. She looked beautiful. She loved feeling beautiful, and I enjoyed seeing her feel beautiful. However, the smile I saw on her face was fake, and anger rose in my body along with my care for her. And then, as if I was dreaming while awake, I pictured a large tub of thick 2 percent milk.

"What happens if you face this anger?" Dr. A asked.

"I honestly, I feel, I see . . . this is weird, but I'm going to go with it. I see a large vat of thick 2 percent milk."

"And?"

"I . . . oh god . . . I picture her facedown. I'm pushing her face in it. And then the milk coming out of her nose." I was horrified by the images coming out of me. "I want to drown her. And not drown her."

"You want to torture her."

"Like waterboarding. God, this is awful. Yet this is what I see. If I let go, I see myself doing that to her, her head in my hand. Her hair between my fingers. I can *feel* myself doing that to her, her gasping for breath."

I felt an urge in my arm to forcefully push down. I leaned into it, letting my arm power up. Dr. A sat silent, waiting for the healing force within me to lead us.

"I . . . I want to milkboard her!"

I sat staring at the image of my mom projected onto Dr. A's carpet. Thick 2 percent milk dripped off her hair and her nose. It collected in her eyes and clumped her eyelashes. She gasped for breath as my hand grabbed her by the back of her head and dunked her again.

"Oh god. I want to milkboard her." While my mind saw the pictures, my body was along for the ride. I sat still in Dr. A's chair while the full experience was coursing through my body. I was free to feel and imagine with no consequence to anyone. My head didn't hurt. I wasn't gaslighting myself or arguing with myself. I had no cause to use cover words or change the subject. I was facing what I had been avoiding: a wish to torture my mother.

Then, the power in my body dropped, the anger exhausted. I shook my head back and forth. I knew what was coming next. We were going to look at what comes after the rage.

"I don't want to look."

"If you look there in her eyes."

A thought raced across my mind: *If I feel my guilt, I won't need opioids anymore.*

My mind knew what came after the desire to torture. Guilt.

Some might say, "But why would you feel guilt if you didn't actually do anything?" While the actions weren't real, the feelings and urges were. If I really did that to my mom, my guilt would be unimaginable. If I left it as rage, I would be disconnected from another part of myself. When we cut ourselves off from real and healthy guilt, we cut ourselves off from our humanity, from our love. Guilt says, "I love, and I am human." Guilt says, "I love you, and I love me." Guilt says, "I hurt you, and we are both human beings, and because of this, I am sorry." Guilt shows us that we are honest and brave enough to be there with the person we hurt. We can bear the pain of guilt for the sake of closeness with one another.

This is not the kind of guilt that punishes. In fact, it is the opposite. Healthy guilt frees us from punishment. Imagine two people who have committed a violent crime. One person denies it, saying it wasn't their fault. The other feels remorse and guilt, showing love and care for the person they hurt. Which one do you trust more? Which one would you make eligible for parole?

Guilt builds trust in ourselves and others. Guilt reminds us we are human, and we have everything within us. Running from guilt causes another part within us, an internal judiciary system, to punish us. When we feel our healthy guilt, we heal. We get out of prison. We are free.

While my actions weren't real, my anger and urges were. And if my anger is real, so is my guilt about these unconscious urges. This guilt was hiding in my unconscious along with my rage, love, and grief.

I did not want to feel guilt for these wishes, for what had been locked in my unconscious mind. Yet if I didn't, I would keep punishing myself with physical pain. And pain meant opioids. Opioids meant comfort. If I faced my unconscious guilt, my pain and the comfort of pills would vanish. No more pain, no more opioids. Avoiding my guilt would help me take opioids, my only comfort.

But then, like a life force refusing to die, guilt rose in my chest and throat.

"I feel guilty looking at her. I know it's not real—"

"And yet the emotions are. Let them all through so you can heal."

And so I cried, feeling my guilt that was previously hidden in the depths of my unconscious, along with a deep love for my mother.

Guilt is the most painful of feelings. Guilt results from our raw humanity. It says we love. It says we can bear our mistakes for the sake of repair and connection and that we don't have to lie to ourselves about being perfect. When we deny our guilt, we set ourselves on a path of pain.

I left the session without sharing my thought about guilt and opioids. I didn't want Dr. A to get his hands on it. I wanted to erase that thought. I wanted to deny the connection between avoided guilt, the resulting pain, and my precious opioids.

And yet during the car ride home, the thought still echoed in my head.

If I feel my guilt, I won't need opioids anymore.

28

Walter: Intergenerational Use

Oh no.

Walter sat on the couch in front of me, his head hanging low. It looked like the first installation of the Pot Plan had been a total failure. I thought of Bion and his "without memory or desire" edict and internally snarled. *Without memory or desire, my ass.* I braced and waited for the bad news.

"I haven't been depressed, but my anxiety has been really . . . really high." This meant that certain defenses weren't functioning, which left him with higher anxiety. What defenses had changed?

I waited.

"And . . . the Pot Plan," he said as if reading my thoughts.

I waited.

"I couldn't do it," he finally shared. "There were two days I couldn't do it, where I smoked before noon." He shook his head back and forth, making eye contact with the ground.

I was stunned. He had succeeded. The defense that had changed was pot. He had decreased his smoking and met his goal for twelve of the last fourteen days. However, his body language didn't match what he said. What was I missing that kept me unaware of why he didn't see his accomplishment?

"You were able to not smoke before noon for twelve out of fourteen days? Am I understanding this?"

"Yes, but I didn't do it. I smoked before noon on two of the days."

I suddenly realized that I had missed the defenses that kept him blind to his accomplishment. First, his defense of self-attack (*You're a screwup!*) wasn't letting him see his strength. His defense of self-dismissal (*Don't look at what I did do, look at what I didn't do!*) wasn't letting him see what he accomplished. His defense of minimization (*It's not a big deal!*) didn't allow him to see what a giant leap he had taken. These defenses kept him from reality. Now that I saw his defenses, I could help him see them too.

"But this is a way to minimize your accomplishments while insulting yourself."

Walter sighed and looked into my eyes.

"And you seem to have forgotten part of the plan," I continued. "The plan was *not* to be able to do it 100 percent of the time, and if you don't, you're a failure. This, what you did, was the plan." I felt an urge to throw my arms up in celebration. I decided to keep them down because while it could be experienced as helpful and exciting, it could also be experienced as excitement he would deprive me of if he failed.

He smiled at me. "Yes, I am minimizing it, aren't I?"

He rubbed his hand over his face and let out another sigh.

"I feel good. But, you know, it's just the beginning, and I really don't want to talk about it and get all excited. I know this sounds ridiculous, but I don't want to let you down."

His defenses kept him from anxiety triggered by hope, excitement, and pride. At least, that was my hypothesis. If my hypothesis was correct, blocking those defenses would yield at least one of three things: increased anxiety, a breakthrough of feelings, or a new defense coming in to do the job for the defenses that were pushed aside. I decided to test it.

"You can't let me down, and you know the Pot Plan is about giving something to you. You say you feel good. What is that like, to feel good about this first try?"

Walter sighed and shifted on the couch. The metal detector was beeping.

"I don't want to get too excited! Plus, this other thing happened this week."

Was this a distraction? A red herring? I had no idea.

"I found out my son has been smoking pot, for who knows how long."

Walter said he never told his son he smoked. I suspected his son already knew. How could he not smell the pot if his father smoked every single day?

"I can't help but think that I caused that."

Of course he contributed to it. Walter was high for his son's entire life. They never talked about it. Walter modeled how to deal with life and feelings: Get high. Deaden yourself. Escape. Don't talk. Hide. Keep secrets. Could we blame his son for doing what he did? Of course not. If a person is raised in an English-speaking household, they wouldn't emerge speaking another language unless they were exposed to someone else who did.

"I never talked to him about drugs or nicotine or whatever. I never spoke to him. I began changing too late."

In many ways, it was true.

Walter hung his head. His wrists went limp, and his body remained still. There was no tension.

"I feel great shame."

"And this makes you want to go bury yourself in a box? Stick your head in the sand? Hide from your son?"

Walter nodded slowly. Walter's shame was part of the problem. Instead of facing his guilt, grief, anger, and love, he learned to turn to shame. Shame hid him away from the world—from his son.

"I'm learning the difference between this punitive shame and guilt, but I can't quite grasp it in this moment." He sighed and picked his head up. "Shame—it isolates me. That's been the problem! I don't want to feel this way anymore."

Without me saying anything to help, Walter was able to do an about-face. Now, he had more of an ability to drive the therapy. Sometimes, a therapist must get in the way of the anxiety and defenses that get in the way of our clients. We also must get out of the way of the healing force that bursts forward from within. As a therapist, it's important to know the difference between anxiety and defenses and the healing force.

"Did you say you're having a problem remembering guilt versus shame right now, but you know you're in shame?"

He nodded.

When it comes to learning emotional material, the 635th time's the charm.

I explained again that shame makes you think you're a shit person who deserves to hide in the corner. Shame says you are bad. Guilt says you are good and have a full, brave heart that can withstand feeling pain over what you've done. Guilt is feeling you're a good person, you love yourself, and you did a harmful thing and want to repair it. The impulse of guilt is to connect, apologize, and mend in some way.

"Shame abandons you and your son because you hide," I said slowly. "Guilt moves you to repair and love. It helps you experience who you really are."

"I didn't help my kid!" Walter exclaimed. "I didn't help him find another way. And now he's suffering like me."

Like his father suffered with alcohol.

Walter began to cry. His chest heaved with wave after wave of painful guilt.

"Let it through. I know it's painful. You've worked hard for this."

"I don't want to hurt my kid," he said. "I have already hurt him so much. My son, I want to be close to him." He unfolded his body and threw his arm toward the tissue box. He grabbed one and blew hard.

"You want to be closer to him," I echoed. Walter nodded into his tissue. "And how does that wanting, that yearning to be closer *feel* inside?" If this wanting to be closer remained only a thought, the feeling would be permanently evicted from his body, and he'd be less likely to act on it. Emotions are a prerequisite for action. A want drives us forward. Our prefrontal cortex helps us decide if action is best.

"I feel it in my chest, arms, and face." Walter gingerly touched each part as he labeled it. "It's like a warmth."

"What's the urge behind the warmth?"

"I want to kiss him and hug him." Walter's arms reached out to a phantom body, and he began to cry. "I don't know if he would want me to hug him!" Walter's son was an adult. I didn't know either. But focusing on his son's wishes was a way to avoid his own.

"Hug him *and* kiss him, you said."

"Did I say that?"

"Yes. Just two seconds ago. You said you wanted to kiss him as well." His brain had already wiped the kiss out. Why?

"And how would you want to kiss him?" I asked. Walter shifted around and looked away.

I could only hypothesize about why Walter's metal detector was suddenly beeping. Was it from sexual feelings toward his son? A reminder of something else? A memory? Cultural norms? What?

"Right on the lips!" Walter proclaimed. "I want to hug him hard and kiss him right on the lips. Not in a weird way, but that's how I feel. I wouldn't actually do it because I wouldn't want to freak him out."

"What would it have been like if your father had wrapped his arms around you and kissed you on the lips?"

Walter stopped moving and locked eyes with me, his eyes filling with tears. "That would have made all the difference in the world."

And with this, Walter's grief burst out like a prisoner breaking free.

He cried and cried, feeling the agony of his guilt for what he didn't give his son and the grief for what his father didn't give him.

If Walter could bear his guilt, he would have a better chance at reaching out to his son, changing their relationship, and ending this intergenerational cycle of drug abuse. When we feel our healthy guilt, we can more easily give ourselves nice things like self-pride, self-esteem, excitement, joy, and intimacy.

When Walter returned for his next session, he shared that he had hugged his son. He was becoming a different father to his son than his father had been to him. We spoke about how the depression was gone and he understood his anxiety. He saw that the depression was a result of his anger toward those he loved going back onto him.

"I can also feel my hope without crushing it," Walter added to his list of changes. "Hope feels like a lifting. It's everything. It's life. I'm alive. I know I have a lot to go through, and no matter what happens, I have hope for me."

29

Michelle: I Love You, Opioids

If I feel my guilt, then I won't need opioids anymore.

By the end of my car ride home from Dr. A's, I knew what to do. Once I saw that I took opioids to manage my emotions, everything changed. It was time to stop taking opioids. I had to. It was not the kind of *had to* that comes from being forced by others but the kind that comes with compassion and a loyalty to oneself. I had to stop being loyal to opioids to be faithful to myself.

My relationship with opioids had changed. I was no longer taking opioids because of a Chiari malformation and incessant pain. I was taking opioids to avoid my feelings. If I didn't let go of the opioids, I would let go of my potential. At first, opioids were a life raft keeping me from drowning in pain. Now, they were the anchor pulling me down.

My headaches had multiple causes.[1] The final surgery for my Chiari had pulled back the curtain as it fixed the structural problem in my brain. Now that we had eliminated a true physical cause, I could also see the psychological causes for my headaches:

- Headaches were a defense against emotions. If physical pain was present, I didn't have to focus on my emotions.

- Headaches were a way to punish myself for unconscious crimes, such as milkboarding my mother. The crimes weren't real, yet the unconscious feelings and self-punishment were. If I faced my unconscious guilt, I wouldn't have to punish myself to avoid my guilt. If I didn't face my guilt, then what better way to punish myself than to do unto myself as I wished to do unto others? An eye for an eye, a head for a head. (I had to see this to believe it.)
- Headaches created the need for opioids, which were my pseudocomforter. Opioids were there for me every time. Since my defenses ignored, dismissed, doubted, manipulated, devalued, and attacked me, I couldn't provide myself comfort.

While I didn't create these headaches or their effects on purpose, I was responsible for changing them.

It was easy to justify taking opioids. When I had a headache, I would take only half a painkiller. I wouldn't get high. In fact, it improved my concentration because there was no more pain. I took less than the prescribed dosage. I took it only when I had head pain. Thoughts like these helped me justify taking opioids.

My defenses kept me from experiencing the feelings my family judged. I was supposed to be peppy, happy, self-confident, pleasant, and perfect. Yet I wasn't that perfect daughter. All the time, I was in conflict with my and my parents' fantasy. My painkillers were another way to hide myself and my feelings. These precious white pills were a solution I could hold in my hand and store in a bottle. They were on-demand comfort.

The defensive systems in us are incredibly adept. They are well-forged armies against the threats we experience in our childhoods, when we are most vulnerable.

All of this hit me on my drive home from therapy.

My body needed a reckoning, a revolution.

I didn't want to tell my husband, Ben, that I had decided to stop taking opioids. I worried he would disagree. And then I realized—this was another defense. I would be hiding from him as I had to hide from my parents. Keeping a secret from him would replicate the relationship I had with my mother. It wouldn't be fair to either of us.

"I decided I'm going to stop taking my painkillers," I told him.

"Well, I don't think that's a good idea," he replied. "What are you going to do if your head hurts? Aren't you cutting yourself off from something that helps you?" He sounded mildly panicked, like I was pulling the plug on my life support.

"I understand why you say that. However, I feel like this is the best thing for me."

I told him about the session, the thought I heard in my head, and what I thought it meant. I said that the pain might be there so I can take opioids, and not taking the opioids was a way to confirm whether that's true.

He stared at me and began to pick at his fingers.

"And if I get an extreme headache," I added to calm his fears, "I'll take one."

He sighed and looked down, avoiding me.

"I don't want to go through life like it's an emotional buffet," I said as anger lifted the words up and out of my mouth, "taking what I want and leaving the rest. It's hypocritical. How can I help my clients face the hardest stuff, to be able to tolerate reality no matter what it is, while I turn my back on myself?"

He looked up at me, then down, and then nodded.

"These little bullshit headaches still come and go. And I still take opioids. I can't keep taking them if I know they're bullshit. My body is up to something, and I'm not consciously pulling the strings. I know that now. I refuse to be at the total mercy of an unconscious puppeteer!"

He looked at me, his eyes wide.

"And I was worried you would say you don't agree," I added, "but I really want you with me on this. It's going to be hard."

He looked up. "I'm sorry I first said that. I'm behind you. I really am."

The next day, I woke up with an extreme headache. I didn't feel I could go to work.

I reached for my pill bottle.

"Wait, you know what?" I said, trying to furrow my brow. "What are the chances I would have this severe pain now? Did my unconscious find the loophole already?"

Ben suddenly looked excited and scooched closer to me. He asked if I wanted to look at the pain "Sarno style."

Before we met and toward the end of his first marriage, Ben had severe back pain after he tweaked it by lifting a log. When it didn't improve, he found a book called *Healing Back Pain* by John E. Sarno. Dr. Sarno's point was revolutionary. Chronic pain is often a distraction from anger, and often, only *knowing* pain's function can take it away. (See the back of the book for literature about and by Dr. Sarno.) Ben's back pain subsided after reading the book. When he first shared that reading this book helped his pain, I had my doubts. *Give me a break. Nothing can go away by reading a book.*

I nodded while holding back an eye roll. I figured there was no way this would work, but he looked excited. I didn't want to turn down his offer.

He leaned toward me and barked: "We can see what you are doing, pain! You're not getting a pill!"

I was startled and felt an excitement rise within.

"You're not getting a med!" I said firmly. "I'm onto you!"

We paused, saying nothing while the words reverberated in our small studio apartment. As we lay silent, the words sank in, and my pain began to change.

After getting up and repeating the phrase "You're not getting a med," I went to my office with lowered pain and sat at my desk. "I'm not getting a pill."

Then, right before my first patient, my pain vanished.

A month later, I sat down on Dr. A's barely padded chair. I told him I had stopped taking opioids since our last appointment. I was going to wait a little longer until I threw away the rest of my opioid stash. I wasn't sure if I would need painkillers again, and I also knew that that type of thinking could make me creep back into it. I had a sense I had to say goodbye.

"I missed them so much it hurt my chest," I told Dr. A. "I yearn for my pills. I don't often cry between sessions, yet every time I thought about opioids not being in my life anymore, I felt a kind of sadness I wasn't familiar with." As I told him this, my eyes searched his office for distracting details to fixate on while my mind searched for a way to describe the heartbreak. "It's like a missing feeling. I miss it. I hate missing. I don't miss things!"

"You understand something new now?"

"Yes, it seems clear as day." When I was in touch with the physical impulse of my anger, I always went for a person's head. Crush the head. Stomp the head. Cut the head. Hit the head. Toes, legs, arms—none of those body parts interested my unconscious. Apparently, I wanted heads to roll. This crucial information was hidden in my unconscious. I had layers of defenses to keep me from seeing it.

He smiled and nodded.

The mind's capacity to inflict harm on the very part of our body that we wish to harm in others seemed like a concept lifted from the pages of science fiction. It took example after example, data point after data point, for me to believe it. I had already experienced this psychophysiological process several times with my own clients. I didn't think it applied to me. Many clients say crying gives them a headache. "It's a natural byproduct of crying," some said. I used to think that as well. I used to say, "I hate crying. It gives me a headache." I even used to say, "Maybe I'm dehydrated because I've been crying!" But no, I was getting a headache because I was holding back my tears or silently berating myself for such an unattractive and ridiculous display. Many people, more women than men, have said something to me like, "But I don't want to ugly cry!" Screw the ugly cry! We demonize this. I was guilty of this too. I used to obsess over my mascara when I cried. Even if I was sobbing, a part of me was trying to stop myself. Since I criticized myself for letting go, I wouldn't.

"And now things are different for you," Dr. A stated. His confidence gave me a sense of accomplishment.

"Exactly."

I could cry and miss something, which meant I had a heart that had experienced love. While my unrequited love was toward a small, white pill, it was still love. It said I was alive. I wasn't dead yet. Even though I didn't want to miss anything, I knew feeling this was good for me. I had started trying to attach to Ben, even if it meant more pain if something bad happened later. I didn't want to lead a life devoid of attachments and the accompanying pain. Attempting to evade such discomfort would be living a falsehood. I saw my self-dismissal and self-neglect and how I minimized and attacked what I was saying by claiming it wasn't important enough. Until a month ago, I didn't see the full connection between my head pain and opioids. How could I? I had a brain abnormality where my brain was coming out of my skull. I knew much of my head pain was from the Chiari and learned there was more going on. Learning this was empowering.

He smiled at me. I felt proud.

"I would even get mad at you when you suggested my remaining pain was psychophysiological. I—a therapist!—would know if that was happening. It's myself, for goodness' sake! Wouldn't I be able to tell? The answer is nope! Or at least, not then."

"And now, it is different."

"Yes, it is. I can get rid of most of my headaches. It's like a superpower. I mean, it doesn't work every single time, but the majority."

"That is sensational."

"Thank you."

"You're welcome."

"Does this mean I'm done with therapy?" I said, smiling.

He smiled back.

"Right, of course," I said, "because god only knows what will come up without the opioids."

A month later, I decided it was time to throw away every pill I had. It was time for the funeral.

Throwing them away made me think of how those small, unused pills would feel without any purpose. I gave them feelings only a living being could have, like I once did with a merry-go-round horse at a mall. After a mom planted her daughter on the plastic horse, the little girl screamed, trying to peel herself off it because it was "so ugly." I marked the abandoned merry-go-round horse and vowed to ride it even if I wanted to ride the tiger two rows ahead. My stuffed animals had rich inner lives. Even stained carpets and broken glass had feelings. And now, as I thought about gathering up all my pills, I saw each of them as sad to be useless and thrown away.

They don't have feelings. These are my feelings. I'm the one who is sad to say goodbye.

I searched through the gallon-sized Ziploc bag by my bedside and pulled out bottles of tramadol and Percocet. Then, stored above the microwave, I pulled out two more gallon-sized plastic bags filled with gabapentin, Zofran, Nucynta, more tramadol, Oxycontin, hydrocodone, oxycodone, and more Percocet. The subsequent moments unfolded like a surreal daydream—retrieving the trash can from beneath the sink, the deliberate twist of the first bottle, and the cascade of pills resonating like gravel spilling from a truck. Tears began to form in my eyes as I watched them land in the trash. My helpers, my saviors for all those years, were going away. I felt the goodbye.

As I came to the last bottle, I picked out a pill and poured out the rest. I took the one remaining pill to the bathroom and turned on the tap. I ran warm water over the small pill cradled in the palm of my hand. My chest ached with loss. I let the water dilute the pill and wash it out of my hand. It disappeared down the drain.

Down the drain also went the greatest of consequences of opioids, which was being unable to nourish myself and receive the nourishment of others. Without pills, I would have to face being imperfect, sad, anxious, and angry. Instead of feeling the comfort of opioids, I would have to face being human.

30

Emma: Hating the Unconscious

When I opened the door to my office, Emma rushed in. She reported she was less depressed and sat down, gingerly placing her bag next to her. Her tenderness toward her bag struck me as unusual.

"That's wonderf—"

"But I still have no desire to date! I'm still alone!"

"And am I hearing you right? That you're no longer feeling depressed?"

"Yes, but—"

"What's happening here? Let's make sure we take an honest look."

Emma clenched her jaw and let out a long sigh. "I'm, uh, totally dismissing myself and this big change." She turned her head and stared out the window before turning back to me. "It's a big, positive change."

I didn't want to dismiss that she was right: she had made no Emma-approved progress with dating. However, if she dismissed successes, she wouldn't get the jolt of energy that successes provide on long journeys to other goals. The puppet strings seemed clear: success (trigger) created feelings (which ones?) that made her anxious (tense) and dismiss the success (defense). This would mean that each time she had success, the strings would pull her to dismiss it within the blink of an eye.

Emma let out a long, exasperated sigh. "I know if I don't acknowledge I'm not depressed anymore, I could lose the drive to feel better at all." Emma was suddenly speaking directly from her wisest self. She began to fidget with her hair, brushing it against her face like a paintbrush. "And I don't want that," Emma said on another long exhale.

"What feelings come up as you look at the fact that you're no longer depressed?"

"I feel . . . happy! Proud." She sighed and refolded her hands in her lap as her chest puffed out. "Uh . . . like uh . . ." She drew her hand across her chest. "I want to, like, actually smile."

"And what's that like, to sit with those experiences in your body, without anything else coming to interrupt them?"

Emma bit her lip and shifted her body on my couch. "I don't know. This is too weird."

"Want to practice so pride and happiness don't have to feel weird?"

Emma moved her butt back and forth on the couch, settling in. "Okay, I'm ready." She paused and sighed again. "I'm no longer depressed."

"No longer depressed," I echoed.

Emma smiled, but then gravity took over the corners of her mouth and pushed them down.

"I just got a headache."

I felt an ache in my chest, bringing my attention to my head. There was no pain.

"It's right here," she said, motioning over her temples, her eyes squinting with pain. The myriad causes of headaches and body pain often leave me feeling overwhelmed with a dizzying array of possibilities to consider. However, I had a hunch about the cause of this headache. Sometimes, headaches and body pains are like sympathy pains. I decided to test out my hunch.

"What does it feel like is being done to you?" I asked.

"Like someone is squeezing my head like this." Her hand made a clamp over her temples.

"What's it like to put that out onto me, to change the direction of that squeeze toward me?" I mimicked her hand motion and turned the clamp to face me.

Immediately, her eyes widened. "It's gone. The pain is gone!" Then, she burst into tears.

Was she finally having a eureka moment, seeing how she puts anger on herself to protect others? Was she seeing the redirection of her unconscious anger toward me?

"I don't like this!" she wailed. "I don't like knowing I have an unconscious. And that it's inflicting this pain! I don't like that we're seeing this! I don't like thinking I have anger toward you! You didn't do anything! This is ridiculous! I'm totally freaked out."

Her defense of rationalization ("You didn't do anything!") was trying to fight the truth she now undeniably saw, which was that she had an unconscious, and it was running part of her life. It put anger toward others onto her in various forms: headaches, jaw tension, self-attack, and perfectionism. She wasn't used to being aware of anger toward others. She was used to being cruel to herself.

She sniffled and snatched a tissue from the box next to her.

"Your being cruel to yourself feels normal," I chose to say.

"It doesn't feel wrong to dismiss myself. That's a good point. It feels normal! I don't want that to feel normal! Like, I'm no longer depressed. I feel better. That's huge. I guess I'm also bummed out that it hasn't translated to dating."

"Headache still gone?" She nodded. "I know you said you didn't want anger. But you do have it, like it or not. That doesn't mean we have to look at it and help you with it. We really don't."

"I know. But what if learning about my anger helps me with dating? I want to know if getting in touch with anger will help," she said, shaking her head in frustration. "Then, I go back to the fact that you've been trying to help me. I shouldn't have anger toward you!" She tensed her entire body, extending her arms and molding her hands into clawlike shapes. Her jaw clenched, leaving no ambiguity about her feelings. As my gaze fell upon Emma's clawlike hands, she, too, became aware of them, drawing attention to the physical manifestation of her inner turmoil. "I can't do this! I don't want to do this!"

And with this, Emma began to tear up. She wasn't sad for herself; she was covering her anger with tears. I knew she was capable. However, I wasn't sure she was willing. And if she wasn't, I wasn't sure how I was going to help her.

Emma had suffered from countless attachment traumas in her family. Traumas that are severe or frequent or occurred at a younger age increase the likelihood that the unconscious wish of anger is to punish or torture. The urges can be quite primitive—biting, scratching, or clawing. No wonder her tears and defenses rose so quickly. No wonder she resisted.

31

Michelle: Moving On

A year went by, during which Dr. A and I diligently worked toward unraveling my emotional barriers and fostering a genuine sense of openness. As time progressed, I had a growing intuition that the moment to conclude therapy with Dr. A was approaching. Initially, I questioned whether this decision was merely a defense, but I had become adept at distinguishing between my self-doubt and the authenticity of my convictions. While acknowledging the undiscovered depths within me, I also sensed that the therapeutic journey with Dr. A had reached its peak, having propelled me as far as it could.

"I am ready to wrap up therapy with you," I said to Dr. A. My stomach was tense. This anxiety told me I still wasn't comfortable *feeling* this goodbye.

"How many more sessions would you like to wrap up?"

"Maybe one, two?"

"I'd say more like three to five."

"How about two more?" I bargained.

"Okay, two. And more if you decide you want it?"

"Yes, that sounds perfect," I said, nodding.

In the wrap-up process, we take time to honor the therapeutic relationship, integrate the therapeutic work, and address what the ending brings up. Dr. A was doing his job, leaving room for anything that might arise by saying goodbye. As a therapist, I knew we needed to say goodbye and feel the loss and celebrate our successes. Yet that didn't mean I wanted to.

I could have ghosted him or sent an email. I could have told him that this would be our last session. I could have avoided saying goodbye.

We don't say goodbye anymore. We ghost. We think it saves us from pain, but it doesn't. I had tried to be the feelingless ghost my parents wanted. I had ghosted others. Nannies weren't part of the family. They were ghosts too. No need to say goodbye. My father was always gone. I had been away from my family since I was fourteen years old. When my mom divorced her second husband of twelve years, she said it never crossed her mind how we would feel.

Before our next session, other thoughts began to cross my mind: *He's going to make me feel sad!* (defense—projection; reality—I am sad about losing him), *I don't want to be sad!* (defense—negation, defiance), and *What if I'm not sad at all?* (defense—denial, argumentativeness).

I found myself in a cycle of denial, projection, and defiance, constructing an image of Dr. A that was not rooted in reality. The emergence of these defenses left me questioning the sudden onset of these protective mechanisms.

I had not only achieved but exceeded my therapy goals. Ceasing sessions with him would translate to both financial savings and a considerable reclaiming of time. Yet these facts drowned out other facts. *Hey, focus on these facts! Not those over there! Let's forget that Dr. A won't be in my life anymore. Let's ignore that I am losing a healing relationship in my life.* I had never sat with someone and honored a goodbye.

Finally, the truth came to me: goodbyes still proved to be a challenge. I steered clear of the emotional weight carried by goodbyes, as the upsurge of grief hinted at the possibility of abandonment or judgment. To my parents, grief was unnecessary, tears a burden. Feeling grief made my parents uncomfortable, confused, and angry.

Despite my newfound awareness, it failed to penetrate the emotional barriers during my second-to-last session. Seated with arms crossed, I engaged in a resistant exchange. As Dr. A invited me to look at my feelings about termination and our experience together, I avoided him like a fly darting away from a slap.

I ghosted him during the session. In the aftermath, I felt a sense of being robbed, yet I recognized that I was the architect of my own deprivation. My body, bearing the aftermath of tension ignored throughout the entire session, felt as if it had endured a relentless beating.

Yet sometimes, errors liberate us, allowing us a clear glimpse into our prisons. The psychoanalyst Charles Brenner once said that the therapist must first help the patient be a "bad" patient.[1] I gained a clear perspective on my actions and their consequences, which jolted me out of the punitive self-torture that had previously consumed me in our second-to-last session. For our final session, I vowed to do more for myself.

At the beginning of the session, I said, "I will miss you. You have helped me a tremendous amount. You have helped me come off opioids. You helped me see what I didn't see without jamming it down my throat. You let me come to my own conclusion about opioids. You were on my timeline and not yours, which was absolutely, and I mean absolutely, required to help me really say goodbye to opioids. If I had sensed, even a little, that you thought I should do something with the opioids, I probably would've bitten your head off." He chuckled. Then, we began to laugh together, knowing the truth of this statement. "Now, I can know I want to bite heads off without biting my own off, huh?"

"Yes." He smiled with kind eyes.

"Thank you for all you have done for me."

"You're so welcome."

We talked about our work together and reminisced. We said more goodbyes and shared more gratitude. When I walked out of his door for the last time, I felt proud. Together, we discovered who I was underneath incessant self-dismissal and neglect. We found the rest of me hidden underneath the incessant head pain. We learned that I could take care of myself without using opioids. He respected and supported my sadness. He helped me say the final goodbye that honors a relationship. And it really was a goodbye. When therapy ends, the relationship ends. The relationship between a therapist and client is completely professional, bound by essential parameters critical to the efficacy of therapy. The relationship is also intimate. No thought or feeling is unacceptable. Discovery is boundless.

32

Walter: The Uselessness of Perfection

After two months of the Pot Plan, Walter had saved his body from over 430 hours of smoking.

"And it doesn't matter that I couldn't do it for a few of those days the last two months," he said as a matter of fact. "I feel good. But I can't get past how much I still smoke."

"Yes, you still smoke a lot. Notice how when you feel good, this 'How much I still smoke' thought hogs the stage? They are both true—you smoke a lot, and you also smoke much less. Why does one hog all the attention?"

Walter laughed. "Yes, I see that. And that part of me that wants to smash my success like it never happened feels strong. I want to work on that." I waited to see what he would lead himself to do. "I gotta say," Walter continued, "I love coming in and telling you how I did on the Pot Plan." My chest popped with warmth and excitement. I liked it too. "I like how you're okay with whatever I come in with, and I like seeing your face when I tell you how I did." Walter could enjoy my enjoyment, but could he enjoy his? "And I want to feel mine too!" he said as if hearing my internal thoughts.

"Let's see what happens when you try." At this point, Walter knew the difference between his feelings, anxiety, and defenses. I wanted to see what he could do without me.

Walter nodded and let out a long sigh. He looked at me. He shifted around on the couch. He said nothing. He let out another long sigh. He squeezed his hands together. It was clear that his anxiety was at the optimal level for growth. His sighs, tension, and body shifts told me that this was a productive (therapeutic) silence. He was working hard to move aside defenses because when a defense dominates, anxiety is low to nonexistent. Walter wasn't comfortable. And who would be? Walter was burrowing down to his depths, where his pride, excitement, and self-appreciation lay alive in their coffins, waiting. He was fighting past his defenses and through his anxiety to try to anchor himself to these precious feelings and pull them up from the depths of his unconscious.

I waited.

Walter sighed.

I waited.

Walter shifted and looked at me.

I waited.

"I feel it. Just a little. It's just a little 'Go, me! Good job, me!' It's just the start of the Pot Plan, you know?"

"Well, look behind you," I said. "The starting line is way behind you."

He smiled sadly. I was happy for Walter, and I also felt a loss. I thought about him cutting back on pot. I thought about him waking up and realizing he had several hours until noon when he could reunite with his best friend. I wanted my pills. That gave me a hunch.

"You miss the pot?" I asked him.

"I do."

There was silence.

"I really do," he added.

In the following sessions, Walter advanced the Pot Plan. Once he found it easy to smoke only before noon, he decided he wouldn't smoke after 8:00 p.m. After he found it easy to smoke only between noon and eight, he decided he would allow himself to get high only two times in that window. He was now the pilot of his gradual and imperfect change.

As he smoked less, he was confronted by the emotions he had been avoiding since he was a young boy. He was lonely. He was angry. He felt immense guilt. He wanted to be loved. He wanted to love deeply.

Less drugs meant more feelings. Like a trainer at the gym, we helped him lift more and more emotional weight so the feelings caused less anxiety. Less anxiety meant fewer defenses. Since he could experience more feelings, he could think about what he wanted to do about his life. He could take better care of himself. He could let feelings guide him. If Walter had continued to smoke in the way he had, he would never have been able to lift the weight of what was to come.

It is nice to think that if we gain emotional strength, those around us will as well. This, of course, is not always true. To avoid the truth of the limited emotional capacities of others, we often sacrifice our own growth to remain with them. Of course, being with someone in this way doesn't mean intimacy. It means being engaged in a relationship of defenses.

Would Walter continue to be able to face the reality of his marriage? I didn't know. All we could see was as he was able to face more of reality, he continued to adapt his plan to meet his own abilities and needs. He understood that the pursuit of perfection would kill his goals of reducing smoking and deepening his connections with others. He saw the uselessness of a perfect score, of a one-to-one trajectory of growth. Thus, like a true hero to himself, he let go of perfection and walked into the unknown.

33

Michelle: The Therapist with the Marshmallow Chair

I broke out into a sweat and nearly blacked out while preparing for my third silent meditation retreat. When I decided to call the leader of the retreat to tell him, I stuttered and went mute. He suggested I see a trauma specialist for what "I had been through medically."

For what I had been through *medically*? The idea had never crossed my mind. I was stunned I hadn't thought to explore this. What else hadn't I thought of?

My work with Dr. A had been quite successful. My headaches were a rarity. I no longer took opioids. I had learned about my buried rage, guilt, love, and grief, and I faced them time and time again.

Although my past therapy had been beneficial, my body signaled that further work was necessary. Engaging in meditation, particularly the stillness it demanded, appeared to activate the medical trauma entrenched within my body.

I reached out to Dr. J. While Dr. A specialized in attachment trauma, Dr. J specialized in trauma. Attachment trauma revolves around disruptions in relational bonds, signifying any strain in the connection between a child and their caregivers that remains unaddressed or unresolved in a constructive manner. On the contrary, trauma is not inherently interrelational, implying that it doesn't exclusively involve experiences between individuals. Trauma can result from a large range of issues outside the norm, such as near-death experiences, rape, violence, disease, abuse, war, and more. Experiencing one of these events doesn't automatically result in trauma for everyone.

I had been curious only about my attachment trauma and how my unconscious dynamics worked. I hadn't thought about medical trauma. I hadn't considered that how I learned to cope with relational loss would impact me in every way, including how I dealt with medical trauma.

"What brings you in today?" Dr. J asked when I first sat down in her padded desk chair on wheels. Compared to Dr. A's chair, Dr. J's chair was one big marshmallow.

Instead of being able to answer Dr. J's question, I flashed to a memory of a doctor finishing a note on her computer. I could see some of the words.

She is becoming increasingly frustrated and hopeless by her headache and does not know what to do next . . . started on long-acting morphine and continues to take Percocet as needed for breakthrough pain . . . This combination has improved her quality of life . . . still in daily pain . . . Going back to square one with her history workup and treatments attempted thus far, discussing whether to repeat studies or to obtain another opinion . . . Consider occipital nerve procedures . . . either pulsed radiofrequency ablation.

A common reaction in individuals with trauma is the struggle to remain present in their own bodies, often stemming from a sense that being fully grounded isn't safe. As a result of my various procedures, particularly those I endured without sedation, coupled with persistent pain, I had acquired a coping mechanism in the form of dissociation. I was with Dr. J, and I wasn't with Dr. J.

My medical trauma was officially out of the Not Important box.

Instead of answering Dr. J's question, "What brings you in today?," I thought about the doctor's note and her recommendation to get an ablation, which is when doctors use electricity to fry your nerves to stop them from sending pain signals. Frying the nerves sounded wonderful. I remembered the thought of my nerves frying like bacon, gasping their last breaths before flames and smoke consumed them, leaving me in peace.

Even though Dr. J was right in front of me, I was on a large table, where a doctor was about to insert needles into my neck and zap the nerves that went to my head with electricity. "DESTRUCTION BY NEUROLYTIC AGENT" read the medical notes. I loved how it sounded—total and sweet destruction of the nerves causing my headache. I wanted to blast all my nerves in one epic mushroom cloud of glory.

There was no sedation.

After the procedure, they said there might be increased pain at first because the nerves in my neck and head might be "angry." The *nerves* would be angry. They wrote that "the patient was comfortable throughout the ablation." Nerves were angry, patient was comfortable. My nerves had feelings, and I didn't.

I suddenly realized I was sitting in front of Dr. J and fought to bring my attention back to her.

"Um, what brings me in today?" I finally answered. "Good question. I'm not sure if you can help. I think I need to process through some of my . . ." The words *medical trauma* were about to come out of my mouth, but they felt so dramatic. I was suddenly back to dismissing myself. "I think I need to process some of my medical experiences," I decided to say. I was still struggling to depend. I still had the same assumption as Emma: *people probably won't be able to help me.*

Dr. J looked out at me under crisply cut bangs that barely touched the top of her glasses, which were made of two multicolored triangles. She reminded me of a sassy-looking Anna Wintour.

"How is your anxiety? Because it can be retraumatizing to pour all of it out, ya know?"

"I don't feel flooded," I said with some relief. If she had asked me to dive into my history with little evaluation of my anxiety, I would have greatly doubted her skills. "I had a ... headache ... for six years." I looked down at my fingers. "And they finally found the reason for it, which was a Chiari malformation. Are you familiar?" I looked back up at her. Her face was horrified. Compared to Dr. A, Dr. J looked like a caricature. I felt my body both warm and harden.

"No, I'm not familiar," she said with the look of horror still stuck on her face. Unlike Dr. A, she didn't seem to hide her facial expressions.

"It's, uh, when your cerebellum, the back part of your brain, comes out of the bottom of your skull, essentially. After it was fixed, I had some headaches, which I dealt with successfully in my past therapy. It's pretty much all gone now. If I get a headache, I can usually get rid of it. I took opioids for about nine years. I don't take them anymore because I realized my relationship with them had become something else. I think my body's rejecting meditation of all things, and that's why I'm here, not to be able to meditate again but to find out what meditation hits on. I freeze up, start to stutter, and sweat. I can't talk."

Dr. J sat there, staring at me with her lips slightly parted. I couldn't take my eyes away from her face. Her eyes were sad, her face in shock. I felt relieved, seeing her untethered expression. It was a validating reality check for which I was thirsty.

"You had a headache for six years?!" she finally blurted out. "Oh my god. I can't even!" Her words felt like a pet to my skin, a pet I both wanted to allow and bat away.

"I want to figure out why I'm ... freezing like this. It's the weirdest thing. I can't talk or think when I ... I know it's what we call cognitive-perceptual disruption. It's severe, and it comes out when I start to think, and I mean really think, about what I've been through medically."

"Is something coming to your mind now?" she asked.

What was coming to mind was a test I had over a decade ago. It wasn't so much a thought coming to my mind as it was a ghost sitting in the periphery.

"Do you feel like you're here?" Dr. J asked, pulling me back.

"Yes and no. I'm back in the angiogram room. Present and past mix a little. And it's weird because I had six cranial nerve surgeries and two craniectomies, had my skull opened and everything, yet right now, it's the angiogram that still seems to haunt me. Maybe the other surgeries are locked further down. Or maybe they weren't traumatic because I was medicated. It's the ones I was awake for that seem to splash across my mind and freeze me up."

"That makes a lot of sense. You couldn't move."

It was only an angiogram. It wasn't even a big deal.

Talk about it.

You're going to look like you want her to feel bad for you. This was not a big deal.

Stop doing this to yourself.

"Um, I'm lying on the table in this room. It's got a lot of white, and it's definitely blurry."

"You are using present tense. Does it feel like you're there now?"

I nodded.

"Okay, so let's help you get back here first," she said as she leaned forward. "Do you feel the chair underneath you? The yellow walls around you as you talk to me now?"

Dr. J was trying to ground me in the present, which is often necessary in trauma work.

I sighed as I looked around.

"I do now, actually. Thank you for that."

I told Dr. J about the procedure. A tiny tube was inserted into my groin and up into the back of my head. For each injection of the dye, I experienced a new sensation: the room spinning, fireworks going off, the taste of metal, and the feeling of urinating.

"Each time, they said, 'Don't breathe, don't even blink.'"

I paused.

"See now, this is where ... things ... got worse," I said to Dr. J. "Um ..."

"Is it happening again?" she asked. I nodded, and Dr. J and I took a moment to reorient myself to the room. "Can you remember the first moment after this experience that you knew you were safe?"

It was when I was back in my apartment with Devon. He was making me soup in the microwave, and I heard it beeping. I felt cared for. He brought it to me in bed with a little towel underneath it so it wouldn't burn my hands.

"Okay, I can continue," I said after I felt safer in my body. I told her about the recovery room of the angiogram, where a numbness began in my left arm. I didn't want to make a big deal out of it. The numbness began to spread, and eventually, I couldn't move my arm at all. It spread up my arm and into my face. My mom was there. I told her I couldn't feel my arm. I'm sure my detached and deflated voice confused her, like someone yawning while they tell you they might be having a heart attack. And then, I went blind.

No longer present in Dr. J's office, I heard voices, concerned tones, a few instances of "No, that's not normal" from the recovery room.

Am I going to die? I think I'm going to die. I leaned forward and vomited, having to sit up so as not to choke on my vomit. I wasn't supposed to move, however, because I could have a stroke.

"I'm not allowed to move! Is this okay?" I asked the air with vomit coming out of my mouth.

"The next thing I can remember," I told Dr. J, "is the sound of the microwave beeping. I regained my sight and feeling, but I don't remember it. I don't remember coming home."

They never figured out what happened to me in that recovery room. I may have reacted to the dye they used in the procedure.

"This is an incredible amount to go through," Dr. J said. She looked at me with wet eyes and enough empathy to make me want to look away. "And does your body feel safe now?"

I took a moment to look around the room. "Yes."

"Did they find out what caused the headache?"

"They did, actually."

I told Dr. J about the surgeries with Dr. B and how a few weeks after Devon and I broke up, Dr. B said there was nothing more he could do.

"After that, I went to see a neurosurgeon, Dr. C, to review recent scans of an unruptured aneurysm found during the angiogram."

When I first sat in Dr. C's office, I was numb. He took a seat at the computer, loaded up my scans, looked at the aneurysm on the scan, and told me it looked fine. Then, he began to scroll through more of my scans.

"I'll never forget that moment," I told Dr. J, trying to make eye contact. "He extended his long index finger out toward his screen and said, 'Now, there, *that's* your problem.' He told me I had a clear Chiari malformation. He sounded casual, like it was no big deal. He told me the Chiari was causing my problems, and we could get me in as soon as possible to take care of it."

I thought back to the morning of September 13, 2013, after 51,288 hours of constant pain, nearly six years after the first night of my headache, when I was wheeled in for my Chiari malformation decompression surgery.

"My official diagnosis was an Arnold-Chiari type 1 malformation with cerebellar tonsillar ectopia," I told Dr. J. "The lower back of my brain was falling out the opening where the skull attaches to the spine."

I imagined how much trauma Dr. J heard about every day and felt grateful that she still had empathy left for me. I felt a zing of warmth in my chest and nestled into her marshmallow chair.

I told her how, under general anesthesia, I was rolled over onto my stomach. They shaved off nearly all the hair from the bottom half of my head. Because of my previous surgeries and scar tissue, a plastic surgeon was called in to ensure the new incision wouldn't result in bone death due to loss of blood supply. After assurance that the planned incision wouldn't cause bone death, they cut into the back of my neck and head. The incision started halfway up my neck, continuing six inches up my head, running north to south. They cut through layers of fibrous skin, vertebrae, and skull at the top of my spinal cord and then wedged in large clamps to keep the back of my neck and head open. Next, they removed a part of my skull and the bony arch of the top vertebrae to create more room for my brain. Last, they opened the dura, the tough outermost membrane that encases the brain and spinal cord. This revealed "an obvious Chiari I malformation with marked descent of the tonsils."

"Obvious," I repeated to Dr. J as I felt the withholding of grief sting my throat.

"After all that searching," Dr. J added.

I looked into her eyes. They carried the weight I felt in my body. It was as if she had been by my side during all the procedures. She was feeling with me.

And then, I cried. I cried for my body and all that it went through.

34

Emma: The Anger Thing

"I don't want to do the anger thing," Emma said firmly after she put her bag down. "I don't think it's helpful. I see what you're saying, that I put the anger back onto me. I've been better at it. And I don't get acid reflux anymore, which is great. I'm not depressed anymore, which is great. I still get headaches and wake up, like, in a knot. I really don't like doing the anger thing with you."

I felt trapped. Her messages were contradictory yet also clear. How could I communicate with her trapped self underneath the surface of her defenses and anxiety?

"The anger thing?" I asked, to clarify.

"Where we look at anger in my body toward you. I don't like where it's going. The trajectory of that specific line of questioning. I don't like thinking of what the anger wants to do." I had yet to ask Emma what her anger wanted to do. She had always stopped us before we went that far. "I don't want to look at scratching or throwing or something." Apparently, Emma had been aware of these urges without sharing them with me. I felt both relieved and annoyed.

"Ah. You don't want to look at how those feelings feel in your body toward me and what the impulses are."

"No. I don't want to look at that."

I didn't either, and thank god I did.

"And you don't have to," I said earnestly, mostly to her but also to myself.

"But it might be good for me!"

I felt my brain hiccup as I realized we were on a seesaw together. If Emma's back-and-forth made my brain lag, I wondered what it did to hers.

"Yes, it might help. It's like eating vegetables. They don't always taste good, but they're good for you. However, you wouldn't feel better after someone jammed vegetables down your throat without your consent or desire, would you?"

Emma smiled and laughed. I didn't want to guide her hand back to the serving dish if she didn't want more. I didn't want to yell at her from the kitchen.

"At least two things are true. You don't have to do a thing. And you protect others with an unconscious mechanism that puts anger back on you in the form of pain, picking, dismissiveness, and criticism. Both are true."

Emma and I sat, looking at each other. Her mouth started to shift back and forth as if she was contemplating something. I also didn't know what to do.

"Is there another way?" Emma asked.

"I was just wondering the same thing!" I said as I slapped my leg. "Does it feel like you can't feel anger or just aren't willing?"

Emma thought. "Both."

Since Emma took a defiant stance, it was important that I not support that stance by defying her. I counteracted her painful defense of I-should-know-everything-and-be-perfect with a stance of do-whatever-you-like-you're-fine-as-you-are. She needed a depressurized therapy to counteract her pressurizing defenses. In someone else's therapy, I might respond in a completely different way based on their defenses.

Emma threw up her hands. "I feel like I'm letting you down. Or failing the therapy. I'm not doing what I'm supposed to do."

"You're being bad and not practicing the violin. You're making a mistake," I said as I moved my head side to side to dramatically illustrate these voices.

"Exactly! This therapy won't work. And it's my fault."

"Yeesh." I cringed dramatically.

"Yeah, yeesh. Super Bitch." She took a deep breath.

"Well, you're not letting me down, that's for sure. I have no agenda here." I stopped, wondering if my words were true. "Well, it's whatever your agenda is. Yes, we both know the anger is going inward, and it would help you to be more comfortable with mixed feelings, including the anger and the guilt it causes. You're putting an important boundary down here, saying it doesn't feel right and that you don't want to. And if you don't want to, you shouldn't." Emma stared at me. "There's no one way. We want to listen to you."

Everything Emma said and did was ideal, a perfect message to us. Every single tiny thing each patient does is sheer perfection. It's one of the only times I'm comfortable using the *P* word. If I ask about feelings, and they change the subject, it's great. I just learned that they diversify (the defense of changing the subject to something unhelpful) to avoid feelings. If I ask what they notice about themselves, and they can't answer, it's great. I know they have a hard time paying attention to themselves and likely experience self-neglect. Each response guides us together.

"You just being yourself gives us information. If you come in with a certain type of anxiety, that's information. If you use a defense, that's information. You can't get any better at giving us the exact information we need. It's exactly what we need to know to help you. And honestly, I had to learn this too. My mentor had to teach me that. I used to hear things clients said and think, *Why aren't they doing x, y, or z! I wish they wouldn't do that!'*

"Yeah, I bet." Emma looked right at me, engaged.

"Therapy is a place where you can't go wrong as long as we're both paying careful attention to you. And everything you do and say is exactly what we need to know to help you. For example, right now, you truly don't want to do the anger thing. And so we listen. I'm with you either way. I follow you."

"To find another way."

"Yes, to find another way. It's based on you, no one else. Not me." I waved my hand toward the window. "Not them."

Emma let out a long sigh. "Okay, that sounds good. Honestly..." She took a moment to think about it, to feel about it. She was more relaxed. Her fingers were left alone. "It feels pretty good what you're saying. I like it. My jaw is looser."

I checked with her other symptoms. She said there was no acid reflux since the first few weeks of seeing each other. She no longer needed her medication. She didn't have a headache.

"If anything," she continued, "there's this little thought that what you're saying is hooey. Like, what you're saying is just trying to make me feel better."

"It's the cheesification defense. It devalues meaningful things as hooey."

"Exactly! That's what I'm doing. Because what you're saying does make me feel better." Emma gazed out the window pensively. "You know, being less depressed and more reasonable with myself makes me different from my sisters and my mom now. I notice the difference. They were speaking to each other kind of harshly, and I was like, whoa."

For someone who wanted to belong, this might be a problem. It might even stop her progress in therapy. If she stops suffering, she no longer belongs to a family group of sufferers. Whether we know it or not, we all want to belong. The people who deny a wish to belong are often the most desperate to belong. This desperation is held deep within.

"I don't want to be where they are. I want to hold on to this."

I nodded, relieved and surprised.

"And you know, I think I tried to be good to avoid my parents finding me difficult."

Eliminating any pressure from me allowed her memories of being pressured to be perfect to come up.

"You tried to be perfect?" I asked.

"That sounds cliché, but yes." Emma looked at her fingers sitting on her lap. "Yes, I did. And I think this was a way to avoid how I felt toward them."

I remained silent.

"I didn't want to, like, want anything, you know?"

I nodded, looking at her intently. *I do know.*

"I didn't want to feel weak, like I was sad. I didn't want to seem affected."

"But you were."

"Yeah, I was."

With the absence of the need to conform to any expectations, whether as the ideal patient or daughter, it was wonderful getting to meet her.

35

Michelle: Cow Parts

Dr. J listened as I continued to tell the story of what my body had been through during the final surgeries. This time, my defenses didn't give a watered-down version of my medical trauma.

"They sewed a protective layer over my brain using a piece of a cow's heart to cover the new hole in my skull," I said, trying to look into Dr. J's eyes. "This expanded the surface of my brain to give it more breathing room."

Drills burrowed into my skull. Layers of my skin, bones, and muscles were sliced through. Now, I had cow parts instead of me parts.

"I can't believe they can do that," Dr. J said, mouth agape.

"I know. Thank you, cow," I said, smiling at her. She smiled back.

"Anyway, after that first surgery—"

"The first surgery?" Dr. J interrupted. "Wasn't it the . . ."

"I guess it was the seventh. I say *first* because it was the first of its kind. For this surgery, the doctor told me it might take time to feel the results. I waited. Relief didn't come."

I was aware that my muscles were tense as I braced for what I was about to share next.

"Only a month after that decompression surgery, my head pain exploded. It was clear that the surgery that was supposed to fix my problem wasn't going to do a damn thing. But that wasn't the problem."

"What do you mean?" Dr. J asked.

"When my pain exploded, I felt the back of my head and neck where the incision was. There was a small bump. I thought it was just swelling. By the next morning, my pain was worse, and the small bump was now the size of a baseball. My neck looked like a tumorous tree trunk."

When Ben and I arrived at the emergency room, the doctor told me I had a collection of cerebrospinal fluid seeping out of the patch from the previous surgery. Brain fluid was leaking through the cow patch into the back of my neck. This was the reason for my pain. I was admitted and scheduled for corrective surgery in a few days. The cerebrospinal fluid pooled in my skull as I lay in the hospital bed for three days, waiting for another surgery to fix the first one that hadn't seemed to work anyway.

Again, I was wheeled into the operating room. Again, they broke into my head with saws, blades, and clamps. They reopened the previous incision and immediately encountered the pooling fluid. They saw the leak from the patch sewn over my brain only a month ago.

"They closed it back up so it wouldn't leak again?" Dr. J asked.

"Yeah. They . . . resewed it, um, layer by layer, closed it back up."

"What do you notice happening right now, Michelle?"

I hadn't realized I was spacing out, which is a sign of high anxiety. My anxiety had increased because I wasn't relying on my harmful defenses of dismissal, minimization, and withholding. It was time to regulate my anxiety together.

"I think, um, I'm getting flooded again. I—we need to bring the anxiety down."

I could ask Dr. J for help instead of using my harmful defenses.

"The anxiety? Can you describe it?" she asked slowly.

"Spacy. I used to do this a lot at the dinner table growing up."

I imagined a glass of milk in front of me.

"And now it's like you're not..." Dr. J said.

She kept speaking, but her words were lost on me. My mind was consumed by the memory of the morning I awoke from the corrective surgery. After getting the royal intravenous treatment, waking up in the hospital after surgery had become one of my favorite experiences. From a painless dream, waking up felt blissful. I could be watching the world end in a spectacular apocalypse—zombies eating people, volcanoes swallowing up cities, tidal waves washing over mountains—and the heavy-duty opioids and postanalgesic haze could make this chaos appear like a bad B-movie I was gleeful to watch. There was nothing to worry about, fix, or do. I even had a catheter to fully take care of business. Pure paradise.

But the eighth time was different. As I lay in the darkness of the recovery room, the worst pain of my life shattered through my unconsciousness. This pain broke the pain scale. I woke up too early and undermedicated. It felt like a chainsaw was hacking into the back of my head and neck. I called for my body to move, yet only stillness answered. I heard nothing but beeps and saw nothing but darkness. I couldn't open my eyes.

I tried to yell.

"Someb!" I could barely push my voice out of my throat.

No answer.

"Somebody!" My voice gurgled, caving in on itself.

"Something... wrong... is happening!"

The sound of two young female voices slowly reverberated in my ears. Nurses.

My vocal cords pushed out two more words. "It hurts!" I began to sob, causing the pain to spread deeper into my body.

"We're getting you more medication, okay? We have to ask the doctor if we can give you more." I felt a hand briefly touch mine, and I grabbed it.

The nurse began to laugh. I sobbed. *Why am I hearing laughter?*

"It hurts!" All I could do was wail and wait, yet I was clear about what I needed.

"Michelle, are you here?" Dr. J asked. Her voice cut through the memory. Flashbacks don't usually take place in normal time. Like a dream, they are sped up. Thus, while I had been through two surgeries and waking up too early, Dr. J could have only been talking for a few seconds.

I took a deep inhale as I heard her voice. I told her where I was and how I woke up from the surgery too early and undermedicated.

"When I woke up in the intensive care unit later, I began to sob," I told her. "I tried to tell my mom and Ben what had happened when I woke up, but I couldn't get the words out."

When I tried, I saw my mom's and Ben's blurry faces hovering above me. I could see they were confused and uncomfortable. I covered my face with my hands to hide my sobs. I wanted to sob, but I didn't want my mom to see me like this, and I didn't want to make Ben uncomfortable. I tensed my body to stop the shudders. I choked down the trauma. It was too much.

"This is an incredible amount to go through," Dr. J said when I was done telling her about the procedure.

"Yeah, so . . . that's what came to me when I sat down. The fuzzy room, lying on that table."

"That's a horrendous amount to go through," she repeated.

"Right, so—"

"A six-year-long headache. Not knowing what was causing it. These procedures." I wanted her both to stop talking about it and to go on forever.

I said nothing.

"It seems like you have some sort of nourishment barrier," she added. "A barrier to you getting nourishment. You reject it."

While I'm sure Dr. A said this to me in many ways, Dr. J's words hit. There is something powerful about hearing something about yourself from more than one trusted person. In this moment, I finally believed and saw the problem. I didn't allow relational nourishment. How I pushed away relational nourishment created problems for me. My chest popped with the joy of being seen and understood. I smiled at her and swung my legs back and forth under my chair. I felt safe.

Then my body took me back to the morning I was discharged, while I waited alone in my hospital room before Ben and my mom arrived to take me home. I looked around the empty space; suddenly, a feeling awakened from deep within. It was painful yet different, unfamiliar.

I wanted a mom.

My chest ached. My arms felt empty. Strange and unwanted, the feeling took a lot of force to shove down. At this exact moment, my mom entered the room. I teared up. She looked at me and put her bag on the chair next to my bed.

"How was your night?" I asked.

"It was fine," she said with a sigh. Were we both pretending not to notice the tears in my eyes? I should have said, *Thank you for showing up in this empty room. Thank you.*

Instead, we talked about the traffic. Ben arrived minutes later, and when it was time to go, he pushed my wheelchair to the car while my mother walked beside us.

"Bye, mom," I said from my wheelchair. I made sure to look into her eyes. "Thank you for being here with me. I really appreciate it."

She smiled, sad but warm, and waved goodbye.

"I think you're right," I told Dr. J after my body returned to her marshmallow chair. "I think I do have this barrier. Can you help me with it?"

Dr. J smiled and said, "Of course."

She said that we would go through these experiences while helping me feel safe in my body. I admitted to her that I hadn't delved much into my medical experiences in previous therapy sessions. I had presumed they were confined to the past, believing they held no sway over me as I rarely thought about them.

"The past is often the present in the body!" Dr. J said, waving her arms in the air.

"Yes, it is. And now that I know that something is locked in my body, I don't want it lurking inside me. It's probably related to my reaction to meditating."

"What kind of meditation?"

"It's the kind where you *cannot* move."

"You weren't allowed to move for your procedures."

Oh my god. I wasn't! I had never made the connection before. The problem sounded obvious.

"You're right. They would even strap me down for the procedures I was awake for. There was a lot of focus on not moving. When all my body wanted was to run or fight, I had to stay still."

"And in the meditation, you're not supposed to move. It puts your body back to all the traumas and uncomfortable experiences. It brings up the pain. I wouldn't recommend that for someone with your trauma history," Dr. J added as she began to get out her calendar to schedule the next session.

"I thought I had to fight through it."

"You can stop doing that now."

And with this, my body loosened.

After I left Dr. J's office, I thought about how the pain did not return after that final surgery. Dr. C was right. The Chiari malformation *was* my problem. The unrelenting pain finally subsided, granting my brain the freedom to breathe. With each heartbeat, there was no longer a collision against the confines of my skull. It dawned on me—my brain was finally freed. It became clear why my pain had persisted unabated.

Trauma frequently emerges from the entrapment of unprocessed emotions that were unsafe to confront during the traumatic experience. Engaging in trauma work does not involve reliving events, as this can retraumatize the body by re-creating the same defenses, limitations, hazards, and fear. Such an approach is counterproductive. Instead, the focus is on reprocessing the traumas within the framework of a safe and liberated body, one that is permitted to experience and process these emotions freely.

Dr. J and I worked together for only a few months. It didn't take long until I could speak or think about my medical trauma without high anxiety. We worked to feel the messages in my body, to feel the rage and grief I repressed when I was strapped down on those examination tables. As a result, I felt better.

"You should write a book about all of this," Dr. J said during our final session.

"You probably say that to most people. Everyone has a story."

She shook her head. "Not yours."

But I didn't know if I was allowed to tell it.

36

Walter: The Mistletoe

A few months into the Pot Plan, Walter told me he had found a sprig of mistletoe in a box in his attic. In a moment of hope for connection with his wife, he put it up in a doorway in his home. He shared that while they sometimes did pecks, they hadn't had a passionate kiss since his wedding over twenty years ago. As he spoke, Walter sounded like a fourteen-year-old boy trying to kiss a girl he liked.

"I tried to walk under it with her, and I said to her, 'Look,' and she was like, 'What?' And I was like, 'Look up!' and she said, 'What's that?' and, of course, *anyone* knows what that is. And I said, 'It's mistletoe, we should kiss.' And she looked uncomfortable, gave me this peck on the cheek, and walked away."

Walter didn't think things were going to change. His wife didn't want things to change. While she was making an effort with couples therapy, he didn't feel it was an effort to know *him*.

"I mean, I don't think she wants to get to know me. Am I nuts for feeling this way? That she's a great person but doesn't want to know me better? To really feel things together? Am I nuts? I mean, am I?" Walter waved his hands in the air and stared straight into my eyes.

I thought about what C. S. Lewis said when grieving the death of his wife. He wrote, "all reality is iconoclastic."[1] The truth Walter faced was an affront to what he wished for and held dear. The reality of Walter's marriage was too painful, so he questioned his sanity.

"Are you?" I asked again. It was his question to answer.

"I want to see what I can do about our marriage. I want to try."

Walter had been in individual therapy and couples therapy for well over a decade. His wife was a lovely woman with a big heart for her child. He loved her dearly.

"Is asking yourself if you're nuts a real question, or is it a way to drive yourself nuts?"

"A way to drive me nuts!" Driving himself nuts was a way to postpone knowing something he might already know, a way to torture himself instead of facing a painful reality about his marriage.

He sat rubbing his face with his palms, then he drew in a deep breath.

"I know it's anger!" he exclaimed. "I know it's anger that comes up inside me toward her. I don't want to be angry with her."

"You're angry whether you like it or not. You're angry with the woman you love."

"It's true! And I'm not depressed anymore. Knowing the difference between guilt and shame and feeling my guilt and understanding that my discomfort was a lot of anxiety, and that there are things underneath the anxiety—these things have really helped me! Feeling has helped my anxiety and depression."

My chest bubbled with joy. I smiled at him.

"You want my help right now to face this anger toward the woman you love?"

"I want to face this so I can know what to do. Feeling will help me know what to do. If I can feel it all."

"How do you feel this anger toward your wife? How do you feel the anger?"

"She doesn't seem interested in truly putting me first." Walter's answer was one of the most common defenses against feelings: thoughts.

"Right, but that's a thought. How do you feel the anger in your body?"

"Oh, I don't feel it. I just feel anxious."

"Right, and if you stop there, you'll never find freedom." We had to look under the anxiety to find the truth. Anxiety tries to distract us from our feelings by grabbing us by the throat and zapping us with electricity.

Walter slammed his body against the couch. This defense is referred to as *discharge*, a process involving actions such as screaming, shouting, loud swearing, or even physically venting frustration, like punching a hole in the wall. It serves as an outlet when we find the intense experience of anger within our bodies too anxiety producing to tolerate. Walter was struggling to contain and experience the rage inside. But then, Walter took a deep breath and looked at me.

"She doesn't understand. She doesn't want to get close." He was back to his thoughts.

"Right, but these are thoughts again. If you keep thinking, you'll only be a thinking man and not a feeling man. You'll be a robot."

"I don't want to be a robot."

"I know you don't. Let's see what you're going to do about that."

Walter sighed and shifted around.

"How do I feel my anger?" His body looked powerful. "I feel it in my arms. I feel it in my chest." I could feel his anger growing as an electric jolt went through me.

This was not the time to back down. This was the time to push forward, to help Walter get comfortable with energy filling his body with strength without hurting anyone. If he wasn't comfortable with it, the anger would go back into him in the form of shame and depression.

"And what does that anger want to do? What does that anger in your chest and arms want to do?"

"It wants to grab." He made fists. "Grab . . . grab . . . grab something that breaks. Because I want to hear it smash! I want it to explode! Like something ceramic!"

"Something ceramic is not what we're talking about. We're talking about your wife, not an inanimate object."

"Right, but I don't want to be angry at her," Walter said while shaking his fists.

"But you are. The question to ask your body is, What does the anger want? What is the urge behind it, without acting it out? That way, you can stop this anxiety, get clear, and have power in your life."

"It wants to grab her by the shoulders and shake her!"

Walter had never placed a hand on his wife. He had no problem with impulse control. In fact, he had the opposite problem. He instantly repressed his impulses and put them back on himself, which caused his shame and depression.

Walter's face contorted into a painful expression.

"And what feelings come up as you look at this picture?" I said, pointing to where his eyes met the carpet.

His arms remained strong, his hands in fists, and another feeling emerged. Walter had worked hard to feel anger in his body without anxiety and depression crushing him.

Walter looked at the image he projected from his mind onto the carpet below. Guilt moved up and through Walter as tears filled his eyes.

"Let it through," I said. "Let this through as much as you can."

We sat as Walter cried, bravely facing his anger and guilt.

"Can you see her face? Your wife's face? After you shook her with all your strength?"

"I don't want to."

I know, Walter. I didn't either.

"This is the problem. You do not want to look at your entire self. There are feelings you cut off by not looking at her face. Let yourself see so you can be free."

He nodded and sighed.

"I see her eyes. I see love. I don't know why, but I see love." Walter paused. "And she also looks scared."

As Walter looked into the eyes of his wife in his mind, he felt a deep love for her. However, this time it was different. He could feel his love and hold on to his anger, which spoke up for what he wanted from her. As this love rose with his awareness of her limitations, Walter leaned forward as the waves of grief and guilt continued.

"And let that all through. The anger. The guilt. The love. All of you."

The sound of sobs filled the room.

"No part of you left behind," I added.

We sat there together as he cried.

For the rest of the session, Walter's mind was clear, and his body relaxed. He didn't need to hide from his feelings because he had faced them. Instead of scaring him, his feelings would set him free. There was nothing to hide. He could finally speak about what he wanted for his life, about what he wanted to do if he left his wife.

He broached the topic of contemplating leaving his wife, reflecting on the intricate life they had woven together. They shared mutual friends and a child and had journeyed through the last two decades side by side. His love for her was undeniable. After twenty years of living in the same house, he would be walking away from pieces of furniture, pictures hanging on the walls, and even carpeting that held rich memories. In his clarity, he knew how much he wanted from her and how little she was able to give. Walter was strong enough to be honest with himself. Throughout this, he cried. He felt grief. He felt guilt. He felt hope. Notably absent was high anxiety, self-hate, and depression.

37

Michelle: The Toxic Daughter

What's wrong with you?
You could have avoided this.
You should have known better.

I was standing over my kitchen sink washing dishes, getting shot by my own emotional bullets. It had been a year since I said goodbye to Dr. J, years since my last opioid, and a month since an attempt to talk to my mom.

Maybe you are a cruel, horrible person.
A toxic person.
Enough. This had to come to an end.

I decided to reach out to a highly recommended psychodynamic therapist, Dr. M. He was an older man in his seventies and had the face of a kind and patient wizard. When he asked what I wanted his help with, he smiled comfortably, looking at me through soft eyes.

"I've been very critical with myself lately," I told him after he asked how he could help. "Something feels terrible inside. I'm guessing it has to do with what's been going on with my mother and this most recent talk I had with her."

Dr. M nodded. He seemed content and comfortable to listen to me talk.

"I've had a lot of good therapy before, but I can tell that there's something I don't quite have a leg up on yet, something I haven't previously addressed. I have a blind spot with what I'm doing to myself. It doesn't feel like simple self-criticism. It's not . . . simple."

"What prompted this most recent talk?" Dr. M asked.

I told him how the talk was prompted by my mother telling me that she wanted a more honest relationship. I wanted one too. I told myself that this time might be different, especially since she was the one who initiated it.

I had also worked on having a more honest relationship with myself. I had learned about my defenses of self-neglect, giving myself head pain, pleasing, dismissal, minimization, and projection. I saw how these defenses hurt me and what they had cost me. My head pain was almost nonexistent, and while I still missed opioids, they were out of my life. I had worked through much of my medical trauma, creating a safer body to live within. I thought that since I had worked on myself, the conversation would finally go well.

"I thought that maybe the conversation between my mom and I would be different. I thought that maybe now I could be clear about what I wanted from her, and she could get to know me. Maybe I could finally make her happy."

I stopped to clear my throat, which felt like it was becoming clogged. I noticed this sign of anxiety and pushed on. Dr. M patiently waited.

"There was one thing I planned to tell her that I knew she wouldn't be happy about, which was that a more honest relationship meant I would no longer keep her secrets that had impacted and involved me. I would share my own experiences."

I told Dr. M that when I arrived at her house, we hugged and sat down in her living room. I was tense. After asking my mom if it was okay if we talked, I took a breath.

I shared that I no longer wanted to keep her secrets. I told her that keeping her secrets had hurt my relationship with myself and my family. I also wanted a better, more honest relationship with her, but for that to happen, I needed her to be aware of her anger toward me so it didn't come out in harmful ways. She adamantly stated that she had no anger toward me, "none at all," and didn't know what I was talking about. I went on to tell her about my anger and love toward her and how facing them both had helped me, especially with my headaches. I asked that she try to listen without arguing against my feelings or experiences, that some things be about me and not her. I wanted her focus and empathy. I wanted her love and attention.

Dr. M kept listening, silent. Did I find his silence helpful or annoying?

Both, I answered to myself.

"I told my mom that I've tried to be there for her, but our relationship would need to be at least two-sided. There needed to be room for both of us."

"You were clear," Dr. M added.

His simple sentence packed a helpful dose of reality: I was clear. I wasn't mean.

"Yes, I was clear. And she said she would try to listen, yet she didn't think she didn't. I asked her if it would be helpful if I gave her examples because I wasn't sure she'd like examples. She said, 'Sure.'"

I didn't want her to be overwhelmed. I told myself that it would be my fault if her anxiety went too high. I had to be the one to monitor it.

"Moments later," I continued, "she changed the subject from something I was sharing to how she was in pain. I cautiously told her that this was an example. She looked at me and frowned. I didn't know how'd she react. She didn't say anything at first, so I told her that I was telling her how I felt, and the conversation changed to how she was feeling and became about her. I told her I needed her to stay with me a little longer."

I held on to the hope that expressing my desires with greater clarity might bring about meaningful change. Perhaps in the past, my communication had left her uncertain about how to connect with me. I attributed our previous misunderstandings to my own blind spots—acknowledging that I may not have grasped how to fulfill the roles of a better daughter and communicator. Maybe I could fix this now.

She nodded her head and didn't say a word.

I told Dr. M how when I left her house, our future felt uncertain. Our long conversation had ended with a mutual hug and her waving goodbye with a large smile on her face. I looked forward to talking more, for her leaving room for both of us. I wondered what it would feel like to have her listen and try to understand me even if she didn't agree with me. I knew it wouldn't be easy. Maybe now, we could finally have the honest relationship we both wanted.

I took a long sigh as I looked into Dr. M's eyes. "I didn't hear from her for two days. I called her. Her phone rang and quickly went to voicemail. Two weeks later, I still hadn't heard anything. Over a month later, there was still no response. Then, moments after my latest unanswered call, she called back. I told my mom that it had been a really long time. I didn't understand. I asked why she decided not to speak to me. She said, 'You know when you called a few days after our conversation? When I saw it was you calling, I dropped the phone. I was terrified of you. I was traumatized by you.' I was speechless."

"She said she was traumatized by you?" Dr. M asked.

"Yes. She said, 'You flayed me,' with this exceptionally grave tone."

My brain had turned to mush when my mom said this, and yet my mind remained clear as I spoke to Dr. M.

"My mom also added that her therapist thinks I'm 'toxic for her.'"

MICHELLE: THE TOXIC DAUGHTER

Dr. M frowned. I wished in that moment that therapists had subtitles.

"I couldn't understand," I went on. "I didn't say it out loud, but I was sitting there wondering, *What are you telling your therapist about our conversation? About me?*"

I imagined her and her therapist talking about setting important boundaries with her toxic daughter, the one who cruelly traumatized her, flaying her like meaningless meat. This was my mom trying to put down a boundary with that daughter. That daughter didn't happen to be me.

The real me didn't stand a chance.

"What did you say?" Dr. M asked with curiosity in his voice.

"I said, 'Well, I don't want you to be traumatized. You shouldn't do what you don't feel comfortable with.' What else could I have said?"

I looked down, playing with the hem of my T-shirt. Dr. M waited.

"It was shortly after that last phone call that I stood at my kitchen sink," I said, picking up my head to look at him, "pelting myself with thoughts about how horrible I was, wondering if I had been cruel."

Some people cut themselves on the outside. I was slicing and dicing on the inside.

"This is why I reached out to you," I told him. "I feel insane. Like, totally nuts. Something about my mom and our dynamics just . . ."

I couldn't explain it. Whatever was happening inside me was a mystery. Both the fact that it was a mystery and the dynamic itself drove me nuts. It didn't feel like self-attack, which was my first guess. I did get the sense that whatever it was, it had been with me for a long time.

"Oh!" I said with a jump in my chair as I remembered more. "After this last phone call. My mom sent me text after text of yellow and pink tulips from around her house."

Dr. M raised his eyebrows.

"I know! And with them, she wrote, 'I thought you'd like to see them.'"

I did not want to see them. I was angry when I saw them. I felt like I had whiplash from a lifelong game of bumper cars.

My anger was quickly replaced with a familiar thought.

Was I horrible?

"She was trying to be nice," I told Dr. M in a pleading voice. "I'm not sure I spoke to her the right way that day we had the long conversation. Was I cruel? She's sending me tulips while I flayed her!"

What have you done? You should have known she would be hurt; therefore trying to talk to her was cruel. You're a therapist. You shouldn't have talked about something serious for such a long time. You should have known what her anxiety was like. It was too much for her, and you hurt her. You should have known she couldn't handle it. This relationship hasn't worked because you refuse to see how awful you are.

What was I missing?

I couldn't stop the cyclone of gut-tearing thoughts. Not only did I believe my thoughts, I also felt them within my body, as if my badness was sewn into me.

"I can't stop ruminating, wondering, puzzling out what I don't understand about how I feel. I feel like I'm either a bad person, or I've been through something bad that has seeped into me. Every time I think it's the latter, I tell myself that I'm just a bad daughter trying to wiggle free of the guilt of being insensitive. I can't stop thinking about it. I puzzled and puzzled. How could I hate her pictures of tulips? Isn't it nice to have a mother sending her child pictures of her tulips?"

I stopped. I had tired myself out.

I was glad to show this inner world to Dr. M. Something about him helped me feel comfortable to share without editing, and because my defenses had stopped telling me I wasn't allowed to share, I made myself feel comfortable to share without editing.

"If this is the repair I've been asking for, why does it make me feel ... dirty?"

"If it was the repair you asked for, you wouldn't feel dirty," he added.

I looked at his face. He had a neutral expression, which carried the confidence of someone who just commented on something as obvious as the weather. It was as if a true self within me knew he was right. Tulips weren't what I asked for. In fact, I had completely forgotten what I had asked for and focused on how I didn't feel grateful when she sent me tulips. I felt relief.

The relief was interrupted with a thought: *Figure out what's rotten in you, and do it as fast as you can to not cause any more harm to your poor mother.*

What about me? another voice answered back.

Selfish, always about you. Maybe that's your problem.

It's not safe to put her first. I've tried that.

She's your mother! Your mom. Your one mom!

Do I exchange my sanity for my mom's comfort? What do I owe my parents? What do I owe myself?

"Actually," I said, cutting off my own internal war. "She sent me another text. It was a cartoon of a unicorn leaping through a flowery meadow with rainbows in the background."

I looked at Dr. M and aggressively moved my arms up by my face as if to say, *What the hell!*

"Well, tulips and unicorns are a little, um, 'Fuck you,'" he said.

An energy rose in my chest. I hadn't heard him swear yet.

"What do you mean?" I knew Dr. M had said something about this before, yet I couldn't grasp it.

"Well, you asked her to get to know you and listen to what's been hurtful so it can change. Instead, you got tulips and a unicorn with a rainbow."

"Why can't I accept these texts? I mean, she's trying to be nice."

He stared at me, causing me to attempt to answer my own question instead.

This was about how she wanted to talk, to communicate. This was not about what I needed from her.

"I had told her that for our relationship to continue in a more honest way, we would have to, you know, be honest! Tulips are completely..."

"Missing the point," Dr. M said calmly, as if commenting again on something as obvious as the weather.

"Yes, but over the phone, when she said she wouldn't talk about how I feel, I told her okay. I can't force her to do anything she doesn't want to do, and I said, 'If that's not right for you, that's not right for you.'"

"And if tulips and unicorns aren't right for you, they're not right for you."

I sat upright. It was so simple. His words felt like puzzle pieces finding their place within my body. That was what I wanted to feel deep within my bones.

"What am I missing?" I asked Dr. M. "There's something I'm not seeing. Something about the subtleties. The dynamics."

"What do you mean by dynamics?"

"They're hard to explain. And I think that's part of my blind spot. I don't quite understand what's going on within her or between us or inside me. I feel nuts. There's something subtle, or maybe not so subtle, I can't see because I'm lost in it. I think I'm getting caught up in something I want to free myself from. Something's inside of me that I want *out*."

I needed an exorcism.

38

Emma: To Feel or Not to Feel

When summer arrived, Emma went on more dates. When it came time for a date at her apartment for a home-cooked dinner, she "totally freaked out."

"I'm nervous about having anyone in my home. I felt like my dog who growls at every new person who enters the apartment."

Emma had unknowingly described her relationship pattern perfectly.

She shared that her acid reflux was still gone, she was being nicer to herself, and she had been more productive. She had more energy to do what she wanted since she spent less energy being cruel to herself.

"I cleaned out an entire closet I've been waiting to clean for years. I'm noticing how I'm mean to myself. And it's much less now. These are good things, and I'm able to feel good about them." Emma smiled and looked at me. She was content.

It's astonishing how the brain can change. With repetitive interventions, it can reorganize and form new patterns. Emma's brain had shifted. By interrupting her defenses, she had effectively created new pathways around the self-attack.

"And I stopped picking at my heels!" she said as she threw her arms up in celebration. "I feel like everything I do is acceptable here, and I realized how much I like feeling that way. It makes a difference. I still don't always feel like that out there." She pointed out the window.

"What's it like to feel good about this accomplishment?"

"I don't know if I'd call it an accomplishment!"

"Well, it is, so too bad," I said as we smiled at each other.

"Good point. I do feel good about it. I don't even need to wear socks anymore, and I'm looking forward to wearing heels this summer. It's just that I still can't figure out what's wrong with me dating!"

"Do you want to focus on this question, knowing we've been successful with the other goals? It's totally up to you. I just want to be clear." Some people move the goalposts as soon as they achieve something and then wonder why they're tired. This is a form of torture. It takes the joy out of accomplishments. Was Emma doing this?

"I really do want to focus on this question," she said. "I want to figure out what my problem is with dating. But I can't feel anything."

I decided not to say anything. Within the silence, Emma flopped her hands into her lap and tensed her neck. She looked toward her bag, out the window, and then back to me. She began to pick at her nails, then stopped. The metal detector was beeping. Was she about to emerge?

"I think I want to feel my feelings," she said. Tears collected in her eyes. "It's really cool to hear me say that. I know it's true too."

"What tells you it's true?"

"I feel sturdy. I feel free. It feels good in my body. I want more of feeling."

"You want to do something good for you," I said slowly.

Emma smiled and took a brief sigh. "I want to do something good for me," she repeated.

"I want to do something good for me," I repeated.

"I want to do something good for me," she repeated. "I want to do something good for me." Emma's voice grew louder. "I want to do something good for me." Her lips began to shake.

"And what feelings are trying to come up if you don't block them?"

"I want to cry, but I'm trying not to."

She wanted to feel, yet another part of her was trying to stop the feelings from coming out of her mouth.

"Let's see if you can help you," I said gently. "Let's see if you can help you do good things for yourself." It was imperative I used *you* instead of *I* or *we*. This was up to her and only her.

"I want to feel my feelings," Emma said slowly.

Emma was trying to feel the reality of these sentences in her body. She was trying to have more than a thought in her head.

"I want to do good things for myself," Emma said again.

I waited.

"I want to feel my feelings," I added.

"I *want* to feel my feelings."

I waited.

"I am proud of me," I said.

"I am proud of me," Emma repeated as she nodded. Tears welled up in her eyes. "I am proud of me. I am proud of me. I am proud of me." She closed her eyes.

"I want to do good things for myself," I repeated. Tears formed in my eyes.

"I want to do good things for myself." Suddenly, she popped open her eyes. "Do you think this will help me with dating?"

"Do *you* feel this will help you with dating?"

Emma sighed and looked at me. Tears returned to her eyes. "Yes. I want to do good things for myself. I want to do good things for myself. I want to feel my feelings. I am proud of myself. I am proud of myself. I am proud of myself."

And then, she added, all on her own, "I don't have to be perfect."
"You don't have to be perfect," I echoed.
"I can't be perfect," she added.
"You can't be perfect."
"We're not perfect," she said.
"We're not perfect."

39

Michelle: Projective Identification and Other Potato Drops

Most who suffer from pain of unclear origins crave an aha moment. An aha moment is like the holy grail. I think of it like being on top of a mountain. When you finally arrive, the view is stunning, you have perspective, and you are momentarily at peace. However, one does not simply beam up to a mountaintop. This one moment requires a tremendous hike with much preparation.

I had hiked. I had worked with multiple therapists, been to multiple meditation retreats, had my head sawed open and sewn back up again and again to fix a brain malformation, had cow parts instead of me parts, engaged in a nearly decadelong relationship with opioids, and experienced many other aha moments before I eventually discovered a whopper of an aha moment.

Dr. M helped me get there.

"This one defense has always eluded me," I said to Dr. M during our next session. "It's the defense of projective identification. I want to make sure I'm clear about my understanding of it because I find it complicated. I'm going to need your help, and I think you can help me."

In my ability to depend on Dr. M, I no longer sounded like Emma when she first started to see me or myself when I met Dr. J.

I shared my understanding that projective identification was a two-step process between two people, unlike other defenses. The first step is basic projection. Person A, whom I'll call Bob, projects an unwanted part of himself, like anger, onto person B, whom I'll call Norma. Bob doesn't want to think of himself as having anger. Bob can't bear the conscious idea or feeling of anger, so Bob projects his anger onto Norma. Instead of Bob simply feeling his anger toward Norma, Bob truly believes Norma is the angry one. This is more comfortable and less anxiety producing for Bob. This can happen with any feeling, thought, or belief that makes Bob uncomfortable.

If Bob can't tolerate his guilt, bam! The guilt can belong to Norma. Problem solved for Bob.

If Bob can't tolerate his grief, bam! The grief can belong to Norma. Problem solved for Bob.

If Bob can't tolerate his judgment, bam! Judgment can belong to Norma. Problem solved for Bob.

However, projective identification involves a crucial second step. Bob doesn't just project unwanted unconscious feelings like anger onto Norma; Norma *actually feels, thinks, or becomes* what Bob projects because Bob acts in a way that would cause that reaction in Norma. This makes Bob feel great! Not only is he free of what makes him anxious, but he can point his finger at Norma and say, *See, you are the angry, bad, cruel, and sadistic one! It's not me. It's you!*

"And Norma feels like a lunatic! Like a goddamn lunatic!" I said, waving my arms above my head. "Something doesn't feel quite right to Norma. Reality isn't reality. The world is upside down. Norma loses herself," I said on a long exhale. "And I suppose Bob does too."

"Right, it's like a game of hot potato," Dr. M added. "Bob can't hold his own anger because it's too hot for him, and therefore he tosses it to Norma, who, instead of dropping it, holds on to it. Bob feels better, yet Norma gets burned."

My skin tightened as goose bumps crept over my body. It was magnificent to hear another person reflect my new understanding.

"And Norma might feel like she must hold the hot potato to help Bob feel better because she cares about him," I added. "Projective identification never made sense to me before. I got it intellectually, but it never *sunk* in. Now, I know why I've never fully absorbed it. It's because I've been in it!"

Dr. M nodded and added, "Adopting their beliefs, thinking their thoughts. The main point being that what you're believing, feeling, thinking, or worrying about isn't *yours*."

Sometimes, people try to rid themselves of their own inner pain and conflict by trying to generate it in others. While some people use words to communicate meaning, others use words to make us feel what they can't bear.

I had taken on my mom's opinions of me. I used her words to describe me. And I believed them. She had been inserted into me. And especially after our big talk, *I* was the one that did all this to myself.

Before this understanding, I'd been searching inside myself for all that my mom accused me of. Then, I could change into the daughter she wanted. Since she saw me as dangerous, I felt dangerous. Since she said I was toxic, I felt toxic.

To make matters more complex, I did have a wish to hurt her, which was seen—and felt—in my milkboarding session and other sessions. I worked to face my feelings so they no longer triggered as much anxiety. Since I had less anxiety about my feelings, my defenses weren't as active.

"The last talk my mom and I had triggered an uproar of this insertion," I said to Dr. M. "It was deeper, more intense. And now I'm understanding it wasn't only a rerouting of anger toward her onto me due to guilt about the rage. It was this insertion, this projective identification."

I sat back in my chair and began to feel the reality that I was not the horror I feared I was. I wasn't the person she saw. I had been holding a bushel of her potatoes. And I was exhausted.

Tears welled up in my eyes as I felt the sensation of truth in my body. Goose bumps continued to flow over my skin. Then, I noticed a sense of belonging to myself, a lack of foreign bodies inside me.

There was something about having a cognitive understanding of this process—that what I felt wasn't mine—that freed me from it. My insults of me were not an insight. What I hadn't seen was that someone else's feelings, thoughts, and opinions of me were inserted into me. This was the aha moment: These weren't mine. They were foreign bodies. I didn't have to carry them.

"Yes, that is exactly what I've been seeing," Dr. M said.

As he reflected an image of myself that I recognized, I felt an unfamiliar peace in my body. It is a sensational feeling to show who you are and to have it accurately reflected by another.

To get to this state, I had to go through multiple layers of defenses and literal body tissue. I had to get multiple surgeries to fix a real physical problem that hid a real emotional problem.

Therapy with Dr. A helped me see how I avoided closeness with others and how I dismissed and minimized myself and my memories—by acting like my mom to myself. Therapy helped me see how when I put aside my dismissal, I found rage, hurt, and pain. When I faced my rage, hurt, and pain, I faced my guilt, grief, and love. I had to face my feelings instead of avoiding them.

Meditation retreats and therapy helped me begin to question my relationship to opioids. I started to see how I created the remaining physical pain to keep taking opioids, punishing myself, and distracting myself from emotional pain. I had to say goodbye to opioids to learn what was deeper inside me. The retreats also helped me become clear about my medical trauma, which allowed me to reach out for help and heal my body.

With opioids out of my system and more insight into my minimization and self-neglect, I could listen to my body's reaction to being told to sit still. Since I listened to my body, I could take care of my body. I reached out to Dr. J for support, and together, we helped me face what my body had been through to let it feel safe again.

Then after my body healed, I could see the other ways in which I was brutal to myself. I could start to see how something deep within me wasn't right. Dr. M served as an honest mirror that helped me reflect who I was, guiding me back to myself. When I felt the truth of being me, I could accurately reflect myself to myself. I didn't have to gaslight myself with defenses. Only when I was honest with myself could I be honest about the gaslighting by other individuals and systems.

A family system.

A medical system.

A cultural system.

A societal system.

With my new understanding of what was me and what wasn't, I realized how hard I had been trying to be what I wasn't. I tried to be the daughter who wanted tulips and unicorn texts. I tried to be the daughter who never remembered anything bad. I tried to be the daughter who never found her mother's Post-it notes. I tried to be the daughter who put her mother first. The daughter who didn't have feelings. The daughter who wasn't insulted when she insulted me or talked behind my back. The daughter who wasn't hurt when she commented on my body. The obedient daughter who agreed with her.

"I had layer upon layer of being mean to myself," I said to Dr. M, not wiping away tears. "There were obvious ways I was mean to myself, and then there were less obvious ways. And I'm still working on many of these defenses. It will be lifelong work. I had to get through all those defensive layers to understand what I'm seeing now, how I swallowed my mother's projections and opinions of me. And how I've been choking on them."

Dr. M nodded calmly. He was giving me space to process.

I knew I had a tormentor in me not because I was broken or sick but because I was human and had a broken heart. I wanted to hurt my mom because she hurt me, and I loved her, and therefore I hurt myself instead by giving myself extra physical pain, ignoring myself, dismissing myself, minimizing myself, shaming myself. Once I saw how these defenses hurt me, I could put aside those weapons and reveal what the defenses hid: my deep anger and the aggression behind that anger. I felt guilt, and I also allowed myself the humanity of those wishes.

Ultimately, the tormentor part of me turned toward me. I acted it out on myself. I was cruel to myself. It was *my* head that hurt. I tortured myself with headaches, neglect, self-doubt, self-attack, self-gaslighting, minimization, dismissal, overanalysis, and questioning and questioning and questioning. I tortured myself with emotional bullets. This was how I protected her and others.

I had inflicted violence on myself. I had hidden me from myself. I didn't mean to, but I did. As I sat with Dr. M, free and clear, I was sad for myself. It was not the kind of sadness that drew pity but the kind that required self-compassion.

I felt guilt for what I had done to myself and allowed myself to feel it as deeply as possible, for I knew that healthy guilt leads to healing. Feeling guilt told me about my love and humanity. Feeling guilt told me about the reality of others, that no person is only bad or only good. It's easy to say people are trash and deserve what they get. Thinking of people as trash protects us from the pain of guilt but propels us into a fractured reality. Feeling guilt was my reaction to my anger and love along with two powerful truths: I'm not bad and neither is my mother.

"You know, I've had patients that'd rather go fight in a war than feel emotions," I said, ending the long silence. "While feeling all these emotions can be painful, it feels brave."

Dr. M sat quietly, looking at me with what seemed like infinite patience. I took a breath. I felt a burn and a lump crawl up my throat. I looked down at my hands and felt Dr. M's gaze upon me. He was still there.

"This feels amazing, to speak without my doubt, my denial, and especially my self-criticism. It feels good to experience sanity!"

Dr. M pursed his lips and nodded his head up and down.

"And for you to support my sanity," I added.

A warm silence filled the room. No one was rushing. We were together, listening to me.

"This is why I needed an exorcism."

I felt a sting in my throat. I was holding back my grief.

"See," I continued as I let tears surface, "if I was the problem, this was good news. Then, I could be the one to change. I couldn't change or make sense of her, so I tried to change and make sense of myself. I hoped that if I could change, she would be happy with me again. Now, I know I can't make her happy. I must mourn the loss of that possibility. I must say goodbye to my hope."

I broke into sobs.

I wanted to make my mother happy. I loved her. I loved her deeply. Yet I couldn't make my mother happy without being someone else. I couldn't make my mother happy without losing myself. I couldn't do what she wanted and keep who I was. I couldn't erase memories, experiences, opinions, and feelings. I couldn't erase that she hurt me.

"I thought I was wrong for still hurting, but how do you stop the pain caused by being unknown to your mother?"

Dr. M nodded, taking in my words. It wasn't a question to be answered, as the answer was clear.

"She tried in her way, you know? I know she loves me. And she did a lot of good. I now know that the way she shows love is not what I need or want, and not because I am bad."

I sobbed again, allowing the sting in my throat to subside and my body to fill with sorrow and the relief that my new understanding brought me.

In my new freedom to feel my own emotions, I thought back to the conversation my mom and I had a few months earlier, when I went to her home to talk to her in pursuit of a more honest relationship. She had told me I wasn't an affectionate baby. I was cold to her, she said. It sounded as if I had deprived her of love, like she was a victim of a cold, distant child. However, I had always been an affectionate person. I touch, touch, touch. We are born with a wish to connect. Was I a cold-hearted bitch baby who was cruelly depriving my mom even as a young infant? Or was I already aware of something unspoken, unknown to both of our conscious minds?

"And how sad you had this issue with your brain," Dr. M said, interrupting my thoughts.

"I got a double dose of shitty reality with that one, huh?"

Dr. M smiled sadly.

"You lose yourself around your mother," Dr. M said.

"Yes. While I act like myself, I don't feel like myself. I feel like an alien. The reflection I see back from her isn't me."

"And then, you lose yourself."

"And then, I lose myself."

"You still had a hope she would understand and be there for you. Because you wanted a mother."

"Honestly, I have a hard time with that," I said. "With knowing . . . I *want* a mother. Since I couldn't ever remember wanting a mother, I wondered if it wasn't in me." I thought of Dr. J's statement about my nourishment barrier. The room around me became blurry.

"What's happening now?" Dr. M asked.

"I'm getting super anxious."

"You look like you're dissociating."

"Yeah, it feels somewhat ... something like that. Just ... like, I'm not ... here."

There was silence, yet the silence no longer felt like a helpful silence. Instead, I felt alone, lost. I needed help, and I didn't want to ask for it. Maybe he knew best?

No.

"I think I need something here. I know you're a quieter therapist, but I think I need more activity from you. It feels like I'm in a hole, and silence makes it worse. I can't always do things alone."

"Thank you for letting me know. You lose yourself again here."

"Yes, I am gone."

"All in the context of wanting a mother," he said.

He heard my request and wouldn't leave me in silence. With his presence, my head cleared, my body warmed, and with it, I felt the yearning for connection.

I didn't want opioids. I wanted a person.

"I'm back now," I said. I could see Dr. M's face clearly. It was sad yet warm. "Maybe I can be there for me. And let others be there for me."

"To connect."

"Yes, to connect."

Then, tranquil silence enveloped us, and within its embrace, I found no sense of being adrift.

"I wonder what else I don't know."

"It seems like now you can be yourself while you find out."

40

Emma: The Impossible Facade

I now understand why I was dizzy the day I met Emma. She had asked me for help after many had failed her and after she had failed herself. She didn't think anyone could help her. We shared this. Emma and I were shrouded in character defenses that asked us to dismiss, neglect, doubt, and attack ourselves. Emma and I had physical pain that took over our bodies, distracting us from the emotional pain we'd both rather ignore. My dizziness that first day spoke to the enormity of my anxiety about the feelings still deep within me.

Emma learned to notice herself enough to notice how much she didn't notice. She saw how she attacked and criticized herself. She found the evidence for the reality of her buried emotional underworld. She stopped berating herself. She stopped hissing at herself. Emma was clear that an entire life was inside of her—one that she and others had previously ignored.

Emma decided to stop her therapy shortly after she learned she couldn't be perfect. A lot of problems go away when we realize we're human, that what we strive for isn't actually possible.

At the end of our work, Emma and I reflected on the success of our relationship. She had fought through her urges to ghost me and dismiss me. She could connect with me. Now capable of a fulfilling relationship, she could allow herself to be seen and helped.

Because of Emma's kind attention to herself, she rid herself of a depression inevitably caused by constant neglect and scorn. Her acid reflux stopped. She still hadn't found someone she wanted to date. I doubt that matters most. She could see the uselessness of perfection, the impossible façade that had taken so much from her.

I wonder if she'll be back.

41

Walter: The Roof Overhead

Walter moved out of the house he had lived in for over two decades and rented an apartment not far away, with a small balcony overlooking the street. He told his son about his drug use and how he was working to change it. He wasn't depressed. He listened to himself. He continued to work on being more honest with himself and his son. He continued to experience his complex feelings, going deeper each time we met for more relief from his defenses and anxiety. He wanted to have a better relationship with his son, who was now struggling with his feelings about the divorce and his father's drug use. Walter kept facing his guilt, anger, grief, and love to be there for himself and his son.

He continued to decrease his pot smoking, altering the Pot Plan each time he felt he was ready. He began each session with a report of how he had done.

"There were twelve days where I met the plan and smoked only once and two days where I didn't smoke at all," he said recently.

"That's incredible," I said, smiling.

He smiled back. "Thank you. I agree."

We both sat in silence, taking in the enormity of his progress.

"By the way," he said, "do you remember that huge storm that went through here a few days ago?"

"Oh yes. There was so much damage."

"I found out I can watch big storms like that from my new little balcony. The roof overhead keeps me dry, even during a huge storm like that."

"That's a great feeling, being outside yet safe from a storm."

Walter looked directly into my eyes.

"It is."

Epilogue

Sometimes, physical pain is due to physical factors. And sometimes, pain results from the ways we avoid the truths of our lives. We learn to reject our feelings to keep from being rejected. Rejecting ourselves and our inner life leads to anxiety, depression, and failed relationships. In therapy, we learn to accept our inner life while being accepted by a therapist. We learn that what was harmed in a relationship must be healed in a relationship. We learn to embrace in ourselves what we rejected. We learn to accept others and ourselves without making them into a perpetual home-renovation project.

After Dr. M and I said goodbye, he sent me a receipt for our last therapy session. He included a letter in which he wrote, "I want to call out the importance of your determination to be you and not to 'lose' yourself."

I am determined. And so are you. That's why you read this book.

Acknowledgments

I would like to thank my clients, who give me the privilege to know them. It is through their bravery that I am inspired each day to orient to the truth and break through resistance. And my students and supervisees, who have helped me become a better therapist. I am honored to be in their army of passionate and dedicated therapists. I want to thank my colleagues and friends Lisa Bendzsa, Kristy Lamb, Diane Byster, Eval Gal-Oz, Teri Scott, and Janet Merkel, who gave me their keen clinical eyes and open hearts. I would also like to thank Elyse Tadich, Natalie White, Candace Bertotti, and Devon Fritz, who read this book when it was a sliver of what it eventually became. Because of your patience at such an early stage, I found a sturdy step on which to climb. And thanks to Janelle Kusch, Djuna Osborne, Victoria Madden, and Kate Love, who gave their input when the book was further along. I also want to thank my dear friend Dr. Katie Golden, whose honesty, expertise, and friendship helped support this book's creation. And to my entire family, who joined me on this roller coaster and did their best to hold on because they love me. Notably, to my sister Erin, who read draft after draft, showing her love and enthusiasm, and to my mother, who ended up giving me her blessing to share my story. To my therapists and Lawson Sachter, who guided me back to myself no matter how many barriers I put up. An immense thank you to Patricia Coughlin, who helped me expand my strength and bravery. A deep thanks to Jon Frederickson, who helped me grow not only as a clinician but also as a teacher, supervisor, therapist, author, and human. My work would not be what it is today without his generosity, insight, and ferocious appetite for clinical thinking. I also want to thank Allan Abbass, whose pride upon reading an earlier manuscript gave me strength to continue. And last, to my husband, who watched me sweat through every page of this book, held me when I cried, and celebrated my voice. As C. S. Lewis said, "the most precious gift that marriage gave me was this constant impact of something very close and intimate yet all the time unmistakably other, resistant—in a word, real."[1]

Appendix

In the appendix, you'll discover additional methods to regulate anxiety, examples of anxiety and its effects, and suggested readings for therapists, couples, and individuals.

Grounding Techniques for Anxiety Regulation

If your anxiety is over the threshold, you can use these techniques as well as those within the book to regulate your anxiety. These can be done in any order. Not all of them need to be done. Feel free to be creative. The most important thing is that these are helpful, not correct.

- Breathe in for longer than you breathe out. Do this at least ten times. For example, breathe in for four seconds, hold for one, breathe out for six seconds, hold for one, and start over.
- Notice your five senses.
    - What do you smell? Nothing? What does nothing smell like? Do you like certain smells more than others?
    - What do you hear? What are the loudest noises? The softest? What is your favorite sound?
    - What do you see? Describe it to yourself as a poet would.
    - What do you feel? The chair beneath you? Your foot on the ground? Your hands on these pages or a reading device?
    - What do you taste? Your last meal? Nothing? What is the taste of nothing?

- Move your body.
  - Do your favorite exercise (walk, run, yoga, etc.).
  - Move your toes, ankles, legs, back, arms, and neck. Notice what each feels like. Do you like moving one part of your body more than another?

- Journal.
  - Write or draw what you feel.
  - Write or draw random associations.
  - Write or draw about your day.
  - Write a letter, even if you don't send it.
  - Write or draw what you're learning.
  - Write or draw what you're struggling with.

- Talk to a trusted friend or family member.

Examples of Anxiety and Resulting Issues

Here are more details about the three types of anxiety and the typical health problems or symptoms they can cause. For more on this, see the book *Hidden from View* by Allan Abbass and Howard Schubiner.

Voluntary/Striated Muscle Anxiety

Voluntary muscle anxiety, also called striated muscle anxiety, is the best state for growth and learning. This type of anxiety is below the threshold, indicating that your body can safely confront what it usually avoids. Below are possible signs of striated muscle anxiety.

Sighing

Fidgeting

Legs swinging

Muscles tightening

Shifts in body position

Skin picking

Hair picking

Tension headaches

Potential Resulting Physical Issues and Psychophysiological Disorders

Below are the common results of temporary or chronic straited muscle anxiety.

Sore muscles

Neck pain

Shoulder pain

Chest pain

Back pain

Teeth grinding

Shortness of breath

TMJ (temporomandibular joint) pain

Tension headaches

Tendonitis

Fibromyalgia

Whiplash that doesn't heal

Chronic abdominal or pelvic syndromes

Tingling in hands and feet

Vulvodynia (unexplained pain around the opening of the vagina)

Piriformis syndrome (a syndrome in which the piriformis muscle in the glute irritates the sciatic nerve)

Sciatic pain syndrome

Repetitive strain injury

Foot pain syndromes

Myofascial pain syndrome

Vocal problems

Tics

Tremors

Jaw pain

Cramps

Involuntary/Smooth Muscle Anxiety

Involuntary muscle anxiety, also called smooth muscle anxiety, is a higher level of anxiety beyond the best state for growth and learning. Smooth muscle anxiety is over the threshold, indicating that your body doesn't feel safe to confront what it avoids, and anxiety usually needs to be regulated until it returns to the striated muscles. Below are possible signs of smooth muscle anxiety.

Acid reflux

Nausea

Diarrhea

Frequent need or inability to urinate

Constipation

Vasoconstriction of the blood vessels

Migraine headache

Creation of excess stomach bile

Burps

Potential Resulting Physical Issues and Psychophysiological Disorders

Below are the common results of temporary or chronic smooth muscle anxiety.

- Irritable bowel syndrome

- Ulcers

- Asthma

- High blood pressure

- Migraines

- Irritable bladder syndrome

- Chronic fatigue syndrome

Cognitive-Perceptual Disruption Anxiety

Cognitive-perceptual disruption is the highest level of anxiety beyond the best state for growth and learning. Cognitive-perceptual disruption is over the threshold, indicating that your body doesn't feel safe to confront what it avoids, and anxiety usually needs to be regulated until it returns to the striated muscles. Below are possible signs of cognitive-perceptual disruption anxiety.

- Blurry vision

- Tunnel vision

Ringing in the ear (tinnitus)

Vertigo, lack of balance, dizziness

Fainting

Pseudoseizure

Memory loss

Loss of train of thought

Loss of normal cognitive function

Hearing loss

Hallucinations (can be in any of the five senses)

Dissociation

Loss of reality, feeling dreamlike

Potential Resulting Physical Issues and Psychophysiological Disorders

Below are the common results of temporary or chronic cognitive-perceptual disruption anxiety.

Vertigo

Postural orthostatic tachycardia syndrome (POTS)

Psychotic disorder

Inappropriate sinus tachycardia (abnormally high resting heart rate)

Reflex sympathetic dystrophy (chronic arm or leg pain developed after injury, heart attack, stroke)

Insomnia and other sleep disturbances

Paresthesia (numbness, tingling, burning)

Tinnitus (ringing in the ears)

Spasmodic dysphonia (involuntary movements of the voice box)

Chronic hives

Hypersensitivity syndromes, such as misophonia (sensitivity to touch, smells, foods, medications, sounds)

Further Reading

For Clinicians

Abbass, Allan. *Reaching through Resistance: Advanced Psychotherapy Techniques.* Kansas City, MO: Seven Leaves Press, 2015.

Abbass, Allan, and Howard Schubiner. *Hidden from View: A Clinician's Guide to Psychophysiologic Disorders.* Pleasant Ridge, MI: Psychophysiologic Press, 2020.

Clarke, David, Howard Schubiner, Mags Clark-Smith, and Allan Abbass. *Psychophysiologic Disorders: Trauma Informed, Interprofessional Diagnosis and Treatment.* Psychophysiologic Disorders Association, 2019.

Coughlin, Della Selva Patricia. *Intensive Short-Term Dynamic Psychotherapy Theory and Technique.* London: Karnac, 2006.

Coughlin, Patricia. *Facilitating the Process of Working through in Psychotherapy: Mastering the Middle Game.* Routledge, Taylor & Francis Group, 2022.

Coughlin, Patricia. *Maximizing Effectiveness in Dynamic Psychotherapy.* New York: Routledge, Taylor & Francis Group, 2017.

Davanloo, Habib. *Unlocking the Unconscious.* Chichester, England: Wiley, 1990.

Davanloo, Habib. *Intensive Short-Term Dynamic Psychotherapy.* Chichester, England: Wiley, 2000.

Frederickson, Jon. *Co-Creating Change: Effective Dynamic Therapy Techniques*. Kansas City, MO: Seven Leaves Press, 2013.

Frederickson, Jon. *Co-Creating Safety: Effective Dynamic Therapy Techniques*. Kansas City, MO: Seven Leaves Press, 2020.

Frederickson, Jon. *Healing through Relating: A Skill-Building Book for Therapists*. Kansas City, MO: Seven Leaves Press, 2023.

Gottman, John. *The Marriage Clinic: A Scientifically Based Marital Therapy*. New York: W. W. Norton, 1999.

Kuhn, Nat. *Intensive Short-Term Dynamic Psychotherapy: A Reference*. North Charleston, SC: Experient Publications, 2014.

Malan, David, and Patricia Coughlin. *Lives Transformed: A Revolutionary Method of Dynamic Psychotherapy*. New York: Routledge, 2007.

McCullough, Leigh, Nat Kuhn, Stuart Andrews, Amelia Kaplan, Jonathan Wolf, and Cara Lanza Hurley. *Treating Affect Phobia: A Manual for Short-Term Dynamic Psychotherapy*. New York: Guilford Press, 2003.

Ten Have-de Labije, Josette, and Robert Neborsky. *Mastering Intensive Short-Term Dynamic Psychotherapy: A Roadmap to the Unconscious*. New York: Routledge, 2019.

For Everyone

Dispenza, Joe. *You Are the Placebo: Making Your Mind Matter*. Carlsbad, CA: Hay House, 2014.

Frederick, Ron. *Living Like You Mean It: Use the Wisdom and Power of Your Emotions to Get the Life You Really Want*. San Francisco: Jossey-Bass, 2009.

Frederick, Ron. *Loving Like You Mean It: Use the Power of Emotional Mindfulness to Transform Your Relationships*. Las Vegas: Central Recovery, 2019.

FURTHER READING

Frederickson, Jon. *The Lies We Tell Ourselves: How to Face the Truth, Accept Yourself, and Create a Better Life*. Kansas City, MO: Seven Leaves Press. 2017.

Gordon, Alan, and Alon Ziv. *The Way Out: A Revolutionary, Scientifically Proven Approach to Healing Chronic Pain*. New York: Avery, 2021.

Hendel, Hilary Jacobs. *It's Not Always Depression: Working the Change Triangle to Listen to the Body, Discover Core Emotions, and Connect to Your Authentic Self*. New York: Spiegel & Grau, 2018.

Kapleau, Phillip. *The Three Pillars of Zen*. New York: Anchor, 2013.

Kuhn, Nat. *Intensive Short-Term Dynamic Psychotherapy: A Reference*. North Charleston, SC: Experient Publications, 2014.

Maté, Gabor. *When the Body Says No: Understanding the Stress-Disease Connection*. Hoboken, NJ: Wiley, 2008.

Maté, Gabor. *The Myth of Normal: Trauma, Illness, and Healing in a Toxic Culture*. New York: Avery, 2022.

Sarno, John. *Healing Back Pain: The Mind-Body Connection*. New York: Grand Central, 2001.

Sarno, John. *The Mindbody Prescription: Healing the Body, Healing the Pain*. New York: Grand Central, 2001.

Sarno, John. *The Divided Mind: The Epidemic of Mindbody Disorders*. New York: HarperCollins, 2009.

Schubiner, Howard, and Michael Betzold. *Unlearn Your Pain: A 28-Day Process to Reprogram Your Brain*. Pleasant Ridge, MI: Mind Body Publishing, 2017.

Siegel, Daniel, Marion Solomon, and Diana Fosha. *The Healing Power of Emotion: Affective Neuroscience, Development & Clinical Practice*. New York: W. W. Norton, 2009.

Van der Kolk, Bessel. *The Body Keeps the Score: Brain, Mind, and Body in the Healing of Trauma*. New York: Penguin, 2014.

For Couples

Gottman, John. *The Science of Trust: Emotional Attunement for Couples*. New York: W. W. Norton, 2011.

Gottman, John. *Raising an Emotionally Intelligent Child*. New York: Simon & Schuster, 2011.

Gottman, John, and Nan Silver. *The Seven Principles for Making Marriage Work: A Practical Guide from the Country's Foremost Relationship Expert*. New York: Harmony, 2015.

Real, Terrance. *The New Rules of Marriage: What You Need to Know to Make Love Work*. New York: Ballantine, 2008.

Notes

Chapter 1

1. Sigmund Freud, James Strachey, and Angela Richards, *Introductory Lectures on Psychoanalysis* (London: Penguin, 1991).

Chapter 2

1. For more detail on the conscious therapeutic alliance, see chapter 6 in Jon Frederickson, *Co-Creating Change: Effective Dynamic Therapy Techniques* (Kansas City, MO: Seven Leaves Press, 2013).

2. For more reading about psychophysiological processes, see Allan Abbass and Howard Schubiner, *Hidden from View: A Clinician's Guide to Psychophysiologic Disorders* (Pleasant Ridge, MI: Psychophysiologic Press, 2020); Allan Abbass, *Reaching through Resistance: Advanced Psychotherapy Techniques* (Kansas City, MO: Seven Leaves Press, 2015); John Sarno, *Healing Back Pain: The Mind-Body Connection* (New York: Grand Central, 2001); John Sarno, *The Mindbody Prescription: Healing the Body, Healing the Pain* (New York: Grand Central, 2001); and John Sarno, *The Divided Mind: The Epidemic of Mindbody Disorders* (New York: HarperCollins, 2009).

Chapter 14

1. Allan Abbass and Howard Schubiner, *Hidden from View: A Clinician's Guide to Psychophysiologic Disorders* (Pleasant Ridge, MI: Psychophysiologic Press, 2020), 171.

Chapter 16

1. For more information on defenses, see Jerome S. Blackman, *101 Defenses: How the Mind Shields Itself* (New York: Brunner-Routledge, 2004); Anna Freud, *The Ego and the Mechanisms of Defence* (London: Karnac Books, 1993); and Jon Frederickson's *Co-creating Change: Effective Dynamic Therapy Techniques* (Kansas City, MO: Seven Leaves Press, 2013).

Chapter 17

1. Waleed Brinjikji et al., "Systematic Literature Review of Imaging Features of Spinal Degeneration in Asymptomatic Populations," *American Journal of Neuroradiology* 36, no. 4 (April 2015): 811–16, http://doi.org/10.3174/ajnr.A4173.
2. Nicole K. Y. Tang and Catherine Crane, "Suicidality in Chronic Pain: A Review of the Prevalence, Risk Factors and Psychological Links," *Psychological Medicine* 36, no. 5 (January 18, 2006): 575–86, https://doi.org/10.1017/s0033291705006859.

Chapter 18

1. Wilfred Bion, *Attention and Interpretation* (New York: Jason Aronson, 1995).

Chapter 21

1. See Alan Gordon and Alon Ziv, *The Way Out: A Revolutionary, Scientifically Proven Approach to Healing Chronic Pain* (New York: Avery, 2021).
2. Martin E. P. Seligman, Steven F. Maier, and James H. Geer, "Alleviation of Learned Helplessness in the Dog," *Journal of Abnormal Psychology* 73, no. 3, pt.1 (1968): 256–62, https://doi.org/10.1037/h0025831.

Chapter 24

1. David H. Malan, *Individual Psychotherapy and the Science of Psychodynamics*, 2nd ed. (Oxford: Butterworth-Heinemann, 1995).

Chapter 25

1. For more information on Zen practice, see Philip Kapleau, *The Three Pillars of Zen* (New York: Anchor Books, 1989).

Chapter 29

1. For more reading about psychophysiological processes, see Allan Abbass and Howard Schubiner, *Hidden from View: A Clinician's Guide to Psychophysiologic Disorders* (Pleasant Ridge, MI: Psychophysiologic Press, 2020); Allan Abbass, *Reaching through Resistance: Advanced Psychotherapy Techniques* (Kansas City, MO: Seven Leaves Press, 2015); John Sarno, *Healing Back Pain: The Mind-Body Connection* (New York: Grand Central, 2001); John Sarno, *The Mindbody Prescription: Healing the Body, Healing the Pain* (New York: Grand Central, 2001); and John Sarno, *The Divided Mind: The Epidemic of Mindbody Disorders* (New York: HarperCollins, 2009).

Chapter 31

1. Charles Brenner, *An Elementary Textbook of Psychoanalysis*, rev. ed. (New York: Anchor Press/Doubleday, 1994).

Chapter 36

1. C. S. Lewis, *A Grief Observed* (New York: Seabury Press, 1980), 66.

Acknowledgments

1. C. S. Lewis, *A Grief Observed* (New York: Seabury Press, 1980), 18–19.

About the Author

Michelle M. May, LPC, NCC, is a psychotherapist based in Virginia and Washington, DC, distinguished for her expertise in Intensive Short-Term Dynamic Psychotherapy (ISTDP). She became a licensed professional counselor and a nationally certified counselor after receiving her bachelor's in psychology from the University of Michigan LSA Honors College and her master's in clinical mental health counseling from Marymount University.

With a passion for advancing the field, Michelle serves as the chair of the ISTDP core training program at the New Washington School of Psychiatry in Washington, DC, and has been on the faculty at the New Washington School of Psychiatry since 2019. She is a certified teacher and supervisor by the International Experiential Dynamic Therapy Association (IEDTA). Her teachings not only enrich the understanding of this specialized therapy but also contribute to the development of future practitioners.

In addition to her academic pursuits, Michelle runs a thriving private practice in Arlington, Virginia, and Washington, DC, where she extends her expertise in intensive dynamic psychotherapy to adults and couples. Her approach is rooted in a deep understanding of the complexities of the human mind, and she employs ISTDP to facilitate transformative change in her clients.

Beyond her clinical and educational roles, Michelle extends her reach into the international community, providing training for health practices, organizations, and universities seeking to enhance their understanding of mental health and intensive dynamic therapies. Her expertise is a valuable resource for professionals seeking to incorporate innovative therapeutic approaches into their practice. Moreover, Michelle is recognized for her supervision of licensed medical and mental health professionals in experiential dynamic therapies, including ISTDP. Her guidance ensures that practitioners receive comprehensive support and mentorship, fostering the growth and development of therapists within the dynamic field of psychotherapy.

In her commitment to intensive psychodynamic mental health awareness and education, Michelle leverages social media to share valuable insights. Her Instagram account, @michellemmaylpc, serves as a platform for disseminating mental health information and engaging with a wider audience, further contributing intensive psychodynamic mental health education.